THE ECONOMY IN QUESTION

Restructuring Britain

The Economy in Question
edited by John Allen and Doreen Massey

The Changing Social Structure
edited by Chris Hamnett, Linda McDowell and Philip Sarre

Politics in Transition
edited by Allan Cochrane and James Anderson

The following are associated Readers published by Hodder and Stoughton in association with The Open University:

Uneven Re-Development: Cities and Regions in Transition
edited by Doreen Massey and John Allen

Divided Nation: Social and Cultural Change in Britain
edited by Linda McDowell, Philip Sarre and Chris Hamnett

A State of Crisis: The Changing Face of British Politics
edited by James Anderson and Allan Cochrane

Open University Course D314 Restructuring Britain
(Details of this course are available from the Student Enquiries Office, The Open University, PO Box 71, Milton Keynes MK7 6AG)

Restructuring Britain

THE ECONOMY IN QUESTION

edited by
John Allen and Doreen Massey

SAGE Publications
in association with

The Open
University

First published 1988

SAGE Publications Ltd
20 Banner Street
London EC1Y 8QE

SAGE Publications Inc
2111 West Hillcrest Drive
Newbury Park, California 91320

SAGE Publications India Pvt Ltd
32, M-Block Market
Greater Kailash – I
New Delhi 110 048

British Library Cataloguing in Publication data

The Economy in question. – (Restructuring
   Britain).
   1. Great Britain. Economic conditions
   I. Allen, John, *1951*–   II. Massey,
   Doreen, *1944*–   III. Series
   330.941′0858

   ISBN 0–8039–8168–6
   ISBN 0–8039–8169–4 Pbk

Library of Congress catalog card number 88–61870

Typeset in Linotron 202 Times by
Fakenham Photosetting Ltd, Fakenham, Norfolk

Printed in Great Britain by Billing and Sons Ltd,
Worcester

Contents

Restructuring Britain: introduction   vii

Introduction   1

1 The UK economy at a crossroads *Laurence Harris*   7

2 What's happening to UK manufacturing? *Doreen Massey*   45

3 Towards a post-industrial economy? *John Allen*   91

4 A crisis of mass production? *Richard Meegan*   136

5 Fragmented firms, disorganized labour? *John Allen*   184

6 What is an economy anyway? *Doreen Massey*   229

References   260

Acknowledgements   268

Author index   271

Subject index   273

Course team

John Allen, Lecturer in Economic Geography
James Anderson, Lecturer in Geography
Chris Brook, Lecturer in Applied Regional Studies
Allan Cochrane, Senior Lecturer in Urban Studies
Chris Hamnett, Senior Lecturer in Geography (Course Team Chair)
Pat Jess, Staff Tutor, Northern Ireland
Linda McDowell, Senior Lecturer in Geography
Doreen Massey, Professor of Geography
Philip Sarre, Senior Lecturer in Geography

Consultants

Joe Doherty, Lecturer in Geography, University of St Andrews
Patrick Dunleavy, Reader in Government, London School of Economics and Political Science
Mark Goodwin, Lecturer in Geography, Goldsmiths College, University of London
Laurence Harris, Professor of Economics, The Open University
Richard Meegan, Senior Research Member, CES Ltd, London
Simon Mohun, Lecturer in Economics, Queen Mary College, University of London
Chris Pond, Director, Low Pay Unit
Mike Savage, Lecturer in Sociology, University of Surrey
Peter Taylor, Reader in Political Geography, University of Newcastle upon Tyne
Nigel Thrift, Reader in Geography, University of Bristol

External assessors

John Urry, Professor of Sociology, University of Lancaster (Course Assessor)
Huw Beynon, Professor of Sociology, University of Manchester
Paul Lawless, Principal Lecturer in Urban and Regional Studies, Sheffield
Andrew Sayer, Lecturer in Urban Studies, University of Sussex

Tutor testers

Cliff Hague, Senior Lecturer, Town and Country Planning, Heriot-Watt University,
    Edinburgh
Mark Hart, Lecturer in Environmental Studies, University of Ulster at Jordanstown
Jill Vincent, Research Fellow, Centre for Research in Social Policy, Loughborough
    University of Technology

Course support

Melanie Bayley, Editor
Ann Boomer, Secretary
Sarah Gauthier, Secretary
Rob Lyon, Graphic Designer
Ray Munns, Cartographer/Graphic Artist
Carol Oddy, Secretary
Varrie Scott, Course Manager
Jane Tyrell, Secretary
David Wilson, Editor

Restructuring Britain: introduction

The Economy in Question is part of a series on the changes which have reshaped the economic, social, political and geographical structure of the UK since the end of the 1950s. Each book is free-standing and can be read on its own, or it can be studied as part of the Open University course *Restructuring Britain*. This book deals with questions about the structure of the economy, production and work; another deals with changes in social structure and culture, including class, gender, race, income, wealth and consumption; and a third with the reshaping of politics and the role of the state. Together with three associated Readers, the three textbooks form an integrated theoretical and empirical analysis of the changing structure of contemporary Britain.

There have probably been few periods in recent history when change of some sort has not been on the agenda; it is one of the defining characteristics of modern society. Yet the last two or more decades do seem to have been marked by transformations of a very different order, and moreover transformations which in different ways and with different timings have affected a wide range of aspects of society. The place of the UK in the international world has changed: its role in the international economic order has shifted quite dramatically and its political position between Europe and the USA has been renegotiated. Within the economy the shift from manufacturing to services has been reinforced, and with it the whole economic geography of the country. The future of cities and of some regions is at stake; and at national level the question must be whether the economy can survive by exporting services. Such shifts, together with wider changes in the labour process, have transformed the occupational structure of the workforce. While unemployment has risen, the most rapidly growing segment of the population in paid work is that of professionals, managers and administrators. But in the less well-paid parts of the economy, many of the new jobs have been in part-time and increasingly in casualized employment. All these changes in the economy have gone along with changes in the social structure too. There has been talk of 'the end of the working class' – certainly of the old image of the male-dominated kind, working in manufacturing – and of the burgeoning of white-collar middle strata: processes that are mirrored geographically in the counterposition of the recent fortunes of different regions of the country. Has women's lot been improved by all this, or are women now caught in an even more contradictory position? And how important have changes in consumption patterns been in moulding the shifting social structure? There have also been changes at the political level, and attempts, some more successful than others, to break the mould of the old party politics and to end the comfortable old consensus. It has, indeed, been the period when the very term 'restructuring', if not newly invented, has been rehabilitated and put to frequent use.

   This series is built around an examination of these changes. Perhaps most fundamentally we wanted to explore the questions: what is the nature of all this change; does it amount to a structural change; are we at some kind of historical turning-point?

In order to get to grips with these issues, a number of different threads have been chosen, which run throughout this series. There are three, and they are necessarily intertwined with each other as their investigation develops.

   The *first* is simply the empirical changes themselves. *Restructuring Britain* covers a wide range of empirical material, and our aim is to investigate it bearing in mind always the questions: what kinds of change have these been; has there been structural change? One point to make from the start is that we want to consider the material geographically, that is, to take the spatial dimension as integral to our whole concern. Thus, while our key question concerns periodization, an underlying hypothesis is that different eras of history are bound up with distinct forms of uneven development. The argument is not that they merely happen together, but that they are integrally related to each other.

   But one cannot examine empirical data for structural change, either social or spatial, without some notion of what structural change might be. So this, too, is an enquiry which runs through the series. How can one characterize distinct historical eras, or spatial formations; how does one assess what are the key relations; or what features can be said to be dominant? Indeed what does 'dominant' mean in this context? This in turn raises questions of the conceptualization of systems, and of structures themselves.

   The *second* concern is to investigate the debates which have taken place within the social sciences about the nature of these empirical changes and about their explanation. Some theories and debates span all three books in this series, since their scope itself ranges from economic to political; the nature of the structural change they postulate or debate involves all aspects of society. Other theoretical debates tend to be more confined in their scope relating to perhaps only one or a bundle of the empirical changes we are considering here. Many of them, too, do not have an explicitly geographical element, and in some of these we have tried to inject our own spatial perspective, drawing out from them what are in some cases already implicit geographical implications. This is not appropriate in all cases, of course; but what we are after in the end is to analyse the nature of the reorganization of economic-social-political relations over space, and the impact of that.

   Thirdly, we stand back even further from the empirical changes and explore how those debates within the social sciences can themselves be assessed. Here we examine the different questions which distinct approaches may address, even when they appear to be examining 'the same phenomena' and to be engaged in the same debate. The different modes of 'self-evaluation' implied by various theoretical approaches are pointed to, and the varying ways in which they relate to 'evidence' are contrasted. Much of this links back quite directly to, and intertwines with, the issues explored under the first heading – different theories, indeed, have quite distinct notions even about what is structural change.

The structure of the series

The Economy in Question introduces some of the theoretical debates over economic aspects of these issues: the definition and importance of deindustrialization, the nature of the international economic order, the characteristics of post-industrial society, the definition of service employment and its links to manufacturing, the changing organization of the labour process, and the concepts of work and economy. *The Changing Social Structure* introduces the debates over gender relations, race and class structure and changing patterns of consumption. Are we witnessing the end of the working class and the emergence of a predominantly middle-class society, dominated by private home and car ownership and a privatized and individualized social ethos? *Politics in Transition* examines the debates over the changing political role of the UK internationally, and the changing structure of politics and state intervention within the country. It looks at, amongst other things, the changing relationship between central and local government, the arguments regarding class dealignment and consumption in voting behaviour and the UK's position vis-à-vis the USA, the European Community and the Commonwealth.

There are, of course, links between all these issues. The division into three groups of issues, and indeed below that into individual chapters within each book, is made for analytical purposes. Although everything may well be connected to everything else, it is nonetheless necessary to hold things apart at certain stages of work in order to be able to explore in more depth the most salient social processes. But the links and interdependencies are still important. Indeed, one of the recent developments in the social sciences generally has been an increasing recognition of their interdependence. When considering questions of sectoral shifts within the economy, for instance, or questions of the location of industry, it is necessary also to be aware of prerequisite changes in the structure and nature of the potential labour force. And the labour force is not constructed by economic processes alone but also through cultural, political and ideological ones. To take another obvious example, neither the economic nor social changes of recent years, nor the changes in gender relations or consumption patterns can be fully considered outside of the context of quite marked shifts in the political climate. Where it is appropriate we have tried to build some of the more important of these interlinkages into the texts.

One issue which does emerge from a consideration of the whole series together, and which raises again the question of the nature of the connections between the processes discussed in each of them, is the distinct timings of those different social processes. Interesting issues are raised by what seem to be the contrasting periodizations of the transformations of different aspects of British society. This raises yet again the question of what is meant by structural change.

Finally, this is very much a course about questions. By no means all the questions are simply answered. This series of Open Texts, and the associated Readers, are meant to be more guides to an exploration and a stimulus to thought, than a treatise which settles the debate. This is true, too, about questions for the future. There are clearly a number of directions in which British economy and society could go. To explore them would take a parallel series on policy. But we hope that enough light is thrown on possible options to provoke further debate about the possibilities.

Introduction

What is happening to the UK's economy? Since the mid-1960s few of the old certainties remain intact. Not so long ago it was virtually taken for granted that the UK was a major manufacturing nation, that the nation's industries would continue to compete in mass markets, both at home and abroad, and that the big cities would remain the centre of economic activity. The settled period of economic growth which was experienced in the UK in the 1950s has given way to a period of instability, an uncertainty over where the economic changes of the last few decades will lead. That the economy is in the midst of a process of change is not at issue. It is the *kind* of economic transformations that have been occurring since the mid-1960s, their impact and breadth, that concerns us here. Some of the changes are very broad indeed, certainly in the questions which they imply. The declining role of the British economy in world manufacturing raises the question of what its future international role will be; long-term increases in levels of unemployment and perhaps more particularly in part-time employment raise the question of how 'work' of all kinds should be distributed as we approach the end of the twentieth century. This book is an engagement with this particular historical moment.

It addresses a number of recent changes in the structure of the UK economy that are likely to have an impact upon people's working lives. In doing so, the book sets out a wide range of empirical material, but the main aim of the text is not to provide a comprehensive or exhaustive account of the major economic trends of the last few decades. There are many other books which set out to provide this type of information. Our major aim is to introduce you to some of the main theoretical debates that have taken place over the significance and extent of recent changes in the economy. Any aspect of economic change requires interpretation and there is no shortage of disagreement over the interpretation of such issues as the decline of the UK's manufacturing industry, the growth of employment in the service sector, the transformation of the geography of industry, the changing nature of work, and shifts in the structure of the labour market.

Each of these topics represents a contested theoretical terrain; they are controversial issues. What we try to do here is to take you through these controversies in a particular way. Rather than set up theoretical debate as a kind of competition between mutually exclusive viewpoints, we have tried to show how the debates are characterized by theoretical viewpoints which exhibit both differences – in their assumptions about economic change, in their conception of how an economy works, and so forth – and a degree of overlap. To be sure, there is a diversity of theoretical argument, but within that diversity there are often shared concerns and shared interpretations. Whether the areas that are held in common are significant or not is, of course, itself open to question.

The emphasis is upon how theories construct their explanations of economic change. Of crucial importance here is the role that evidence performs in supporting different theories. None of the changes identified above – in the structure of the economy or the types of work that people do – can be understood by reference to evidence alone, for different theories select certain kinds of evidence to support their interpretation. In this sense, theories are partial interpretations; they offer an explanation of what has been happening from a particular viewpoint, one that has been informed by a set of assumptions about how society is organized and how it changes. What counts as evidence, therefore, will often vary from theory to theory. Some theories prioritize statistical evidence, whilst others rely heavily upon qualitative aspects of change, and others may opt for a combination of the two. In many cases, the same piece of evidence is subject to varying interpretations and we have to consider which is the most fruitful or plausible interpretation. In doing so, we start to see how different theories put their explanations together, the connections that they draw, and the emphases they place upon particular characteristics of the economy and urban and regional economic change.

To examine the process of theorizing – to unravel how theories 'work' – is not, however, an end in itself. Theories are the vehicles through which we attempt to make sense of the changes that are happening around us. Each chapter of this book sets out the contours of a continuing theoretical debate – in some cases debates – over aspects of the economy that have attracted attention precisely because they are held to be in the throes of some kind of radical change. The issue of radical change is important here. In much the same way that our selection of topics has been guided by the presence of a theoretical debate, it has also been guided by the *kinds* of economic change that may be taking place. Particular attention has been paid to economic changes which are seen to be of a *structural* nature.

The issue of what is and what is not a structural change is, as was pointed out earlier, a challenging one and itself open to theoretical interpretation. A minimal definition of a structural economic change would be one that represented a fundamental shift in the way that the economy has hitherto been organized. Candidates for the label 'structural change' would be the shift in the economy from manufacturing to service-based employment, the decline of big cities as the prime foci of production, the growth in the dominance of multinational corporations in the running of the economy or the shift from full- to part-time employment in the labour market. None of these changes, however, has occurred in isolation from the others. Each in some way has had an effect upon the other or contributed to its formation. The growth of part-time work, for example, is an integral aspect of the rise of employment in the service sector. Equally, multinational companies are now major employers within the service sector – in areas such as cleaning, catering and leisure. When considered together, you start to get the idea of a *period* of structural change, a historical moment, rather than a discrete set of changes. Each of the chapters takes a different slice through the contemporary period of change and explores the new directions that are appearing on the horizon.

Thinking of structural change in this way, as a kind of break with the past in which new directions are taken, has a number of attractions. First, it enables us to consider the temporal characteristics of economic change, the periodization of change: the periods of decline, the break with the old, the transition to the new, the emergence of a new structural formation over time, and the different tempos of change. Second, it draws our attention to the spatial characteristics of economic change, the uneven development of the economy which leads to different outcomes, in different places, at different times. You have only to think of the uneven impact of the process of manufacturing decline across the UK and the economic significance of the divide between north and south to gauge this point. Periods of economic change in the UK have not affected the country in a uniform geographical manner; they have affected different places in different ways partly because the processes themselves operate unevenly and partly for reasons related to the specificity of particular areas. National economic changes, in this sense, take a variety of forms across the country. A period of structural change in the economy may mean also a new form of uneven development. In this book, we have deliberately focused upon economic changes which not only possess a geographical dimension, but for which a changing geography is an integral aspect of how such changes work themselves out. They are part and parcel of the wider processes of structural change that are transforming the economy.

In order to come to grips with what is happening to the UK's economy it is important to explore both the geographical and the historical dimensions of structural change. And to move in this direction requires a starting-point not within the country itself, but outside of the UK, at the level of the international economy. Chapter 1 therefore begins there. Starting from the notion that the UK economy is at some kind of a crossroads, it shows that this is not the first such period of structural change and that each has been embedded in wider international shifts. It then examines the ways in which the UK economy's relation to the international economy has been changing, looking at deindustrialization, at patterns of international trade and of foreign investment. What emerges is a picture of an economy which historically has been open and is becoming more so while at the same time shifting its role in the international world. And these changes can be set within international processes of internationalization and multilateralism. But if these are the main lines of the changes which have been under way, how are they to be explained? Long-wave, world-system and regulationist theories are each introduced in Chapter 1 and explored in terms of how they deal with an economy's international relations, its internal structure and its history.

These international changes have been reflected in the restructuring of the UK economy itself. Chapter 2 begins our examination of this by looking at manufacturing. It starts by looking at that much-used but often ill-defined concept – deindustrialization. The question of what deindustrialization is, and why clear conceptualization is important in the social sciences, runs through the chapter. But however it is defined, deindustrialization has had a very unequal geography. The spatial organization of manufacturing has undergone a major transformation since the mid-1960s. There has been massive decline in the old manufacturing heartlands, especially the big cities; there has been decentralization from urban areas to more rural ones and, for a period, from central regions to periphery; there has been growth of new manufacturing sectors often in new areas very different from the old. The challenge of explaining this re-working of the geography of manufacturing has provoked productive debates between different theoretical positions, and these are examined here. It also raises the wider question of the definition and explanation of one of the central concepts of this text: uneven development. There are, moreover, those who would set the specific changes in manufacturing in the context of wider social transformations, and here Chapter 2 picks up from Chapter 1 the discussion of long-wave and regulationist theories and examines what they have to say about the emergence of a new era of manufacturing (and its geography) in the UK.

In Chapter 3 a different kind of turning-point is considered. The question here is not what kind of manufacturing sector is likely to emerge out of the economic downturn of the 1970/1980s, but what kind of service economy is being established. The debate centres on the view that the UK is in the process of adjusting to a new kind of economy, a post-industrial economy in which services are dominant. Deindustrialization, in this context, is a predictable aspect of the transition from an industrial to a post-industrial economy. As with previous chapters, the theoretical controversy around this view is set out, and particular attention is paid to the kinds of evidence that the theories appeal to in support of their arguments.

Much of this debate has taken place at the level of the national economy, but more recently there has been a growing awareness that the service industries, alongside manufacturing, are also reshaping the UK's economic geography. What is more, not only are the expanding service industries reinforcing and reworking the divide between north and south, clustered as many are around London and in the South East, they are also reproducing the unequal division of labour between regions, with the managerial and control functions located in the southern regions. These developments have led to speculation that the UK is becoming a 'dual economy', with a 'deindustrialized' north and a 'post-industrial' south. The growing debate around this conjecture is outlined in Chapter 3.

The first three chapters therefore examine broad sectoral changes in the British economy, as well as the changing role of the UK in the international economy. Chapters 4 and 5 adopt a rather different focus. Chapter 4 sets out a debate over another kind of turning-point, a turning-point in the way things are produced and in what is produced. In recent years much has been written about the decline of mass production and standardized markets –

Fordism for short. The question now is, if that was dominant and is now declining, what is emerging in its place? Despite differences in their approach to this question, the two theories which are addressed in this chapter share the view that some kind of 'flexible' economy is being sought. Companies are seeking flexibility from their technology, their suppliers and their workforces. The nature of these changes, their extent and their implications for the way production is organized, is explored through the contrast and connections between the two accounts.

Geography has been central to this debate, for the shifts in the organization of production are also laying down a new pattern of uneven development, both within the UK and at the international level. The shape of this pattern is far from clear, ranging from a move towards a greater dispersal of industry to signs which indicate a recentralization of production in regional centres. It would appear that the geography of neo-Fordism is every bit as flexible as the production processes that mark it out.

The question of 'flexibilization' does not end with the debate over the rigidities of Fordism and the future of mass production. One of the major difficulties with the concept of 'flexibility' is its vagueness; it can be stretched to cover a wide range of changes that are said to be taking root in British industry. Some of the changes that have been referred to as a sign of increasing 'flexibility' within industry are explored in Chapter 5. They include the break-up of the large factory in the urban centres and the transfer of production to smaller, dispersed plants and small firms, the erosion by companies of established skill demarcations between jobs, the increased use by employers of a peripheral, casualized workforce, creating a divide between them and a permanent core group of multi-skilled workers, and changes in union recognition and collective bargaining procedures. The extent of these changes is subject to debate and so too is the interpretation of what such changes add up to, both economically and geographically. Are they representative of a new, 'disorganized' phase of capitalism, a structural shift in the organization of the economy or merely a reworking of older trends? And if a series of more disaggregated and varied changes is under way in the organization of British industry, what are the spatial implications of such developments? Do such changes herald the demise of large factories in the older, industrial urban centres and the growth of peripheral, rural locations? Or have such developments been exaggerated?

The wide and varied set of economic changes explored in Chapters 1 to 5 together indicate that there may be some more fundamental issues at stake. Chapter 6 therefore steps back a little to examine some of these issues. If this is indeed a historical break-point of some form, then it is throwing up questions about the whole shape of the economy. This is so in a number of ways. There is the question of the future role of the UK economy in the international economy – does the decline of manufacturing matter? Instead of workshop of the world could not the UK successfully become banker to the world, for instance? Could it not survive by exporting services? To explore the debate around this, Chapter 6 looks at arguments over what sectors can provide the necessary engines of growth for an economy and which are more likely to provide an adequate basis for exports. The arguments are shown to have distinct social and geographical implications.

But that question in turn raises issues about the causes of decline and about the whole conceptualization of the economy. In particular it forces us to think about the categories used in conceptualizing the internal structure of the economy – manufacturing:services, marketed:non-marketed, productive:non-productive, public:private and waged:unwaged. Each of these divisions throws a different light on the economy, on its potential futures and on its social form. Indeed, it raises the whole question of the relation between what we customarily call 'the economic' and 'the social'; it leads us, in other words, to the point where we hand over to *The Changing Social Structure* (Hamnett *et al.*, 1989).

1 The UK economy at a crossroads

Laurence Harris

Contents

1.1	**Introduction**	8
1.2	**Periods of structural change in the UK economy**	10
Summary of section 1.2		14
1.3	**Deindustrialization and the international context**	14
1.3.1	Deindustrialization and the long boom	14
1.3.2	Exports and imports: the 'workshop of the world'	17
1.3.3	Direct foreign investment	20
1.3.4	Financial (portfolio) investment	21
Summary of section 1.3		22
1.4	**The changing international economy**	22
1.4.1	Internationalization	23
1.4.2	Multilateralism	24
1.5	**Theoretical frameworks**	26
1.5.1	Long-wave theories	27
1.5.2	World-system theories	29
1.5.3	Regulationist theories	32
Summary of section 1.5		35
1.6	**Conclusion: the international economy and structural change**	36
1.6.1	The international economy	36
1.6.2	Structural change	38
Further reading		43

1.1   Introduction

Throughout the United Kingdom at the time of writing – the late 1980s – there is a sense that profound changes are under way in the economy. It is not that a major shift is suddenly taking place, although the stock market crash of October 1987 did make people feel as if the ground was unexpectedly moving beneath them. It is more a general feeling that the ways in which we work and consume, trade and invest, obtain our salaries, wages or profits, own property and have entitlements to welfare, are all changing dramatically. Those changes appear to be so great that they will certainly still be affecting readers of this text in the 1990s.

This book explores the idea of major economic shifts being on the agenda. The title of this chapter captures that sense of a change in direction in the concept of a *crossroads*. The chapter's main aim is to examine the nature of that crossroads and how best to analyse it. There is also a word absent from the title that specifies the subject of this chapter: the word is *international*, for here I am mainly concerned with changes in the international position of the UK economy, while the following chapters deal with the internal changes to which they are linked.

Before going on to the detailed issues, let me begin by discussing some general aspects of what we mean by a crossroads and by the international position of an economy.

To say that the UK economy is at a *crossroads* suggests that it is a time for important decisions to be taken leading to a change in direction. To understand what is happening to the economy we have to be able to explain why we have reached this crossroads, to describe the new path the economy is taking and explain why this new path rather than another direction has been taken. We shall be discussing these matters throughout the chapter.

The idea of a crossroads is a difficult concept to pin down because we have to distinguish between different types of changes. All economies are continually changing, but in saying that the economy is at a crossroads we are dealing with a change in its whole direction. How can we distinguish these major changes from more minor ones? In what sense do these mark a crossroads while the others are no more than a widening of the road? One answer is that in the late 1980s we have been witnessing *structural changes*, whereas in more normal times we see only adjustments and changes within a set structure. But what is meant by a structural change? I intend to approach this problem piece by piece and in the final section (section 1.6) I shall attempt to outline a general concept of what is meant by structural change.

The second main concern of this chapter, as we have said, is with changes in the UK's *international* position. The idea of the country's international economic standing is well established, for over several decades we have all been confronted with frequent and regular comparisons between the UK and other countries. For example, we all know that productivity growth in the UK has been inferior to West Germany's over the post-war decades; that product development has been behind that of Japan; and that over many years the rates of growth of South Korea, Italy and East Germany were higher than the United Kingdom's. But such league tables are not what is meant here by the UK's international position. Rather it is the character of the links between the UK and the rest of the world, the influence of the UK economy on others and, of greatest importance, the influence of the international economy on the UK.

It is generally assumed that international forces have a great influence on the UK so that it is the **international economy** which determines the character of the crossroads now facing the UK. Let me elaborate on that assumption. The impoverished quality of life in, say, a depressed industrial town breeds a closed-in local feeling. But however much that sense of a *local* spiral of depression exists, there is an ever-present sense that the economic crisis has been part of broader international changes and problems. That international impact on local affairs is true for all economies. However, since the UK economy has historically always been a highly **open economy**, it is especially true that what happens locally is strongly influenced by international changes. It is an open economy in the technical sense that the ratios of both imports and exports to Gross Domestic Product (GDP) have historically been high compared to other advanced industrial countries and in the broader sense that UK firms' investments overseas are high, foreign firms' ownership of UK enterprises is high, and the financial sector, the City, which is a major sector of the economy and dominates it in several ways, is essentially international in outlook.

But exactly how should we define an economy's international position? One common way is to think of the United Kingdom's economy as a national entity where the different parts – the various industries, banks, sections of the labour force and so on – are bound together by relations and institutions which are internal and national. On that view its international position consists of relations (exports, imports, financial and other flows) with other countries which are also cohesive national entities. An alternative way, however, is to see national cohesion as secondary and to think of the UK economy as simply one site where the forces of a worldwide, supranational economy are in play. If, for example, a firm with its headquarters in London is running manufacturing plants in the UK, Third World countries and elsewhere, if it is using parts and even designs originating abroad, if its shares are owned by people and institutions of all nationalities and are bought and sold on the New York Stock Exchange as much as in London, why should its output and its profits be counted as part of the United Kingdom economy? Surely, it may be argued, its board and owners have more in common with the board and owners of a similar firm with headquarters in New York than with workers or self-employed professional people in the UK. And, equally, it could be argued, the workers in Ford UK have more in common with workers in Ford's Spanish factories than with British shareholders in Ford. An extreme form of this alternative view is to argue that an economy such as the UK's has no national cohesion at all and our attention should therefore be focused on the way in which supranational world economic forces affect us.

At this point we shall not attempt to choose between such alternative concepts, to pin down the meaning of the 'international position of the UK economy'. We shall discuss it in a variety of ways throughout the chapter and consider how it differs between theoretical frameworks. Sections 1.2, 1.3 and 1.4 outline some of the changes that have occurred in the UK economy and its international position over recent history. Section 1.5 discusses some of the theoretical frameworks that could be used to analyse the UK's structural changes and its international position. By concentrating on the international dimension of the UK's crossroads we are saying that the structural changes are conditioned by the UK's international position – however we conceive it – and are at least partly determined by structural changes in the international economy.

1.2   Periods of structural change in the UK economy

Economies like ours are, by their nature, continually changing; however problematic those changes are, they are marks of the dynamism that characterizes the economy. But although change is ever-present, some periods seem to see greater and more significant shifts than others. Those are periods of structural change and they recur after substantial periods. There is no easy, obvious way to distinguish structural from other changes in the abstract, so let us approach the issue from an empirical, historical perspective. Which periods of UK history seem to have been periods of major structural change?

I would say that there have been four since the early nineteenth century. The most recent has been from the late 1970s through the 1980s, and if we think of those years as one of only four periods of major structural change in nearly two centuries we can appreciate that we have been living in interesting times. The four periods I would identify are these:

- the 1830s and 1840s
- the 1880s and 1890s
- the 1930s and 1940s
- the 1970s and 1980s.

These periods do not have precise starting and finishing dates but instead roughly span some part of the decades I have mentioned. In each of these periods there was poverty and unemployment associated with the break-up of old industries and patterns and there was also the development of new industries, methods of production and new sources of profitable business. I shall now outline some of the main features of those periods, that is some of the main structural changes that occurred. The list is not comprehensive or detailed but tries to focus on the most salient points.

Activity 1.1

Look at the items listed as the main structural changes in each of the four periods. Make a note of which changes are national and which are part of the UK's international position.

- *1830s and 1840s*

development of railway transport

mass urban and rural poverty in the 'Hungry Forties'

growth of new engineering industries

rise in foreign lending from the UK to Europe, Latin America and North America

- *1880s and 1890s*

development of electricity and telegraph communications

new industries such as electrical engineering, large-scale chemicals and steel shipbuilding

competition from newly industrialized countries, especially Germany

colonization of Africa and other areas by Britain and consolidation of the Empire including India

establishment of London as the centre of the world's international monetary system based on sterling and gold

- *1930s and 1940s*

decline of the cotton, textile, shipbuilding and other large-scale industries especially in Scotland and North of England. Mass unemployment

development of new industries during the 1930s mainly in the Midlands and South East: radio engineering, motor vehicles, domestic appliances, aircraft, plastics, rayon and others

state rationalization, funding and provision of welfare services in founding the welfare state in second half of 1940s

nationalization and state planning of coal production, rail transport and other industries

large-scale assembly-line production fully established as the most productive method of production

sterling ceased to be at the centre of the world's financial system. In the mid-1940s the US dollar became the dominant international currency and new institutions (the Bretton Woods institutions) were established to supervise international finance, trade and investment

the economic ties of the old British Empire were tightened during this period and Britain remained at the centre of that group of countries' trade and finance

- *1970s and 1980s*

decline of industries manufacturing motor vehicles, vehicle components, other engineering, steel and others. Mass unemployment

growth of industries based on information technology, growth of employment in consumer services, growth of financial sector

new productive methods based on fragmented labour force and flexible labour established in leading industries

partial dismantling of state ownership of major industries and state provision of services

consolidation of the strength of manufacturing industry in newly industrialized countries such as South Korea. Increased trade between the UK, Western Europe, North America and new industrialized countries

historic expansion in volume of international finance and financial dealing coinciding with instability in financial markets and collapse of the Bretton Woods system based on the dollar's pre-eminence

---

At first it seems easy to make the distinction between changes which are national and those which are international. The following are all clearly international: the rise in foreign lending from the UK (1830s/1840s); the colonization of Africa and consolidation of the Empire and the establishment of London at the centre of the world's monetary system (1880s/1890s); the new dominance of the US dollar and the establishment of the Bretton Woods institutions (at the end of the 1930s/1940s period); and the growth of trade between manufacturing nations and the expansion of international financial markets (1970s/1980s). And the following appear to be structural changes which are internal and national rather than international: railway development and mass poverty (1830s/1840s); mass unemployment associated with the decline of textiles, shipbuilding and other industries; full establishment of large-scale, assembly-line production (early part of the 1930s/1940s period); new production methods based on a fragmented labour force and flexible labour (1970s/1980s).

But is the distinction really so easy to make? The changes I have suggested as national and internal actually have a very strong international dimension. The connection illustrates the view discussed in section 1.1 that what happens in the UK economy, and other economies, is inextricably linked with international developments. Consider those apparently national changes again. The railway boom in Britain in the 1830s and 1840s was more than national: it formed the basis for vast projects of British railway construction abroad and the expansion of overseas lending to finance railway enterprises. The poverty and hunger in that period was exacerbated by the high import duties on foreign corn which kept the price of food high for the urban working class, and which led to the campaign to repeal the Corn Laws: this success assisted the subsequent development of industry on the foundations laid in this period. The mass unemployment of the 1930s was precipitated by the collapse of export markets for textiles, ships and other products and this, in turn, was caused by the collapse of world trade and the chaos in the international monetary system. The new, large-scale, assembly-line industries established in that period were highly international, for their scale required large export markets and the new products themselves were often derived from foreign innovations. The new production methods based on a fragmented labour force and information technology (computerization of design and production) have been established in the 1970s and 1980s on an international rather than purely national basis. They are employed by multinational companies which, during this period of structural change, have organized or reorganized their production on a worldwide basis with different parts of the production process carried out in different countries.

I do not wish to imply that there is no distinction between internal forces and changes and international ones. Some of the main developments in the UK economy have resulted from economic and social developments within the country. The establishment of the welfare state and a large nationalized sector (at the end of the 1930s/1940s period of change) was due to the political balance in the country at the time and the need of UK industry for a rational provision of education, health and economic infrastructure at the core of the economy. Similarly, the relatively slow growth of labour productivity and high level of unit costs in the post-war period of growth (between the crossroads of the 1930s/1940s and those of 1970s/1980s) were largely attributed to the character of management and labour, employers and unions, within the UK and to the internal policies of the state.

All changes in the UK are influenced by international factors, but domestic factors are far from irrelevant; for some changes domestic factors have a relatively great influence and international factors a relatively smaller role, while others are arranged on a scale of increasing influence of international factors. The presence of international factors even in the most domestically oriented changes can be seen by considering again the establishment of the welfare state. Even this was influenced by international conditions. The establishment of a welfare state and the state purchase of major industries would have been almost impossible in many other years of the twentieth century for they would have precipitated a sterling crisis as bankers and firms switched their assets out of sterling and into foreign currencies. This is what had happened in 1931 when Ramsay MacDonald's Labour government had attempted a very small expansion of spending. In the years immediately following 1945, however, foreign exchange markets were so disrupted and so strongly under the control of government that the post-war government could establish its own internal programme while relatively insulated from international financial forces.

Thus the economy is continually changing even between the four periods that I have suggested are periods of structural change. The dramatic shake-ups during those periods do not suddenly appear out of nowhere but should be seen as resulting from the more gradual and less fundamental changes that had been occurring within the old structure's context over previous decades. In the following section we shall examine the changes that have occurred in the UK economy in the decades leading up to the latest period of structural change, the changes over the post-war period culminating in what is often called the deindustrialization of the UK. Since, as has been argued here, international forces are a factor in all the structural changes in the UK economy, we shall also focus on the international side of the economy in the years leading up to the 1970s/1980s crossroads.

Summary of section 1.2

- Although the economy is continually changing, some periods experience marked upheavals as *structural change* occurs.

- Four periods of structural change can be identified: 1830s/1840s, 1880s/1890s, 1930s/1940s and 1970s/1980s.

- The changes that occur in those periods all have an important international dimension, but in some the international factors interact with strongly influential, internal developments while in others the international side has greater relative weight.

1.3   Deindustrialization and the international context

1.3.1   Deindustrialization and the long boom

The structural changes completed in the 1940s were followed by almost three decades of prosperity and growth in the UK. Rising levels of output, high employment, rising living standards and expanded trade within a relatively stable framework of international finance marked the 'long post-war boom' that stretched from the mid-1940s through the 1950s, 1960s and part of the 1970s. Nevertheless, the performance of the economy, while historically remarkable, was inferior to that of other capitalist countries. Not only were West Germany, Japan, the United States and Sweden recording much better economic results than the United Kingdom, but European countries such as Italy, France and Spain experienced 'economic miracles' which passed Britain by. This relative weakness centred on manufacturing industry.

Reviewing the four decades that followed the Second World War, Rowthorn and Wells concluded:

> There is not the slightest doubt that the cause of Britain's relatively poor economic record lies in the thoroughly unsatisfactory performance of large parts of her [sic] manufacturing industry. When confronted with the challenge, posed by an increasingly integrated world economy, of growing competition in international markets for manufactures large numbers of Britain's manufacturing enterprises failed to perform satisfactorily. They failed to invest and invest efficiently on a large enough scale; they failed to develop sufficient numbers of new products and they failed to raise productivity rapidly enough. (Rowthorn and Wells, 1987, pp. 1–2)

By the time of the 1980s crossroads years this record of relative weakness during the 'long boom' had its impact on every aspect of the economy. Real income per head of the UK population was lower in the mid-1980s than in eleven other advanced capitalist countries, while even in 1953 only three (the US, Canada and Sweden) had been ahead of the UK. Unemployment in 1984 was 13 per cent and although many of the country's competitors were also experiencing historically high levels of unemployment, only Belgium and Holland surpassed the UK's unemployment rate.

Overall figures such as these, however, are less illuminating about economic life in the UK than are shifts between different parts of the economy. The most marked shift has been between different sectors: the percentage of output (Gross Domestic Product, or GDP) accounted for by manufacturing has decreased while the proportion attributable to service industries has increased. Manufacturing was 30 per cent of the UK's GDP in 1950, but had fallen to 25 per cent by 1984. The shift from manufacturing to service industries has been even more marked in terms of jobs: in 1950 manufacturing employed 35 per cent of the total in civil employment but this had fallen to 26 per cent by 1981; at the same time, jobs in the service sector rose from 47 per cent to 60 per cent of total employment. In concrete terms this means that people entering the workforce in recent decades, and especially since the early 1970s, have increasingly taken jobs in banks, offices, shops, restaurants, schools, hospitals and other service enterprises instead of following their parents into working in factories.

This change in the UK economy has come to be known as Britain's **deindustrialization**. This is a broad, catch-all term which 'gatecrashed the literature, thereby avoiding the entrance fee of a definition' (Blackaby, 1979, p. 2); the question of definitions is taken up in Chapter 2 but for the moment it is important to note that it is a misleading term for it is often used to describe the relative decline of *manufacturing* industry rather than industry as a whole which includes primary industries like mining, quarrying and oil and gas production and also includes construction and transport. Nevertheless, despite its vagueness, the term 'deindustrialization' has a real meaning to all who have lived in the UK in the 1970s and 1980s.

The argument advanced in section 1.2 would suggest that we cannot explain or understand these changes in the UK economy without understanding the international forces that have acted upon it and which the UK has itself shaped. Explaining the poor development of UK manufacturing industry, Rowthorn and Wells located the causes in its response to a changed international system: 'an increasingly integrated world economy [with] growing competition in international markets for manufactures'. To understand the UK economy and the restructuring of Britain that has been occurring we have to consider not only the *response* of British industry to changes in the world economy, but the character of those global changes themselves and the forces that have produced them. It is worth noting that this task of putting the UK economy in its international context is *quite different from that of making international comparisons*. We have already noted the differences between the UK's output per head and its unemployment and those of other countries, but such league tables do not themselves imply that there is any connection between the UK economy and global forces. It is precisely that connection to which we now turn. Later we shall consider three different theoretical frameworks which attempt to identify the motor-force of changes in the world economy and of nations within it, but first we shall look in general terms at the historical characteristics of the international economic system in which Britain operates.

Britain's connections with the rest of the world's economy have three dimensions:

1 *Foreign trade:* the export and import of goods and services

2 *Direct investment:* the inflow of foreign investment directly into UK enterprises (as when Ford, a UK company, builds a new plant in the UK or takes over a UK firm) and the investment of British firms in foreign plants

3 *Portfolio investment:* the inflow and outflow of finance.

Each of these has changed substantially in the post-war period, but the central argument of this chapter is that such changes cannot be seen as the result only of changes within the UK. The changes in exports and imports of manufactures, for example, cannot be attributed only to a failure, or in some cases success, of British managers and workers; and the rise in (portfolio) investment overseas by UK banks and finance houses is not explicable in terms of the propensities of British bankers or the character of the UK banking system alone. Instead, these phenomena and others result from changes in the international economic system as a whole and the manner in which the UK has interacted with that global system. In line with that perspective, section 1.4 goes outside the description of the UK's trade, direct investment and portfolio investment covered in the preceding subsections and moves on to give a summary description of the developments in the international economic system within which those changes in the UK's position have occurred.

1.3.2   Exports and imports: the 'workshop of the world'

At the start of the twentieth century the UK's **foreign trade** and balance of payments fully justified the stylized but powerful description of this country as 'the workshop of the world': the country was a net importer of primary products including food and industrial raw materials (such as rubber and cotton) and a net exporter of manufactured goods. In the simplest version of this concept the UK imported raw materials which, together with indigenous materials (especially coal and iron), were transformed by British workers whose diet depended on imported staple foods (especially cheap grain) and who produced high quality and low cost manufactured goods which were sold abroad to pay, in part, for the primary imports.

The recorded statistics on UK trade provided some basis for the continuation of this picture through most of the twentieth century. Even in the years immediately following the Second World War, when its manufacturing capacity was weak by any standards, the UK's net exports of manufactured goods (the surplus of sales of manufactures after deducting imports of such goods) was 8.6 per cent of the country's output (GDP) while net imports of primary products were 11.4 per cent of GDP. Over the next four decades, however, the balance gradually changed, with the surplus on net exports of manufactured goods declining as a proportion of GDP and the deficit on trade in primary products declining. These trends are recorded in Table 1.1.

Table 1.1   UK balance of trade on selected items (as % of GDP), 1946–86

	Manufactures	Primary products
1946–59	+8.6	−11.4
1951–55	+8.8	−12.4
1956–60	+8.0	−9.1
1961–65	+6.4	−7.1
1966–70	+4.9	−5.7
1971–75	+3.5	−6.2
1976–80	+3.2	−4.6
1981–82	+1.6	−0.4
1983	−0.5	+0.3
1984	−1.1	−0.3
1985	−0.7	+0.1
1986	−1.3	−0.9

Source: Central Statistical Office (1987) *UK Balance of Payments*, London, HMSO

As Table 1.1 shows, 1983 witnessed a significant and much-noted milestone. In that year the UK imported more manufactured goods than it exported; it appeared to mark the end of its role as the workshop of the world. In fact, of course, the table shows it was not a particularly sudden turnaround but another small step along the worsening path established during the 'long boom'. But that year's and subsequent years' deficits on trade in manufactured goods brought into sharp focus the realization that the 'workshop of the world' tag is completely out of date and has sharply posed the question of what new role is the UK taking in the international economy.

One important concern should be cleared up before proceeding. The powerful notion of the UK as the workshop of the world was always accompanied by the exhortation 'export or die' or, in other words, 'export manufactured goods or be unable to afford to buy imported food'. As a result, at the back of people's minds there is frequently the notion nowadays that since 'we' are now net importers of manufactured goods, 'we' are not able to compete successfully in the international market for manufactured goods, so the country must be impoverished and only able to avoid facing up to this through luck or a trick. But is this fear justified? Does the worsening trade balance in manufactured goods over the 'long boom' and through the point where the UK imports more manufactured goods than it exports mean that the UK's export industries have failed?

Activity 1.2

Examine Table 1.2 and consider for the period 1946 to 1983:

(a) whether exports have fallen or risen;

(b) whether exports of manufactured goods have fallen or risen;

(c) if either has risen, whether it has failed to rise as fast as Gross Domestic Product.

Table 1.2   The changing pattern of exports in relation to GDP, 1946–83

Volume indices for UK 1963 = 100	GDP	Total exports	Exports of manufactures
1946–49	67.5	59.9	62.7
1950–59	92.6	77.6	78.9
1960–69	105.6	107.6	108.8
1970–73	128.1	156.4	160.2
1974–79	140.4	201.9	202.2
1980–81	144.8	225.4	208.4
1982–83	149.6	230.9	202.0

Source: Rowthorn and Wells, 1987, p. 186

The figures in Table 1.2 tell a story of export success. The United Kingdom's total exports by 1983 were nearly four times greater than at the end of the 1940s. This refers to the increase in the volume of exports after allowance has been made for inflation; it does not simply reflect the increased prices of goods. By 1983 exports had doubled even compared with their average during the 1960s. Of course, that increase may be due to the expansion of sales of primary products such as the boom in North Sea oil sales, so it is pertinent to consider the performance of manufacturing industry's exports. Despite deindustrialization total exports of manufactured goods increased substantially: by 1983 they were more than three times their level in the late 1940s and almost twice their average during the 1960s. Moreover, both total exports and exports of manufactured goods increased more than GDP, which more than doubled over the whole period.

It seems that, although some substantial and long-standing export industries declined, others expanded their export sales over the post-war period (although the rise slowed down in the early 1980s). Nevertheless imports of manufactured goods increased even faster. And the economy, always open, became even more so.

The new phenomenon of a deficit on manufactured trade has not, however, created any crisis in the UK's international position: even the decline in *net* exports of manufactures has not fulfilled the prediction implicit in the adage 'export or die'. Instead, trade in other goods and trade in services has moved increasingly into surplus to offset the worsening balance on manufactured goods.

A steadily more favourable balance on the UK's trade in primary products has been a particularly important offset: it generated a surplus in 1983 when manufactures went into deficit. This trend is shown very clearly in Table 1.1, but what lies behind it? The primary products in which the UK has most obviously become a net exporter are oil and gas. Before the Second World War the UK with its huge coal exports was a substantial net exporter of fuel, but coal exports did not recover from wartime disruption and the UK became a net importer of fuel. After the shortages of the 1947 fuel crisis, net fuel imports rose steadily until 1974, but started a steep decline after OPEC quadrupled the price of oil between 1973 and 1974. By 1981, with the expanded production of North Sea oil and gas, the UK had become a net exporter of fuel again. But in addition to fuel, the UK greatly reduced the dependence on food imports that had characterized 'the workshop of the world'. As UK farm production rose, the economy became nearly self-sufficient in many foodstuffs and a net exporter of others so that between 1958 and 1983 the UK's net imports of food almost halved in quantity.

When we turn to trade in services it is no surprise to find that the UK's net income from financial services has grown dramatically as the City's banking and financial business has grown. This net income represents the profits, fees and commissions that UK-based banks, finance houses, insurance companies and related activities receive from their international business. After allowing for inflation the net income of the City within this category (which excludes interest and dividends received) tripled between 1966 and 1977, but then it was almost stationary until rising by a further 20 per cent in the three years preceding 1983.

We shall try to put into perspective these changes in the UK's trade when we consider their international context in section 1.4. Before doing so, we should look at what has happened to direct investment and portfolio investment, for all three are related.

1.3.3   Direct foreign investment

In quantifying the UK's foreign trade it is easy to think of it as being carried out between independent British and foreign firms. Firms in the UK, it can be assumed, import goods and services from foreign firms and export merchandise to others. But to a large, and increasing, extent that is a false picture. In many cases imports and exports take place between the different branches of international firms; they occur *within* firms rather than between them. A typical example would be a decision by Ford to manufacture cars in its German factory and ship them to its UK enterprise for sale in this country. More than this, such transactions involve the production and movement of parts, for example gear-boxes from one country will be imported for cars being assembled in the same company's factory in another country.

Multinational corporations build up their global networks through **direct foreign investment**, that is, by building factories and warehouses in foreign countries and taking over or establishing companies in them. That direct investment is itself controversial. If a British multinational invests in plant abroad, it is often argued that it weakens British industry because the resources could have been used to invest in new production in the UK. Against these criticisms of direct investment abroad, it is sometimes argued that the profits generated by the foreign factory will be a long-term benefit to all UK citizens. A third view could be that such investment is not an element in a zero-sum game: investment abroad is not a simple net loss to UK plants but, instead, creates productive facilities which complement and are integrated with UK production.

Multinational corporations have an unusually large role in the UK's economy. The UK's stock of overseas direct investments is second only to that of the United States, considerably ahead of West Germany's and Japan's, although those countries' enterprises abroad have grown considerably since the 1960s. At the same time, the UK is also the 'host country' to an unusually large stock of assets owned by foreign multinationals, ranking third behind Canada, which has a large presence of US companies, and the US itself (Ietto-Gillies, 1987, Table 3.1). The outward flow of direct investment by British multinationals is high in manufacturing industry: moreover it has recently been increasing. At the same time, however, there has also been a large, but lower, flow of inward investment. This does not directly tell us anything about the 'weakness' or 'strength' of UK manufacturing, but it is interesting to note the sectoral distribution: UK multinationals in the food, drink and tobacco industry export more capital through this route than comes in; in mechanical engineering the inflow greatly surpasses the outflow, while in electrical engineering UK multinationals export more capital than foreign firms bring in.

1.3.4 Financial (portfolio) investment

The third major link between the UK and the international economy is **financial or portfolio investment**. This consists of money that banks, finance houses, pension funds, insurance companies and other financial institutions invest outside the country in which they are based, and it is invested in financial instruments and securities of all kinds ranging from bank deposits to bonds issued by governments and corporations. In principle, therefore, it is different from direct investment: while the latter is associated with multinational corporations' overseas plants and enterprises, portfolio investment relates to the international borrowing, lending and investment of the City.

At the height of Britain's imperial role, at the end of the nineteenth and beginning of this century, there was a considerable outflow of investment, in the form of both direct investment and financial investment by the City in foreign bonds and securities. Whole strata of the British middle classes lived on the income received in the form of interest and dividends from such investments. By the end of the Second World War, however, that had greatly changed. There were strict controls over the export of capital and the City's ability to invest abroad (outside the group of countries known as the Overseas Sterling Area and consisting to a large extent of former members of the Empire) was restricted. Throughout the 1950s, '60s and '70s these restrictions were reduced or became a less important hindrance to the City's international operations, but they remained partially effective until they were completely abolished in 1979. Until then, financial institutions had to pay a premium to obtain dollars from a restricted pool in order to invest finance overseas. As a result, pension funds, insurance companies and other institutions held relatively few of their investments in foreign securities, but as soon as these restrictions were lifted the City embarked on a huge outflow of funds.

Between 1979 and 1986 the UK's portfolio investments overseas rose as the annual outflow increased. The role of pension funds in this outflow is often taken as indicative for, since the mid-1960s, pension funds have become the main channel for employees' long-term savings and their overseas investment is sometimes seen as a 'diversion' of savings that could otherwise have been used to finance productive investment in British industry. Whether one accepts that view or not – and I do not think that it is valid in its simple form (see Fine and Harris (1985)) – it is a powerful one; in that context, the fact that the proportion of foreign assets in UK pension funds' total investments has risen is a mark of the power that the post-1979 boom in the City's foreign investment has had.

It is important to note, however, that portfolio investment is a two-way affair. At the same time as the City has increased its foreign investment, financial institutions in other countries have increased their financial investments in the UK, buying UK bonds, securities and bank deposits. Portfolio investments into the UK have increased strongly. Once again, the economy has become yet more 'open'.

Summary of section 1.3

●   During the 'long boom' the UK's economy did not perform as well as those of other advanced capitalist countries and this was due to the relative decline of manufacturing industry. That phenomenon is known as *deindustrialization*.

●   In international trade the UK's net exports of manufactured goods declined until imports eventually came to exceed exports. However, the level of total exports and of exports of manufactures rose throughout the long boom and the 1970s.

●   In direct foreign investment the UK is marked by a high proportion of multinational companies having their headquarters in the country. In the other direction, the UK also hosts a high proportion of branches of foreign multinational companies. Over the post-war period the flow of direct investment out of and into the UK has grown.

●   In portfolio investment UK banks, pension funds and other financial institutions have invested a high proportion of finance abroad. This is particularly true for the period since 1979. At the same time increased inflows of financial capital have occurred.

1.4   The changing international economy

The changing international position of the UK economy described in the preceding section reflects changes in both the UK itself and the international economy. This section outlines some of the main characteristics of the changes in the international economy over the post-war period and starts to draw out some implications for our understanding of the UK's position in it. A thorough and more extensive review of these changes in the global economy is given by *Thrift** (1986). Two concepts are key to these developments: internationalization and multilateralism.

* An author's name in italics indicates that this article has been reprinted in the Reader associated with this book (Massey, D. and Allen, J. (eds) (1988)).

1.4.1 Internationalization

Internationalization is the notion that each country's economy has become less self-contained and more a part of a global process of production and change. This has been particularly marked in production as multinational corporations organize their processes on a worldwide scale and 'source' parts for their finished products from factories, workshops and even domestic labour ['putting-out' or 'homeworkers'] linked in an international network. Associated with this internationalization of production, sales and purchases have become increasingly international as products are made for a world market rather than for 'local' national buyers. And the accumulation of capital has been internationalized by the internationalization of production: it has generated flows of direct investment as multinationals expand their enterprises in different countries and it has also indirectly generated flows of portfolio investment as the multinationals' cash and financing needs have been channelled through the financial markets of the City, New York and Tokyo.

This internationalization is a worldwide phenomenon and the changes in the UK's foreign trade, direct investment and portfolio investments have occurred within that context; they differ from the experience of other countries in the face of these global changes because the particular history and structure of each country is distinct.

Saying that worldwide internationalization is a key concept in explaining the changes in the UK's position may sound like stating the obvious. But, as was explained in sections 1.1 and 1.2, it differs markedly from the alternative, commonly held perspective which sees each country's economy as essentially an integrated whole, exporting any surplus of goods, capital or finance, or importing in response to a deficit. That perspective generally sees the UK's international performance as stemming from its internal strengths and weaknesses. At any one time, both types of force are in play and the UK's international economic position reflects both its internal dynamic as a definite, structured, national economy and the changes which reflect the internationalization of economic processes across the world and hence, in different ways, affect all countries. But, although both are in play, internationalization has become increasingly important and, in some senses, the dominant dimension over the post-war period.

The counterposing of internationalization and national economic forces is not a purely theoretical issue, for it has a definite concrete implication. If the UK economy were principally a national economy, its external relations would result from internal surpluses (or deficits) and broad specialization. If there were an excess of saving in the country, capital would be exported, either as direct or portfolio investment. Trade in goods would arise from broad specialization of the 'workshop of the world' type, for example exporting manufactures and importing primary goods. Any overall surplus of exports over imports would result from an excess of saving and a lack of consumption and investment within the economy. By contrast, if the economy were highly internationalized there would be strong two-way flows in all categories. There would be direct investment both inward and outward as different multinationals arrange their operations on a global basis instead of direct investment only in one direction resulting from the overall balance of the economy. Trade in goods and services would, similarly, be a two-way flow in all categories. Instead of the UK being especially good at manufacturing, say, chemicals and bad at producing food, it would both import and export chemicals and food as a multitude of purchasers and sellers made their decisions as 'world citizens'. As production is internationalized, an increased proportion of trade in manufactures would be accounted for by manufactured parts being shipped between branches of multinational corporations. The flows of trade and capital discussed in sections 1.3.2 to 1.3.4 indicate that the growth of these complex two-way flows has become the most important factor in the UK's international position. The deficit on the UK's trade in manufactures is in the context of a rise in exports and imports as manufacturing is internationalized. And the rise in overseas investment is the *net* result of an increase in both inflows and outflows.

1.4.2 Multilateralism

Together with internationalization, multilateralism has helped to shape Britain's economic position in the post-war world. The growth of internationalization has not been purely autonomous and spontaneous. It is the result of conscious planning by multinational corporations and banks and it results from the conscious actions taken by the US and UK governments in building the post-war world. The institutions and arrangements they built were driven by an idea of **multilateralism**. Basically, this is the principle that the transactions between the UK and other countries take place without restriction so that trade and investment with any country is as possible and open as with any other. Multilateralism is the opposite of bilateralism under which a country's trade and investment is arranged on a reciprocal basis with specific partners. A point of greater relevance to the UK is that it also differs greatly from trading and investment blocs under which a country's trade and investment flows to countries within the bloc are free but there are restrictions between the bloc as a whole and the rest of the world. At the end of the Second World War the US and UK set out to construct a new order for international trade and investment, a set of institutions and arrangements that became known as the Bretton Woods system. Its watchword was multilateralism.

The Bretton Woods institutions are the International Monetary Fund (IMF), the World Bank, and the third, which emanated indirectly from the negotiations at Bretton Woods, is the General Agreement on Tariffs and Trade (GATT). The multilateralism they sought to construct was a reduction and eventual abolition of all countries' restrictions on trade and investment, such as those on the convertibility of one currency into another and on foreign investments, as well as import duties and import quotas. The strongest motivation for inscribing multilateralism in the new world order came from the United States and had definite implications for the UK. A large part of the world had special trading and investment relations with the UK stemming mainly from the ties forged during the earlier days of the Empire. These countries could trade with Britain without being subject to the import duties and restrictions that applied to other countries and British capital could be invested in Sterling Area countries without restriction. The results were evident in people's everyday lives. We ate New Zealand lamb and dairy products; British factories used Malaysian rubber and tin; British machines were sold to India; and British capital was invested heavily in South Africa. The American push for multilateralism in the new post-war order was designed to enable US firms to break into this protected British sphere of influence and other protected blocs.

The principle of multilateralism has been pursued with varying degrees of success and sincerity in the post-war world. To take two extreme examples, while Third World countries have been pressured to dismantle barriers against imports in the 1970s and 1980s, the United States and the European Community have built and maintained high protective walls against agricultural imports. What has the overall result been? I think that, if we concentrate on trade first, there have been two trends, operating simultaneously:

1   A general opening up of economies to multilateral trade. This has resulted: from a succession of negotiating rounds within the framework of GATT to reduce tariff levels on a wide range of imports (with important exceptions); from the policies the IMF and, more recently, the World Bank and other aid agencies have imposed on poor countries to liberalize imports; and from the policies several countries have pursued (especially under World Bank tutelage) to expand their export sectors.

2   The creation of new trading blocs as the old ones are dismantled. Within the context of the overall expansion of multilateral trade, some old trading blocs with preferred trading arrangements between the members, such as the system of Commonwealth preference, have been dismantled, but new ones have been constructed, such as the European Community.

Both of these forces have had a powerful impact on the UK's trade. For example, the overall move toward multilateralism has enabled countries such as South Korea and Taiwan to emerge as major manufacturing economies exporting their products to growing markets throughout the world. These newly industrialized countries have, in turn, sharply changed the degree of competition in world trade faced by UK manufacturers in sectors as varied as clothing and shipbuilding. At the same time, the construction of new trading blocs and dismantling of the old have greatly shifted the pattern of the UK's trade: as the Commonwealth's preferential trading system was dismantled and the EC trading bloc was constructed, the proportion of UK imports and exports traded with Commonwealth countries declined while the proportion traded with the six initial members of the EC rose strongly.

The strategy of multilateralism concerns capital movements as well as trade, and, in some sense, has even greater significance there. As it has been pursued, shifts in the internationalization of capital in the UK have occurred. When we look at UK multinational corporations' direct investment we again see the impact of the break-up of the Commonwealth as an economic bloc: in the early 1960s Commonwealth countries accounted for 60 per cent of the UK's overseas direct assets, but by 1984 this figure had declined to 32 per cent (taking account of current and ex-Commonwealth countries). As capital flows became more open and multilateral, this shift away from the Commonwealth was matched by a shift toward direct investment in Western Europe and the US. Thus, the internationalization of the UK economy has increasingly meant investment in the advanced capitalist countries of Western Europe and the US until they have come to far outweigh UK investment in the Third World or in other Commonwealth countries.

1.5   Theoretical frameworks

So far, we have looked at some of the features of four periods of structural change in the UK economy and some of the main developments in the international connections of the UK economy from the 1940s until the recent period of structural change. Now, in this section we look at three distinct theoretical frameworks that attempt to explain the nature of these changes.

The theoretical frameworks we will consider are 'long-wave' theories, 'world-system' theories and 'regulationist' theories. They differ in the ways in which they approach the economy along three dimensions and emphasize each to a different extent:

1   The economy's *international* relations. Broadly, this means a concern for the position of the country in the international economy and the ways in which that international economy should be conceptualized.

2   The economy's *internal* structure. This includes the relations between different sectors of the economy, the relations between classes and between different social groups, and the geographical pattern of industry, employment and other economic phenomena.

3   The economy's *history* over time. This includes a concern with the distinction between periods of major structural change and other periods, and a concern with cyclical patterns.

Long-wave theories are concerned with how the economy fluctuates over long time periods. To the extent that their international dimension is explicit, many exponents of those theories view these fluctuations as embracing

all the advanced capitalist countries simultaneously. The main internal relations they are concerned with are those which generate waves of innovation by industrial enterprises.

World-system theories emphasize the international character of the capitalist economy. The capitalist world-system is viewed as all-embracing so
that the internal structure of each nation's economy is of secondary importance in explaining developments. This world system and its evolution are
seen as providing a historical framework, an account of world history.

Regulationist theories, by contrast, see the internal relations and structure of each nation's economy as primary. The international economy consists of relations beween these national entities and is shaped by them
rather than by a world system which dominates and determines national
conditions. The changes in the ways in which these national economies are
regulated account for their historical development.

The long-wave, world-systems and regulationist theories are broad
frameworks to which several writers have contributed and each has given a
new twist to the framework they use. Let us look at them in more detail.

1.5.1   Long-wave theories

The name most associated with long-wave theories is Kondratiev, a Soviet
economist, who is widely believed to have been the first to develop the
theory. Kondratiev's basic proposition was that the advanced capitalist
economies as a whole (although he concentrated on a selected few only) go
through cycles of booms and slumps in a regular pattern. From beginning
to end, each cycle of boom and slump lasts, Kondratiev argued, for about
fifty years.

There is some doubt about whether historical data do show the existence
of a regular cycle of approximately fifty years, but the idea has attracted
much attention in the 1980s. At first sight at least, it would appear to fit
with experience. The UK's factory closures, high unemployment and dislocation of trade of 1980–1 came with surprising exactitude virtually fifty
years after the slump of 1931–33. Surprisingly, that is, for mainstream
economists, who had assumed that Keynesian economic management
would abolish such crashes, but without surprise for the few who had remembered Kondratiev's ideas.

Such excellent timing does not settle the matter, however. It still leaves
room for doubt about whether a fifty-year cycle is evident from the data.
Assuming one is evident, Kondratiev's discovery alone does not add up to
a theoretical framework. Even if the early 1980s mark the trough of the
latest Kondratiev cycle we have little idea of what is happening to the UK
economy unless we can explain what gives rise to these long waves. Long-
wave theorists rely upon fluctuations in **innovation** by firms for most of
their explanatory power. They argue that major innovations in products,
or production techniques, are bunched together every fifty years or so and,

when they occur, they have pervasive effects, generating a long boom which eventually peters out and turns into a slump. For example, it could be argued that a boom and slump lasting in total from about 1790 to 1840 was initiated by the Industrial Revolution's typical innovations (cotton spinning and weaving; new methods of iron production; steam power); that from the mid-1840s a new boom was generated by the development of railways which initiated a fifty-year cycle; that from the 1890s a new boom and long cycle stemmed from electrification.

If those historic innovations did, in fact, launch long booms and subsequent slumps, similar innovations would, within this framework, be central to our understanding of the position of the UK economy in the 1980s. The rise in unemployment and the fall in output at the start of the decade could be seen as the low point of a cycle which started with the 1930s' innovations in chemical industries and light engineering and generated the new consumer durable industries that fuelled the long post-Second-World-War boom. On this view, the 1980s are to be followed by a new long boom initiated by a series of innovations. Information technology, electronics and genetic engineering are the obvious candidates.

The long-wave framework, therefore, has considerable appeal for interpreting modern structural change. The theoretical view seems to offer a convenient framework for a broad division of history into periods which can be described by innovations that appear to be characteristic of each. But is description enough? If long waves exist and are caused by the bunching of innovations, how can we explain that bunching? Moreover, how do the bunched innovations have their effect on the economy as a whole? Long-wave theories have devoted most attention to the question of why the bunching exists.

Schumpeter (1934, 1939) explained the bunching of innovations which generated long-waves by the characteristics of entrepreneurs as industrial leaders. Innovation requires people with the special qualities of 'entrepreneurship', although their psychology is such that innovation is greatly affected by the state of the economy. A major recession makes innovation risky and discourages it, but in such a period the more adventurous entrepreneurs see the opportunity to profit by investing in new innovations. From their example, people with less entrepreneurial ability will see that risks have been overcome and profits made, and they will follow the leaders generating a swarm of innovations. They will be concentrated in the same industries and come on stream as the economy is beginning its recovery from the depression.

A modern writer, Mensch (1980), has argued in a rather different way from Schumpeter that innovations are bunched. He and others such as Freeman, Clark and Soete (1982) concentrate on what generates the bunching of major or 'basic' innovations. In Mensch's theory the cluster of innovations comes in the depths of recession and is sparked by the low level of profits. He argues that the depression marks the exhaustion of firms' ability to obtain profits from the last generation of innovations and their low profit rates force them to take radical steps. Across a range of industries, major innovations are implemented in attempts to stem the decline in profits. This does not necessarily involve a search for new inventions, but, rather, a concerted shortening of the lead-time between the inventions and their implementation in the form of new innovations. Although Mensch's theory is in the same tradition as Schumpeter's, the mechanism that triggers the clustering of innovations is industry's common experience of low rates of profit as the profitability of the old family of technology that fuelled the last boom is exhausted.

The principal focus of long-wave theories is historical, offering a framework for conceiving the movement of economies over time so that, if they help us understand the modern UK economy, they do so by locating the present in a pattern that covers the past and the future. Thus the 1980s are seen as marked by the wholesale adoption of new technology replacing the legacy of the past and setting the terms of a future long boom. Writers in this tradition do touch on some spatial dimensions but they are not central. For example, although Kondratiev saw long waves as international, embracing all the advanced capitalist societies simultaneously, that was more of an empirical observation than an attempt to understand spatial relationships. His theory did not attempt to explain how long waves are generated at the international level or the mechanisms by which national economies' cyclical movements are linked. Nor does it show how the international sphere affects the long cycle; no consideration is given to how the international structure of industry affects innovation and the propagation of long waves or how innovation affects industry's internationalization.

1.5.2 World-system theories

'World-system theory' refers to one school of social scientists. Its main exponent is Wallerstein (1974), but the term is used here to describe a slightly broader group (including writers like Amin (1976) and Frank (1967)) whose work shares some similarities with Wallerstein's. The main characteristic of their theories is the idea that an individual economy or country is only one part of a complete and structured world system. In order to understand what is happening in that country we have to see its internal developments as the effects of what is happening to the international economy as a whole. In the words of Wallerstein:

> I abandoned the idea altogether of taking either the sovereign state or that vague concept, the national society, as the unit of analysis. I decided that neither one was a social system and that one could only speak of social change in social systems. The only social system in this scheme was the world-system. I could explain changes in the sovereign states as consequent upon the evolution and interaction of the world-system. (Wallerstein, 1974, p. 7)

This view appears disarmingly general but widely acceptable when it is stated as the idea that any economy has to be seen as only one part of a structured world system. But, as the quotation from Wallerstein shows, his world-system approach is more narrowly defined than that, for what happens in the UK (or other countries) is seen as *wholly subordinate* to changes in the world system. The world system is the unit of analysis for understanding all changes, even local changes.

World-system theories did not originate in the study of phenomena like the modern UK economy. Instead, writers like Wallerstein, Frank and Amin were principally attempting to understand Africa, Latin America and the Third World within this framework. Their perspectives were strongly historical with Wallerstein in particular applying his theoretical framework to understand the historical creation of the world system. Nevertheless, the main ideas in these theories are frequently found in studies which relate more directly to the changes in the UK economy in the 1980s.

A prominent example is the research conducted in the 1970s on the development of a new international division of labour. Frobel, Heinrichs and Dreye (1980) start from a basic proposition that: 'These national economies are organic elements of one all-embracing system, namely a world economy which is in fact a single worldwide capitalist system ... the structural changes in individual national economies are interrelated within this single world economy' (p. 8). They go on to argue that the 1970s saw a new phase in the world economy, a development they call the *new international division of labour*.

> ... for the first time in the history of the 500-year-old world economy, the profitable production of manufactures for the world market has finally become possible to a significant and increasing extent, not only in the industrialized countries, but also now in the developing countries. Furthermore, commodity production is being increasingly subdivided into fragments which can be assigned to whichever part of the world can provide the most profitable combination of capital and labour. (ibid., p. 13–14)

According to Frobel *et al.* this new international division of labour has come about through two global networks. One is the network of the world market and the other is the multinational corporations that operate plants worldwide. The commodities produced in the new international division of labour are, above all, to be exported and imported either by trade between merchants on the world market or by transfer (as semi-finished parts of finished articles) from one branch of a multinational corporation to another branch. Moreover the multinational corporations are responsible for the investment in plants around the globe, establishing new capitalist, industrial operations in each country with each plant performing a part of the labour that goes into producing commodities. What changes in the 1970s set up the forces, working through the world market and multinational corporation networks, to generate a new international division of labour? Frobel *et al.* identify three factors which are the culmination of long historical forces coming together in the 1970s:

1   The growth of a huge reserve of labour available in Third World coun-

tries to be employed in new industrial processes at low wages and under poor terms of employment.

2   The division and subdivision of production processes have reached a stage where each operation can be performed with minimal skills.

3   The development of transport and communications techniques enables corporations to plan their production on a worldwide basis.

The results of these forces are, they argue, felt in Third World countries and simultaneously in the UK and other European and North American economies (their empirical research relates mainly to the Federal Republic of Germany). In industries of all types, ranging from textiles to automobiles and electronics, multinational corporations have transferred work to the Third World by setting up plants where cheap labour performed the most labour-intensive sub-processes in manufacturing. What hitherto had been integrated plants in countries like the UK, carrying out complete manufacturing processes, are closed down and rationalized in order to manufacture products more cheaply from parts manufactured by workers divided between a number of countries. In the UK this had led to high unemployment and the overall decline in manufacturing that marked 'deindustrialization' in the early 1980s.

There is considerable evidence to show that manufacturing in multinational corporations has been reorganized along the lines described above. And there is little doubt that the run-down of whole sectors of UK industry has been associated with it, but the interpretation given by world-system theories is a particular one. In terms of the three dimensions of theories identified earlier, world-system theories hold a particular interpretation of each. They have a strong historical dimension, but their treatment of the new international division of labour indicates that it is limited by its generality. Why, for example, did the three forces mentioned (the growth of a reserve of cheap labour; the subdivision of manufacturing processes; the new methods of communication and transport) culminate together in the 1970s? What was their history: had they progressed smoothly or with fits and starts? What other forces bore upon the changes in manufacturing? They also have a strong *international* dimension since they argue that these forces are aspects 'of the continued development of world economy, an economy which can only be understood as a single, integrated system'. But this is only one kind of international dimension, only one way of understanding the geography of the international economy. In this account the world is seen as one where individual countries are completely subordinate to the general world system, in contrast to an international economy being created by the interplay of different countries which are themselves prime actors. Consequently, the *national* dimension is not strongly present in these theories.

For the UK this means that the run-down of many sectors of manufacturing is treated as if it is unconnected with the policies of successive UK governments, with the qualities of management and the character of British trade unionism. Moreover, in the example looked at here – the theory of the new international division of labour – there is a concentration on one type of economic activity – large multinational capital in manufacturing – whereas the study of the national economy of the UK would require distinctions to be made between different types of capitalist enterprise. Small and medium-sized firms as well as multinational corporations interact in UK manufacturing, and manufacturing firms interact with financial institutions and other enterprises in the growing service sector.

1.5.3   Regulationist theories

The theoretical framework of regulation was developed in France in the 1970s and first published as a coherent and comprehensive approach to studying the dynamics of capitalist economies by Aglietta (1979). In a more recent application of this framework, Aglietta (1982) has explicitly brought out the underlying spatial conception of his theory. In direct contrast to the world-system perspective he starts from 'the primacy of the national dimension'. International economic developments have a central role, but he 'regards the world economy as a system of interacting national social formations'. From this viewpoint, the regulationist theories give a rather different account of economies like the UK's from that of world-system theories.

  The central question in this framework is how the production and growth (*accumulation*) of the advanced capitalist economies is regulated. Instead of assuming that their development progresses along a smooth and unproblematic path it is assumed that there have to be mechanisms and policies to overcome constantly recurring disequilibria and attempts to gain some sort of balance (for example, between agriculture and industry; between the amounts available for consumption and for investment in new capital; between money and financial capital on one hand and production on the other; and, especially, between capital and labour). Taking the national economy as the basic unit of analysis, regulation is analysed at two levels: the mechanisms of regulation *within* the country's economy, and those mechanisms that regulate the economic relations *between* countries.

  The mechanisms within each economy regulate the relations between labour and capital on one hand and between different types of capital on the other. The former include: the system of management, the labour process and the system of wage payments; the role of market forces in determining prices and wages; and also the policies of the state toward incomes control and welfare provision. Some countries in particular periods have flexible wages and prices which, at times of unemployment, change so as to reduce the real value of wages. The US in the first half of the 1980s appears to have had such a mechanism whereas in the UK the real wages of employees did not respond flexibly to high unemployment by falling. During the long post-war boom, argues Aglietta, such flexibility had not been an important regulating mechanism. The internal mechanisms regulating relations between different enterprises and industries during the long post-war boom had less to do with price competition between enterprises and, in countries like the UK, more to do with state policies. In the UK, as compared with the state planning and support of enterprises carried out in, say, Japan and France, these state policies were half-hearted and failed to generate high rates of industrial growth by international standards. But they were pervasive, ranging from policies on the taxation of profits to regional assistance schemes. Another mechanism regulating the industrial post-war boom was the banking system (in West Germany, for example), although in the UK neither the banks nor the financial markets of the Stock Exchange played that role. If they did have an effect, it was in a negative direction discouraging long-term planning (Fine and Harris, 1985).

At the international level Aglietta argues that the principal mechanism regulating the economic relations between national states is the international financial system. This system in turn rests on and reflects the domination (or hegemony) of particular nations. The growth of international trade during the long post-war boom and the internationalization of production which have given rise to the new international division of labour occurred under a system where exchange rates were stable over long periods of time, and international finance was dominated by the US dollar, the US economy and Washington's policies. By contrast, the regulation of the international economy in earlier periods had been under the domination of London, pivoting around London's capital markets and the pound sterling which acted as the main form of international money.

The regulationist approach explains periods of structural change such as the 'crossroads years' of the 1970s and 1980s in terms of the breakdown of one mode of regulation and the possible shifts toward a new one.

The most fundamental shift identified by these writers for the 1970s/1980s period is in the structure of production: this embraces the methods of production (or labour process), the strategies of management and the relations between unions, management and the state. One of the main theses of the regulationist school is that in the 1970s/1980s there has been a decisive shift from *Fordism* (named after the company in which its introduction is most famed) to *neo-Fordism*. Central to Fordism is the mass production of particular models (of cars, textiles, tools or washing-machines, for example), manufactured in long runs on assembly lines which involved massive investment in inflexible fixed plant. This was accompanied by corporatist relations between unions, management and the state under which, although conflicts existed, there was consensus on the state's tasks in managing the economy's overall balance. The state was responsible for full employment policies. At the heart of neo-Fordism is the development of flexible specialization to replace the rigid assembly-line system of production. Technological changes such as computer-assisted design and computer-based inventory and production control have made small-batch production economical and facilitated the decentralization of production. Parts can be produced in many different locations and ordered for assembly in batches thus avoiding the need for large, inflexible holdings of inventories. As a consequence, labour has become decentralized, less tied to large factories and rigid hours. Large-scale unionism has declined and management has been able to organize the labour process directly without concern for unions' power. The state has made labour markets more flexible by abandoning both its commitment to full employment and corporatist arrangements involving consultation between unions, management and the state. Regulationists argue that Fordism was part of and was sustained by the United States' dominance at the international level and the shift to neo-Fordism has coincided with a challenge to the United States' domination of the international economy.

Aglietta argues that several developments brought the post-war structure of Fordism to an end, and in particular undermined the international mechanisms of integration upon which US hegemony was based. One was a technological convergence which raised productivity levels in European and Japanese industry and thereby diminished the absolute superiority of US industry. Another, and most potent force, was the development of new forms of international money and international debt (summarized by the term Eurodollars) which are outside the control of any national economy so that the hegemonic power that the US exercised through the international use of its currency was undermined. That structure of international regulation broke down in the 1970s and has been followed by a period of instability where it is uncertain whether US hegemony can be re-established or whether a different mode of regulation under Japanese or European domination will be constructed. A corollary of the breakdown of the old structure of international regulation would appear to be the breakdown of internal, national mechanisms. In the UK the new instability of exchange rates and international financial markets was followed, in 1976, by the abandonment of Keynesian policies to sustain full employment and, since 1979, by changes in the roles of the state, management and trade unions in influencing (regulating) the pace and direction of production and growth.

The regulationist approach, therefore, would view the major changes in the UK economy in the 1980s as resulting from a breakdown of the old structures of international and national regulation. Its future direction depends on what new structures are constructed and, in particular, on whether European, Japanese or US hegemony is established at the international level. This theoretical framework clearly has a strong *historical* dimension. Because it considers that capitalist economies are fundamentally in disequilibrium and each regulation system which controls them breaks down eventually, its view of history does not include the regular and predictable cyclical pattern of long-wave theory. And because it is always uncertain whether a new system of regulation can be smoothly established when the old one breaks down, the regulationist approach does not share worldsystem theories' perspective of inexorable capitalist expansion in which all developments are seen as functional for and planned by capital as a whole.

The regulationist approach also has a strong *international* dimension, regarding the mechanism by which the international economy is regulated as important for every part of it. But its conception of the international economy is different from that of world-system theories because it sees it as created and conditioned by the rivalry between different nation-states. The competition between the US and Europe, for example, and the long hegemony of the US have determined its character rather than the general laws of an undifferentiated world economy. The rivalry and interaction between advanced capitalist economies is a feature of this theoretical framework which is absent from world-system theories.

Finally, the regulationist theories' emphasis on the nation-state makes it amenable to studying the *internal* structure of a country. Thus, the respective roles of the state, labour and different types of capital (such as large industrial enterprises, other enterprises and financial institutions) can be distinguished, and the ways in which they have interacted to produce recent economic changes can be analysed. Those economic changes, in turn, have implications for the changing urban and regional structure of a country.

Summary of section 1.5

Long-wave theories

• The central idea of long-wave theories is that advanced capitalist economies go through a regular cycle of boom and slump with each trough or peak occurring approximately fifty years apart.

• An explanation advanced for this is that industrial innovations generate expansion. These expansions are compressed into booms, followed by slumps, over the fifty-year cycles because innovations are bunched into compressed periods.

World-system theories

• World-system theories treat the world system as the fundamental unit of analysis. Each national economy is not only seen as part of that world economic (and social) system, it is treated as subordinate to its global forces.

• An empirical application of this theoretical framework is the work of Frobel *et al.* on the new international division of labour. This has arisen, it is argued, through the operation of the world market and multinational corporations. The factors which made it a reality in the 1970s are a pool of cheap labour, new production processes and new communications methods.

Regulationist theories

• Regulationist theories assert that advanced capitalist economies are marked by a succession of distinct historical stages which differ from each other in terms of the organization of production within each economy. For a long period before the 1970s they were Fordist; in the 1970s/1980s period of structural change neo-Fordism came to dominate.

• At the international level regulationist theorists argue that the national economy is the basic unit of analysis. The international economy consists of relations between coherent national economies and the hegemony of one national economy over the international economy is an important aspect of it.

1.6   Conclusion: the international economy and structural change

How do the three theoretical frameworks help us to understand the international aspects of the latest crossroads of the United Kingdom economy? How do the theoretical frameworks relate to the UK's experience described in sections 1.2 and 1.3? In this section we address this question by examining how the differing theories approach, first, the international dimension and, second, structural change.

1.6.1   The international economy

Each period of structural change in the UK economy has involved major changes in its international position. However, as noted in section 1.1, there are two possible interpretations of an economy's international position. Either we can think of the UK and every other economy as a coherent whole with a dynamic of its own or we can think of it as subordinate to the world economy such that its parts are the cogs of an international economy and have no coherence on a national basis. The theories reviewed in the previous section clearly divide along these lines, with world-system theories using the latter concept while regulationist theories use the former. How do they relate to the UK's experience of periods of structural change?

Regulationists' view of a coherent national economy with international links is, in my opinion, consistent with the 1830s/1840s crossroads. Recall from section 1.5.3 that the regulationist school sees the international economy as having one national economy in a hegemonic position; a period of structural change can thus be one in which that hegemony is consolidated or challenged and undermined. Equally, it is one in which the pattern of uneven development at the international level changes in line with the shifting relations of domination and subordination between countries. At the time of the 1830s/1840s crossroads, for example, the UK economy dominated all others and the changes in that period helped to consolidate its hegemony. From the end of the Napoleonic Wars in 1815, England had been the dominant financial and commercial power in Europe and, on that basis, in the global economy; the structural changes in the 1830s and 1840s were to consolidate that hegemony. Apart from the impetus that new railways gave to British industrial strength, railway-building abroad was the means for an expansion of British capital overseas, through loans to railway companies and states, and the export of British capitalism itself in the establishment of British enterprises and railway companies abroad.

The regulationist school could give a similar interpretation to the hegemony of national economies in each of the other periods of structural change in the UK economy. The 1880s/1890s were marked by an early challenge to the UK's hegemony by the industrialization of Germany, other European countries and the United States. They were also marked by the rivalry between these growing capitalist powers for colonial markets and sources of supply in Africa and other non-industrialized regions. The 1930s and 1940s saw the collapse of UK hegemony and the consolidation of the United States' hegemony over a new international economic system. The subsequent decades saw a growth of internationalization and multilateralism within this system until the crossroads of the 1970s and 1980s where the United States' hegemony over the international system was interrupted. Its end was marked by the instability of the dollar and the end of US financial domination, and much of the chaos of this period was attributable to the fact that no other country had come to take a hegemonic role.

The regulationist school can, therefore, give a cogent account of the international economy in periods of structural change; and its concept of the international economy as consisting of the relations between coherent national economies with one dominant over the others appears credible.

The conception of the international economy held by world-system theories is, in my view, less effective, although it gives a forceful account of contemporary changes in comparison with earlier periods. That theory's notion of a world economy is, in its simplest form, based on the view that, since the inception of capitalism in Europe, every part of the globe is linked together through a world market and, thereafter, all that happens obeys the logic of that world market so as to generate profits for enterprises in the advanced capitalist countries. That conception makes it difficult to address sharp unheavals in the international system that occur in many periods of structural change, the rivalry between different countries that occurs in international trade and finance, or the impact that a country's internal conditions (such as the structure of its unions and management) have on its international position. In the case of the UK's crossroads, for example, that approach pays scant attention to the break-up of the UK's position at the centre of the Sterling Area and Commonwealth trade in the 1970s, or to the responsibility of unions, management, the financial system and the state for manufacturing industry's poor productivity growth and hence declining international competitiveness during the long boom leading up to the structural changes of the 1970s/1980s period.

It is difficult to strictly demarcate the two approaches since each has been used and interpreted in a variety of ways. For example, the world-system perspective outlined here is its simplest version with the basic features that its proponents put forward. But the writers who use world-system theories in empirical studies of particular countries' economic history include features that draw it closer to regulationist theory: for example, the uncertainty, problems and changes associated with conflicts over international hegemony are often studied. The two approaches, therefore, are not hermetically sealed units, impenetrable to each other. They are distinct, but they overlap in certain respects, albeit in areas that do not challenge their basic theoretical viewpoints.

1.6.2   Structural change

What is it about the changes that occur in a crossroads period that mark them out as structural changes, distinct from the movement and change experienced during the intervening years?

One possible answer is that in periods of structural change major upheavals and dislocation are felt – a crisis is obvious – whereas in the intervening years changes occur smoothly and are felt to be less dramatic. There is some validity in that idea. Great crises do occur in the midst of structural change and, in fact, are part of the process helping to carry those changes through. The financial crises of 1929 and 1931 and the following years' dramatic collapse in trade and production helped to lay the foundations for the new industries and the new international trading blocs that began in the 1930s and 1940s, and for the new international financial system established in the 1940s. The foundations of the post-war boom in Britain were laid in those crises at the start of the 1930s. Similarly the sharp collapse of factory production in 1980 was a real crisis which could be interpreted as laying the foundations for new industries in Britain and a new set of international trading and investment relations for the UK in the 1980s.

But is it enough to say that periods of structural change are marked by crises? For events that appear to be crises at the time (although not in a longer perspective) occur even in the intervening years. In Britain the apparently smooth growth during the long boom was marked by dramatic events that, at the time, seemed to be crises: for example, the 1957 credit squeeze and record interest rate jump, the sterling crisis and cuts in government spending plans in 1966, and the devaluation of 1967. We need some way to distinguish such events from the crises that mark structural changes. One possible way to distinguish periods of structural change from others is to view structural change as involving an upheaval and *crisis in production* and *a change in the direction and structure of production*. Let me develop this view.

On this interpretation, some sectors of the economy are more fundamental than others. For example, the strength of industrial production could be judged as more fundamental than retailing and the City's financial dealing. They all affect each other – the growth of industry would be hampered if marketing were inadequate and industry can be disrupted by financial disruption – but on this view industrial production has a more fundamental or determining effect on the whole economy than the other sectors have. A superficial illustration of this view would be that while the collapse of the UK's steel industry, car industry and others at the end of the 1970s and early 1980s affected the whole economic landscape of the UK, generating mass unemployment in the north, the midlands and in all inner cities, the Stock Market crash in the international financial crisis of October 1987 had an impact on few people.

What does it mean to say that periods of structural change are marked by changes in the direction and structure of industrial production? One way of getting to grips with this question is to look at how the three theoretical frameworks interpret the structural changes identified in section 1.2. Each theoretical framework gives a rather different account of the meaning and significance of major industrial changes as marks of structural change.

Long-wave theories focus on changes in industrial production to the exclusion of all others and even within that sphere their subject matter is restricted to changes in material aspects of production, the hardware that is used in production or in the material goods that are produced. Recall from section 1.5.1 that these theories are concerned with innovations in production processes and products. The innovations in production processes they deal with are those embodied in new types of machinery, transport and instruments rather than innovations in the organization of labour even though the former are, in fact, closely linked to the latter. This concentration on hardware is, I think, partly responsible for the rather limited international view taken by this approach: it envisages that the bunching of innovations which generates long cycles also generates international ripples so that the innovations are diffused through the leading capitalist countries and the long cycle is international.

I call that a restricted international perspective because it does not explain or attempt to explain how production is organized internationally and, to my mind, a theory cannot do that unless it says something about the changes in the organization of labour that go along with innovations in machinery, transport, instruments and products. In the case of the structural changes occurring in the 1970s/1980s the UK's crossroads was not characterized only by computerization, information technology and the new machinery and new products that have arisen. What counts for the UK's international position is that these innovations have enabled production to take place with new types of labour, new ways of organizing labour and in new areas of the world, but long-wave theories do not consider those changes. Nor do they consider the changes in the spheres of international finance and trade that result from these changes in industrial production.

World-system theories also interpret structural change in a manner which suggests that changes in the character of industrial production are fundamental and, therefore, a defining aspect of structural change. The empirical study of the new international division of labour outlined in section 1.5.2 illustrated the importance of industrial change within this framework.

However, it differs in two ways from the approach long-wave theory takes to industrial change.

First, the world-system account of the new international division of labour argues that there is an international mechanism which links all parts of the globe into industrial shifts. In a sense that mechanism is the cause of the industrial change: the shift to a new international division of labour occurs *because* of the international market and the multinational corporations, or because they set the framework for profit-oriented production and investment. Second, this account is not solely or even primarily concerned with innovations in machinery and instruments: a central part of the analysis is the organization of labour. The way labour is organized – *the division of labour* – is itself seen as depending upon the wage levels, the availability of different skills and the extent of unionization. In other words, this approach uses a concept of industrial change which is *broader* than that used in long-wave theory.

What can this theory tell us about the changes in the UK economy's international position in the structural changes of the 1970s/1980s? It does not appear to offer any definite predictions for the future, the road that lies ahead of the crossroads. In fact its implications are, in my view, rather ambiguous and this can be shown by considering some of the basic features of the UK economy that were outlined in sections 1.3 and 1.4.

The most relevant feature is the high proportion of multinational corporations in Britain. The world-system theorists of the new international division of labour see multinational corporations as the key agents of change, so the fact that Britain has a high proportion of multinational corporations must place the country at the centre of that new international structure of industry. But there are two *possible* directions this could take. On one hand, the multinationals with their headquarters in the UK increasingly organize their worldwide production to gain the benefit of cheap labour in the Third World to carry out those parts of the manufacturing process that are labour-intensive, while the parts that are capital-intensive or rely on skilled techniques such as design are carried out in the UK. This was clearly the role that Frobel *et al.* (1980) envisaged for West Germany as its multinationals in the textile industry participated in the new international division of labour.

On the other hand, the foreign multinationals with branches in the UK could reorganize their production so that the UK itself occupies the sub-ordinate role. Labour in the UK is low-paid compared to West European and other advanced capitalist countries, so there is an incentive for multinationals to locate the labour-intensive, relatively low skilled parts of their manufacturing processes in the UK and the highly skilled or capital-intensive parts of their production processes in West Germany, Japan or the United States. For example, in the 1980s the UK appears to have hosted parts of an international car industry because it could provide a relatively cheap, disciplined and flexible labour force and, as a result, the parts of the production process it could host were similar to those found in some Third World countries.

Regulationist theories also consider industrial change as the key or fundamental aspect of structural change. Like the previous framework, regulationist theories analyse industrial change both in terms of the strongly international driving force behind it, and in terms of the social and organizational restructuring that accompanies technical change and innovation. We will look at these two aspects of the regulationist framework in the context of the UK economy, before considering how it differs from world-system theories.

This approach would interpret the UK economy's international position in the 1970s and 1980s as one in which British multinationals are engaged in a formidable rivalry with foreign-based competitors. These companies' activities on the Stock Exchange during the 1980s could be taken as evidence of this as foreign companies have mounted massive takeover bids for British ones. UK companies have themselves taken over foreign companies and, within the UK, companies have been restructured to strengthen their international position. That rivalry, however, is deeper than Stock Exchange battles. It is seen as competition between multinational corporations which requires each to adopt the most profitable organization of its production and that invariably affects the international structure of its operations.

According to this framework the late 1970s and the 1980s are a period of structural change partly because this new international structure of production has been put in place. It involves a new subdivision of manufacturing processes on an international basis under which multinational corporations based in the UK, Europe, Japan and the US have established manufacturing plants in the Third World to produce parts which are combined in branches of the multinationals in other countries.

Associated with this new international structure, the regulationist approach argues that the emergence of neo-Fordism (described in section 1.5.3) is a structural change which affects a wide area of economic and social life. Within production, computerization has produced 'automatic production control' in integrated and self-monitoring plant and machinery which has required changes in the labour process. These have occurred both within the UK and abroad in the recent period of structural change and have affected the international position of UK manufacturing. For example, new car assembly plants (such as Nissan) and electronic goods assembly plants (such as JVC) have been established in the UK by foreign multinationals and employ labour processes based on job flexibility instead of craft demarcation and specialization. The regulationist school, however, sees the structural changes that are associated with the changes in 'hardware' (the computerization) as broader than changes in the labour process. The new job flexibility has required a break-up of old trade union structures and attempts to emulate in the UK systems of labour relation based on Japanese and some US examples. On a still broader scale, this has meant that governments in the UK have decided to abandon full employment and corporatist policies, especially since 1979. Arguably this has led to the break-up of the old trade union structures and increased management's ability to obtain flexibility of labour. It also has a strong international dimension, for the abandonment of full employment policies was associated with policies on exchange rates and interest rates which greatly increased the UK economy's openness to international competition. And these high exchange rates and interest rates were particularly responsible for the 1980 collapse of manufacturing production in the UK. Another of the wide-ranging structural changes the regulationist school identify with the technical developments of neo-Fordism in the UK is a sharp increase in concentration of economic activity in the hands of multinationals.

How does this account of structural change in the UK economy in the 1970s and 1980s differ from the world-system account?

To my mind they are remarkably similar. At the centre of each is a new division of labour, a new structure of the labour process, which is based on technical innovations, especially computerization. And each would agree that this places UK manufacturing at the centre of a new international structure of manufacturing. So in what ways do they differ? In section 1.6.1 a major difference in the way they conceive of the fundamental forces that generate these changes at the international level was identified. Whereas the regulationist approach emphasizes the rivalry between each major capitalist economy and between the multinationals headquartered in each, the world-system approach, in principle, locates the driving force in a supranational international economic system. In this section we have been considering their respective accounts of structural change. The main difference, in principle, is that the version of world-system theory addressed concentrates on structural change in terms of technical innovation and the division of labour, whereas the regulationist school locates those aspects in the broader framework of changes in the structure of industrial relations, the state's economic policy, the financial structures and the concentration of industry.

There is no formal summary to this section. As many of the points developed here arise from the fuller accounts of the three theories in section 1.5, I have opted to end this chapter on an activity which highlights their points of divergence, their points of overlap and their respective view of the UK crossroads.

Activity 1.3

Turn back to the summaries of the three theoretical approaches at the end of section 1.5 and read through them again. Now place yourself inside the regulationist framework, that is, adopt the stance of a regulationist in relation to the other two theories. From the summary in section 1.5 and the last section it should be evident that the regulationists hold particular views on:

●   The structure of the international economy – that it is shaped by relations between national economies, each with their own dynamic, and it is characterized by one national economy in a hegemonic position.

- The 1970s/1980s period of structural change in the UK – that there has been a breakdown of the old structures of international and national regulation. In particular, the shift from Fordism to neo-Fordism has wrought a series of structural changes:

  – in the organization of production (from mass production to flexible specialization)

  – in management/labour relations (towards greater flexibility in the labour market)

  – in state policies (the abandonment of full employment policies and corporatist strategies), and

  – in the organizational structure of industry (increasing concentration of economic activity in multinational corporations).

From this viewpoint, what criticisms would the regulationist school have of the other two approaches in respect of:

(a) The *international perspective* held by long-wave theories (section 1.6.2).

(b) The conception of the *international economy* held by world-system theories (section 1.6.1 and summary of section 1.5).

(c) The *focus* adopted by long-wave theorists. Which features of the economy, from a regulationist standpoint, are neglected by long-wave theories in their account of structural change? What features do they both address? (section 1.6.2)

(d) The *focus* adopted by world-system theories in their account of structural change in the UK economy in the 1970s and 1980s. Which features of economic change, according to a regulationist, receive excessive attention? (section 1.6.2)

At this point, you may find it useful to turn the activity around. Put yourself in the position of either the long-wave or world-system approach to assess how they would view the regulationist approach, its account of structural changes in the UK economy and its changing international position.

Further reading

The main item of further reading I would recommend is Nigel Thrift's 'The geography of international economic disorder', in R.L. Johnston and P.J. Taylor (eds) *A World in Crisis* (Oxford, Basil Blackwell; 1986). This chapter was written with Thrift's article very much in mind; it provides a wealth of empirical material and concepts which complements this chapter's theoretical discussion. For this reason you will find it reprinted in the associated Reader (Massey, D. and Allen, J. (eds) (1988)).

Thrift's article is not specifically concerned with the UK but discusses the world economy as a whole. On the other hand, Doreen Massey's article, 'The legacy lingers on: the impact of Britain's international role on its internal geography' (Ch. 2 in Martin, R. and Rowthorn, B. (eds) (1986) *The Geography of De-Industrialisation*, London and Basingstoke, Macmillan), is concerned with the impact on the regional economy of the UK of its changed international position.

A stimulating book which carries further this chapter's discussions of the regulationist and world-system theories is Alain Lipietz' *Mirages and Miracles: The Crises of Global Fordism* (London, Verso; 1985). This book explains and extends the regulationist school's concepts of Fordism and neo-Fordism, and applies them in an analysis of the structural changes in the international economy of the 1980s. In the process, world-system theories, and particularly the idea of a new international division of labour, are critically evaluated.

The most comprehensive further reading is J. van Duijn's *The Long Wave in Economic Life* (London, Allen and Unwin; 1983).

One puzzle that stands out in considering the UK's position is what makes the UK's experiences different from those of other countries in the context of an international upheaval like that of the 1970s/1980s. This question is addressed by B. Fine and L. Harris in *The Peculiarities of the British Economy* (London, Lawrence and Wishart; 1985). A major element in the international position of the UK economy, which was partially discussed in section 1.3, is the international role of the City, as the centre of the UK's banking system. There are two other books that I co-authored which cover this aspect. The changes that occurred in the City's international role over the 1960s and '70s are explained and discussed in J. Coakley and L. Harris, *The City of Capital* (Oxford, Basil Blackwell; 1983); the international role of the City over a longer period is discussed in depth in L. Harris, T. Evans, J. Coakley and M. Croasdale, *New Directions in the Financial System* (London, Croom Helm; 1988).

2 What's happening to UK manufacturing?

Doreen Massey

Contents

2.1	**Introduction**	46
2.2	**Deindustrialization**	47
2.2.1	The economy as a whole	47
2.2.2	The relative decline of manufacturing	50
2.2.3	The absolute decline of manufacturing	52
2.2.4	Employment or output?	53
Summary of section 2.2		54
2.3	**Geographical changes**	55
2.3.1	The broad regional trends	55
2.3.2	Processes of change	57
2.3.3	Another look at deindustrialization	59
2.3.4	Within the regions: the urban-rural shift	60
2.4	**Explaining the changes**	62
2.4.1	Location factors	62
2.4.2	'Restructuring'	65
2.4.3	Urban decline	68
2.4.4	Debate	71
Summary of sections 2.3 and 2.4		72
2.5	**Explaining the changes: uneven development**	72
2.5.1	Changing patterns	73
2.5.2	Underlying relations	75
2.5.3	Change over time	77
2.6	**A historical turning-point?**	79
2.6.1	Regulationist theories	80
2.6.2	Long-wave theories	82
2.6.3	Debate	87
Summary of sections 2.5 and 2.6		88
Further reading		89

2.1   Introduction

Chapter 1 looked at the UK in an international context, but the changes that it examined have had major implications for the internal structure and organization of the economy. It is with these internal changes that the rest of this book is concerned.

This chapter focuses on manufacturing and on the current state of that part of the economy which once made the UK the workshop of the world. Very broadly, the chapter begins from recent preoccupations about decline in British manufacturing, encapsulated in the term *deindustrialization*, and ends with a major historical turning-point, for manufacturing and for the economy more widely. On the way, between these debates, the chapter examines the major changes which have recently taken place in the geography of manufacturing in the UK, and explores the important and continuing debates over how to explain them.

The relation between shifts in the national economy and changes in its geography is a central concern of the course, and runs throughout this chapter. Its exploration involves the development and use of some fundamental concepts. One of these is the concept of *structural change*, which was introduced in Chapter 1 and will be taken up again in Chapter 3. Another is the concept of *uneven development*, a term designed to capture the fact of inequality between geographical areas. This chapter introduces that term and devotes a section to the beginnings of an exploration of what it means.

Another concern of the book is indeed with concepts and with theorizing, and throughout this chapter concepts – from deindustrialization to uneven development to full employment – will be held up to scrutiny. One such concept is manufacturing. Although the term is not examined in detail here, it will be clear from both this chapter and Chapter 3 on services, as well as Chapter 6, that the division between manufacturing and services has always been blurred and is becoming, perhaps increasingly, problematical.

The chapter begins, then, by focusing on a phenomenon about which there has been much recent discussion – deindustrialization. Section 2.2 explores different definitions of deindustrialization, looking at each of them in the context of data on what has actually been happening to manufacturing in this country over recent decades. Section 2.3 turns to an examination of the geography of deindustrialization. It sets out the basic patterns, and looks at how they have changed over the years. It looks at the north-south divide, and at the shift of jobs out of major cities. It also begins to look at some of the processes which together make up these overall trends. One thing which emerges is that it is not all decline. There are also sectors of growth, and the geography of these is explored. Clearly, one issue for the future is whether this is 'terminal decline' or a decline before a new burst of growth, but of a different kind, and probably with a different geography.

Section 2.4 begins to examine the debate about how the dramatically changing geography of manufacturing can be explained. It is a debate which reveals contrasting notions of what is an adequate explanation and different views of the interrelationship between an economy and its geography. In section 2.4 the focus is on explanation at the level of the individual firm. Section 2.5 broadens the discussion to consider the whole concept of uneven development. Why is it that societies are so frequently marked by geographical disparities? How can such geographical inequality be assessed and explained? The empirical evidence in the earlier sections certainly indicates that there has been a structural shift – though its causes and its form may be disputed – in UK manufacturing. Over the same period there has also been a transformation in its geography. One issue which is raised is how important a shift this is. Is it a major historical turning-point, implying the complete re-fashioning of the economy, of production and of the geography of production? A number of theories argue that it is, among them two of the schools of thought which were introduced in Chapter 1: long-wave theories and regulationist theories. In section 2.6 we pick up these theories again and examine what they have to say about the shifts currently under way in British manufacturing and its geography.

2.2   Deindustrialization

There is debate about the definition of **deindustrialization**. For some, deindustrialization refers to the level of activity in the economy as a whole, and the economy's ability to reproduce itself. For others, probably the majority, deindustrialization is concerned with the decline of manufacturing. The most common definition is the absolute decline of manufacturing employment. But relative decline is used as an indicator by some; and output can be used as a measure rather than employment. Each definition implies a slightly different underlying concern, and each gives a slightly different answer to the questions 'when did deindustrialization begin?' and 'how important is it?'

2.2.1   The economy as a whole

Rhodes (1986) writes: 'De-industrialization is defined as the failure of a country or region to secure a rate of growth of output and net exports of all kinds sufficient to achieve full employment' (p. 138). And Singh (1977), who has been an important protagonist in the debate over deindustrialization, defines it in terms of the economy's ability to sell enough of its products abroad to pay for the nation's import requirements, and to do these things while maintaining 'socially acceptable levels of output, employment and the exchange rate' (p. 128). This definition of deindustrialization establishes the link between the international trading position of the UK economy, discussed in the last chapter, and the internal structure of the economy, which is the subject of this chapter.

With this definition of deindustrialization a range of indicators can be used to assess whether or not the UK economy is deindustrializing. Britain's position within the international division of labour and its trade balance were examined in Chapter 1, where it was seen that there have indeed been major shifts over the post-war period. But what of measures internal to the UK economy? One set of important data concerns levels of employment and unemployment within the economy as a whole. This indicates whether production in the UK economy, and the economy's international trading position, are healthy enough to provide sufficient employment for people within it. These data are given for the post-war period in Figure 2.1.

The graphs indicate that on these measures there have been substantial changes over the post-war period. A break-point can be picked out from the graph of employees in employment (Figure 2.1(a)): 1966 was the peak year for the total number of jobs in the economy. Having risen strongly over the post-war period until that year, growth stopped; there have been major fluctuations since, but the total has never been so high again. Unemployment, in contrast, has risen sharply during the latter part of the period, in terms of both numbers and rate (see Figure 2.1(b) and (c)). Here there is not such a clear break-point in the trend, though it is perhaps important to note that until the mid-1960s there were fairly regular fluctuations up and down, but since then no downward fluctuation has ever dipped significantly below the *peak* of preceding cycles. Since the mid-'60s, in other words, the overall trend has been upwards. In both employment and unemployment there is evidence of an exacerbation of the trends in the late 1970s.

On the basis of these data, there has been a shift in the economy in recent decades. On the basis of this definition, it looks as though there has been deindustrialization.

But let us examine this definition itself more closely. There are two points which are important to note. Both are of fundamental significance, and will be discussed fully in Chapter 6. We shall just introduce them now, but try to bear them in mind as you read on.

First, Rhodes' definition refers to **full employment**. But what *is* full employment? Before the mid-'60s, when unemployment was lower, was there full employment? There were between a quarter and a half a million people registered as out of work. Of course, many of these people may well have been 'between jobs' – that is, their unemployment may have been what is called 'frictional' unemployment, a part of the continuous and necessary process of adjustment within the labour market. On the other hand, many people who do not have a job but who in principle would like one do not, for one reason or another, register as unemployed. There have been numerous changes recently to the way unemployment figures are counted, producing a downwards adjustment. But even in the 1950s and '60s the unemployment figures may not have reflected the 'true' number

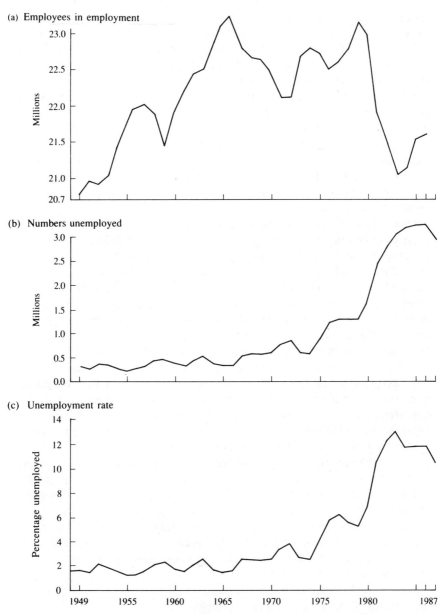

(a) Employees in employment

(b) Numbers unemployed

(c) Unemployment rate

Figure 2.1 Employment and unemployment, United Kingdom, 1949–87
Source: Based on Hudson and Williams, 1986, p. 16; updated with Department of Employment data

unemployed because of people's failure to register. In particular this applied to women, and one indication of it is indeed the change over the postwar period in economic activity rates among women. The **economic activity**

rate is the percentage of the relevant population either in work or registered as unemployed. For married women this rate increased dramatically over the post-war period, from about 22 per cent in 1951 to nearly 50 per
cent in 1979 (Central Statistical Office, 1978, 1982). Much of their employment, however, has been part-time, which raises the issue: what is a job?
The second peak in employees in employment in Figure 2.1(a) includes far
more part-time workers than the peak in 1966 (see Chapter 5): so is the figure comparing like with like? Unemployment and employment statistics
have to be *interpreted*.

In addition to this, what counts as 'full employment' is socially determined and changes over time. The quotation from Singh makes this point
by using the phrase 'socially acceptable levels of . . . employment'. In the
1960s the fact of more than *one* million unemployed would have been
heralded as foreboding 'the end of civilization as we know it'.

None of this invalidates this definition of deindustrialization. But it does
point to the need to examine carefully the social processes registered by
apparently simple concepts. This definition of deindustrialization is concerned with the ability of the economy to produce a socially acceptable
level of employment (full employment) in a context where the unemployment level is itself a product of government regulations about definitions
and individuals' propensity to register.

Secondly, given this definition, why in so much discussion of deindustrialization is the emphasis placed on manufacturing? In considering this
question, Rhodes relates it specifically to the case of the UK: 'prominence
is given to manufacturing only because Britain, as most other advanced
countries, has relied heavily on manufacturing activities as a source of net
exports and employment' (1986, p. 139). This raises the question whether,
if manufacturing industry is collapsing, that implies the collapse of the UK
economy. Could not the economy survive by other means? Rhodes argues
that 'if Britain had alternative sources of net exports which were growing
rapidly, then the relative decline of manufacturing industry would not matter. But . . . the growth in net exports (of) services and food cannot be relied on to replace the loss of manufacturing and oil net exports and secure
further growth sufficient to achieve full employment' (p. 139). This question of how much deindustrialization matters is an issue to which we shall
return in Chapter 6.

It is certainly the case, however, that most definitions of deindustrialization do equate it with *manufacturing decline*.

2.2.2   The relative decline of manufacturing

But what is manufacturing decline?

First of all, are we talking of relative or absolute decline?

Figure 2.2 shows the changing *relative* importance of manufacturing in
employment terms. On this definition, deindustrialization started in the

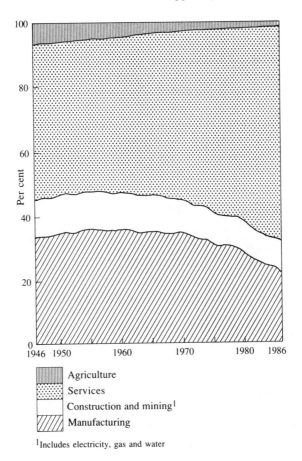

Figure 2.2 Employment in the major sectors of the UK economy as a proportion of total employment, 1946–86
Source: Data from Ministry of Labour and Department of Employment

mid-1950s, since which date the importance of manufacturing as a source of employment in the economy has been declining fairly consistently.

This second definition is concerned with changes in the *sectoral* structure of the economy. This can be important. In part it is simply descriptive of the employment foundations of the economy, and is sometimes related to theories of economic development which argue that national economies evolve through a series of stages dominated in turn by agriculture, manufacturing and services. This view of advanced economies as moving into a service-dominated phase, and the recent theoretical arguments about it, will be examined in Chapter 3. Note, however, that, in spite of what was said earlier, at *no* time since the Second World War has manufacturing employed as many people as services. This raises further issues about what is meant by the 'importance of manufacturing', and how it should be measured, to which we shall return later. Deindustrialization, defined as the declining relative importance of manufacturing, brings changes in the kinds of places many people work in, changes in the skills which are demanded of them, in the unions they belong to (or do not), and a whole range of other social changes consequent upon the shifting balance of employment opportunities. Some of these implications will be explored in Chapter 5.

On the other hand, this definition does not concern itself with whether the declining importance of manufacturing is a problem for the economy, since it does not examine what is happening to total employment or to unemployment. Nor, indeed, does it say anything about what is happening to manufacturing itself.

2.2.3   The absolute decline of manufacturing

It is on this last issue that the third, and the most popular, definition of deindustrialization focuses: the *absolute* decline in manufacturing employment. Figure 2.3 plots the data from Figure 2.2 in absolute rather than relative terms.

Figure 2.3 shows that manufacturing employment reached its peak in

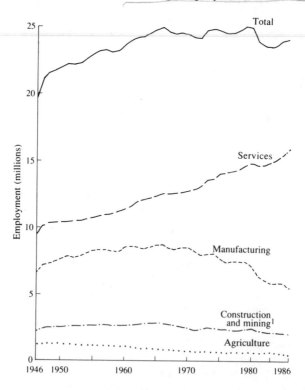

Includes electricity, gas and water

Figure 2.3   Employment by sector in the UK, 1946–86
Source: Data from Ministry of Labour and Department of Employment

1966. Thus, between the mid-'50s and the mid-'60s, while manufacturing was declining relatively within the economy, the number of people it employed was still increasing. In other words, while there was deindustrialization in terms of the second definition, there was not in terms of this third definition. Manufacturing employment was increasing, but employment in services was going up even faster. On the other hand, in 1966 when manufacturing employment turned down, so did total employment. Neither services nor any other sector increased sufficiently to compensate for the loss of jobs in manufacturing.

2.2.4 Employment or output?

Let us return to the question raised above: what is manufacturing decline?

So far, we have focused on the different implications of relative and absolute decline. But there is one further issue to be addressed: what index should we use to measure decline? The discussion up to now has focused on employment as our index. This certainly accords with the concerns about full employment in the first definition of deindustrialization, but is employment level the only way of measuring the health of an industry? There is a range of other measures which could be used. Perhaps the most obvious other measure is *output*.

Figure 2.4 shows UK manufacturing output since the war. It is a different

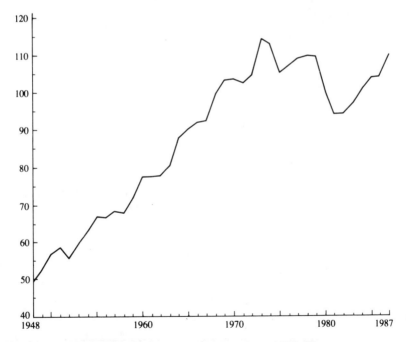

Figure 2.4 Manufacturing output, United Kingdom, 1948–87
Source: Treasury, 1987

picture from that for employment, in that from 1966 to 1973 manufacturing output continued to grow even while employment fell. This is the phenomenon of **jobless growth**. It means that changes in productivity have more than wiped out any potential for increased employment through growth in production. Such increases in productivity might be due to new investment in existing industries, to speed-up and other kinds of changes on the shop-floor, or to a change in balance between low and high productivity sectors. Many of the changes will have resulted from attempts to keep manufacturing profitable. Yet they have resulted in job loss. What is good for profits is not necessarily good, at least in the short term, for the employees.

So, once again, the measure which is adopted in the definition of deindustrialization must reflect the underlying concern behind the question. In this case, the issue is between a concern for levels of manufacturing output and a concern for jobs. Nonetheless, the picture for output in manufacturing does indicate a shift after 1973, away from the trend of steady post-war growth.

Summary of section 2.2

- There is debate about the definition of *deindustrialization*. One definition relates to the health of the economy overall; another group of definitions is concerned with the decline of manufacturing. Within the latter group, decline may be measured relatively or absolutely, and a number of different indices may be used.

Table 2.1   Definitions of deindustrialization

Definition	Possible measures

• The failure of a country or region to secure a rate of growth of output and net exports of all kinds while maintaining socially acceptable levels of employment.	• Measures concerning the country's international position:
	  – balance of trade
	  – exchange rate.
	
	• Measures concerning internal state of economy:
	  – employment
	  – unemployment.

• The relative decline of manufacturing, i.e. the decline of manufacturing as a part of the economy.	• Manufacturing's share of employment (usually) or (occasionally) output in the economy as a whole.
• The absolute decline of manufacturing.	• Absolute levels of employment (usually) or (occasionally) output in manufacturing.

- Issues of definition are significant. In any social science, one of the most important building-blocks is careful *conceptualization*. Thus:

    - there is often a relation between the way in which a phenomenon is defined and the wider concerns of the analysis, the questions to be asked

    - contrasting conceptualizations may produce different answers to questions

    - many accepted terms (full employment, a job) may change their content as social conditions change

    - similar results in terms of statistics (e.g. a decline in the share of manufacturing) may be the result of different causes

    - a whole range of social processes may underlie apparently simple numerical shifts.

- Nonetheless given all the complexity of the above, and consequent disagreements over dates and magnitudes, there has been a major change in the importance of manufacturing within the UK economy. Most analysts agree that there has been 'deindustrialization'.

2.3 Geographical changes

The shift in the importance and growth of manufacturing within the national economy has been bound up with a similar change in the *geography* of manufacturing. The reworking of the manufacturing economy at a national level has gone hand in hand with a reworking of its urban and regional geography.

2.3.1 The broad regional trends

In the context of urban and regional geography the debate has focused mainly on employment and the concern has been primarily with the definition of deindustrialization as an *absolute loss of manufacturing jobs*. It is on this, therefore, that we shall concentrate.

1966 not only marked the year in which manufacturing employment began to fall nationally; it also marked a year of significant spatial change. Keeble (1976) identifies 'the pivotal date of 1966'. He demonstrates how in the 1950s, during this peak period of the post-war boom in both international and national economies when total manufacturing employment was still increasing in the UK, the bulk of that growth took place in the central regions: that is, the South East and the midlands – in and around the major conurbations of London and Birmingham. From 1966, however, that pattern changed.

Activity 2.1

Table 2.2 provides basic data on regional manufacturing employment changes since the mid-'60s:

(a) Which regions have lost most manufacturing jobs over the period as a whole?

(b) Try comparing 1966–1973 with 1979–1984 (or 1974–79). What contrasts are there between the sub-periods?

This can be done using a number of different comparisons:

• For 1966–71–73 which regions increase absolutely?

• For 1966–71–73 which regions increase their share?

• For 1974–79 and 1979–84 which regions lose more and which lose less than the national average?

Table 2.2
Regional manufacturing employment change, United Kingdom, 1966–84

	1966		1971		1973		1974–79 % change	1979–84 % change
	Total	% UK	Total	% UK	Total	% UK		
N. Ireland	183	2.0	170	2.1	164	2.1	−12.8	−30.1
Scotland	731	8.1	669	8.3	657	8.4	−10.6	−27.6
Wales	323	3.6	324	4.0	329	4.2	−7.1	−32.8
North	457	5.1	448	5.6	450	5.8	−12.3	−29.9
Yorks & Humberside	884	9.8	779	9.7	768	9.8	−7.9	−27.7
North West	1344	15.0	1163	14.5	1116	14.3	−11.1	−29.4
W. Midlands	1243	13.9	1104	13.7	1074	13.7	−9.7	−27.6
E. Midlands	617	6.9	595	7.4	591	7.6	−1.1	−20.2
E. Anglia	186	2.1	190	2.4	200	2.6	+1.0	−14.2
South East	2603	29.0	2206	27.4	2069	26.4	−7.2	−17.3
South West	400	4.5	407	5.1	409	5.2	−1.3	−17.8
UK	8971	100.0	8055	100.0	7828	100.0	−7.6	−23.8

Source: Department of Employment

At the most general level, what Table 2.2 demonstrates is that the absolute loss of manufacturing employment has not just been 'reflected' in the different parts of the country. Rather, different regions have been affected in distinct ways. The national change has also been marked by a shift in the geography of manufacturing employment.

The period 1966–73 saw both national manufacturing decline and spatial dispersion. Both the South East and the West Midlands reduced their shares of national manufacturing employment, while that of most other regions increased.

These latter regions consisted of two rather different groups. First there were the regions of the south and east which lie outside the major industrial centres (the East Midlands, East Anglia and the South West). Secondly, there were the regions of the old industrial periphery – the North, Wales and Scotland – which for half a century had suffered higher than national rates of unemployment. Comparing this with the earlier period, Keeble (1976) wrote: 'During the 1960s, and especially the later 1960s, concentration has been replaced by increasing spatial *dispersion* of manufacturing industry, both to relatively unindustrialized subregions and to the peripheral areas' (p. 15, emphasis in the original).

By the late 1970s, however, some elements of this dispersal had in turn been reversed. And once again this geographical change coincided with shifts in the economy at national level. From the late '70s manufacturing employment nationally went into even steeper decline. And the new geography of this steeper decline can be picked out from Table 2.2. Between the late '70s and the mid-'80s, while the share of the three more rural regions of the south and east continued to expand, that of the old peripheral regions declined. In complete contrast the South East began to recover relatively. Geographical concentration, having been interrupted by the decentralization of the '60s and early '70s, seemed to have reasserted itself.

But this was *not* a reversion to the pattern and processes of concentration typical of the 1950s. The West Midlands continued to decline as a manufacturing region throughout the period, for instance. And the re-concentration of growth, and the much smaller impact of decline, in the south since the mid-'70s has been very much focused on the previously *less* industrialized regions (and parts of regions). East Anglia is the prime example. This is a rather different 'north-south divide'.

2.3.2 Processes of change

What have been the processes producing this shifting geography? From the statistics alone it is impossible to tell. But most research agrees about the kinds of processes that were in operation.

During the period from the mid-'60s to the mid-'70s, while there were closures and redundancies in most regions, deindustrialization was most marked in the old manufacturing areas. At a regional level, this meant that the North West and West Midlands were particularly badly affected. On the other hand, any new growth in manufacturing jobs tended to take place away from these regions, and also away from the huge London conurbation industrial area. But another element, not large in quantitative terms, but distinctive to this period, was *locational change* (Keeble, 1976; Massey, 1984). In other words, as well as relative decentralization through different rates of growth and decline, there was also actual movement. This movement mostly originated in the central regions (the West Midlands and the South East) and went to the peripheral regions and to the 'outer' southern regions. Industry was moving out of its old bases. In some cases whole firms moved, but this was usually in the shorter moves to nearby regions such as East Anglia, often by smaller companies. In many cases the headquarters were retained in the central region and only the production processes were decentralized. Nonetheless such decentralization contributed to a degree of evening-out of unemployment rates between different parts of the country. It was not to last.

From the mid-'70s to the mid-'80s it was increasing *in*equality which was to dominate the changing geography of manufacturing, and indeed of employment more generally. Martin (1986) calculated that, 'Regional percentage-point unemployment differentials are now wider than at any other time since the inter-war period' (p. 269). This time the key to understanding the changing pattern is the starkly contrasting geographies of decline and of growth. As far as decline is concerned, a census published in 1987 showed that of the jobs lost between 1979 and 1984, 94 per cent had been lost in 'the north'. The north was defined as all regions outside the South East, East Anglia and the South West (the omission of the West Midlands from the south was itself an indication of just how much the geography of manufacturing industry had changed).

But not everything, even within manufacturing, has been employment decline. While most of the sectors which are expanding employment in the economy are services, there is also a group of new and growing manufacturing industries. In particular, these are related to the emerging 'high-tech' sectors of electronics, sometimes referred to as the 'sunrise' industries, in counterposition to the 'sunset' industries of the rest of manufacturing. Yet they, too, have a very unequal geography. Table 2.3 gives the South East's share of employment in some of these leading growth industries. The significance of these percentages can be gauged by comparing them with the South East's share of total manufacturing which stood then at about 27 per cent.

Martin* (1988) aggregates employment in a wider group of growth sectors and calculates that the South East region's share of employment is over 41 per cent, with East Anglia and the South West together claiming over 10 per cent more. The 'south' of the country is clearly claiming 'more than its share' of the so-called sunrise sectors. Moreover while electronics is seen as a growth industry, it is in fact nationally a sector of 'jobless growth'. Between

Table 2.3 The South East's share of employment in the electronics industry in Britain, 1981

Sector	South East % employment
Telecommunications	34.4
Components	45.9
Consumer electronics	64.0
Computers	59.0
Capital goods	64.5
Total share	53.2

Source: Department of Employment, *Employment Gazette*

1975 and 1984 total employment in the electronics sectors declined by 19 per cent. But it declined differentially. The biggest job losses were in the semi-skilled operator groups, while at the other end of the skill and status spectrum, jobs for technicians, managers, scientists and engineers increased markedly. It is these latter, higher status, jobs which are most concentrated into the south of the country (*Martin*, 1988; *Massey*, 1988). This points not only to a severe differential in the *quality* of jobs between north and south but also to a differential in their rate of job growth over time.

Thus, while the north has suffered most of the job loss resulting from deindustrialization, the south is gaining most from the rise of new sectors. The last section of this chapter will ask if what we are witnessing is not some 'final' deindustrialization but a shift between types – or even different eras – of manufacturing. If so, the geography of the new will be very different from the geography of the old.

2.3.3 Another look at deindustrialization

So far this section has focused on deindustrialization as *absolute loss of manufacturing jobs*. But, as was seen in the last section, deindustrialization can be measured in different ways.

1 *Output* only declined during part of the period, but when it did the geographical pattern was the same as for employment. The fall in output between the late 1970s and mid-'80s in the South East, East Anglia and the South West was less than half the rate of fall nationally and less than one third of the rate of decline in the three worst-hit regions: Wales, the West Midlands and the North West.

During those years, in other words, there was a faster decline of manufacturing in terms of both output and employment in those areas of the country where manufacturing had been more important in the regional economy.

2   In turn this relates to the definition of deindustrialization as the *relative* decline of manufacturing. The regions of the north have seen a faster deindustrialization in these terms than have the regions of the south. This is partly because manufacturing has declined faster in the north. But it is also because of the geography of growth of the service sector, which has also been very uneven. This is less true of public sector services than of the private sector, but in recent years it is in the latter that growth in employment has been concentrated. Moreover that growth has been greatest where the decline in manufacturing employment has been least – that is, in the regions of 'the south'. Thus *Martin* (1988) talks of a clear inverse relationship between deindustrialization and tertiarization: those regions that have suffered most from the decline of manufacturing employment have gained least from the expansion of jobs within the private service sector. The decline of manufacturing and the growth of services therefore *both* contribute to deepening inequalities between British regions.

However, the geography of service employment growth is less uneven than that of manufacturing decline. This means that in terms of proportions of total employment there has been a faster shift away from manufacturing in the regions of the north than in the regions of the south; there has been faster deindustrialization, measured in these terms also, in north than south. For the future, that leaves the different regions of the country more equal in their balance of dependence on manufacturing and services.

3   It is, however, an equality in inequality, for the net result in terms of the definition of deindustrialization *as a failure of the economy to provide jobs*, is that 'full employment' is far further away in the north than in the south.

2.3.4   Within the regions: the urban-rural shift

It is not just at the regional level that the geography of British manufacturing industry has been changing. Indeed categorizing data on a regional basis can conceal almost as much as it reveals. Certainly, there is much local variation within all regions: there are areas of severe deindustrialization in the south and of industrial growth in the north. The focus of much recent research has in fact been on the significant differences which exist between 'localities', with the focus on the subregional level.

At this more detailed level of analysis, the most important shift in the geography of manufacturing since the mid-1960s has been the decline of the inner cities and the conurbations and the relative growth of outer metropolitan areas and smaller towns. Indeed Fothergill and Gudgin (1982) argue that this *urban-rural shift* was the main component of change over those years (more important, that is, than changes in balance between regions). *Fother-*

gill, Gudgin, Kitson and Monk (1986) write: 'The industrial city in Britain is the product of nineteenth-century capitalism . . .', but 'all this has changed . . . there has been a complete turnaround in the fortunes of the industrial city: in the late twentieth century the city is the principal location of deindustrialization'.

Indeed, at this intraregional level, too, there has been a very definite geography of deindustrialization. Inner London and the inner areas of a number of industrial cities suffered first, but the loss of manufacturing jobs then spread to the outer areas of cities and to wider regions, such as the West Midlands and the North West, where these were based on manufacturing. Tables 2.4 and 2.5 show this process of the 'spreading' of deindustrialization, from the inner areas of some of the great cities, outwards to more rural

Table 2.4 Percentage change in manufacturing employment in the inner and outer areas of the conurbations, 1951–1976

	1951–61	1961–71	1971–76
Inner areas ⎫ conurbations	−7.5	−20.2	−15.0
Outer areas ⎭	+4.8	−16.5	−13.7
Rest of Great Britain	+9.6	+8.8	−6.2

Source: Adapted from Dicken, 1982

Table 2.5
Manufacturing employment change by type of area, Great Britain, 1960–1981

	1960–78 (as % of 1960)	1978–81 (as % of 1978)
London	−42.5	−15.5
Conurbations[1]	−26.5	−22.7
Free-standing cities[2]	−13.8	−17.2
Large towns[3]	−2.2	−16.0
Small towns[4]	+15.7	−15.2
Rural areas[5]	+38.0	−10.0
Great Britain	−11.5	−16.8

Classification after Fothergill, Gudgin, Kitson and Monk, 1986:

[1] Manchester, Merseyside, Clydeside, West Yorkshire, Tyneside, West Midlands

[2] Other cities with more than 250 000 people

[3] Towns or cities with 100 000 to 250 000 people

[4] Districts including at least one town with 35 000 to 100 000 people, plus coalfield areas

[5] Districts in which all settlements have fewer than 35 000 people

areas. In contrast, there has been less decline – and some growth – in certain areas outside the major cities. Once again, the geographies of growth and decline are almost mirror-images of each other. At this intraregional scale the result has been a major shift in the urban-rural balance of manufacturing industry.

2.4 Explaining the changes

The last section identified some of the processes which have contributed to the overall shift in the geography of manufacturing. But we have not yet broached the *explanation* of these changes.

In fact the search for an explanation has provoked one of the widest-ranging and most interesting debates of recent years in economic geography. Part of its fascination has derived from the number of levels at which the debate has taken place. There has been difference of opinion not merely over the content of any explanation, but also over what would *count* as an explanation. Part of what was at issue was the nature of 'theory' and 'explanation' themselves. As such, the discussion was part of important debates within the social sciences as a whole. We shall focus here on two issues to illustrate the terms of this debate.

The first issue is the relative decentralization of manufacturing jobs which took place, particularly between the mid-'60s and the mid-'70s, from previously urbanized and industrialized central areas to peripheral and pre-viously less industrialized areas. What was *not* in dispute was that major changes were under way. The debate started from agreement about the outcome to be explained – the kinds of data given in the previous section – and about the broad changes, also described in the last section, which had been involved. The disagreement was about how this decentralization was to be explained.

2.4.1 Location factors

One interpretation focused on *location factors*. This approach attempted to identify what was problematic for manufacturing industry in those areas where it was declining fastest and, on the other hand, what was attractive about the areas where it was growing, at least relatively. The exploration was pursued by statistical analysis relating the amount of manufacturing change (the phenomenon to be explained) to characteristics of areas which it was hypothesized might explain the change. Characteristics which were found to be statistically significant in their relation to manufacturing employment change were deemed to be contributory causes of it. In some of the most detailed work in this vein, Keeble (1976, 1980) identified a number of factors as important causes of the relative decentralization of manufacturing employment. He distinguished between the 1960s and the 1970s, arguing that the balance of significant factors had shifted between the two periods. For the '60s he identified the most important factor as being government assistance, that is regional policy in all its forms. This was indeed a period, under the Labour government of Harold Wilson, when regional policy was strong. It largely took the form of financial incentives to companies to move to, or expand within, certain parts of the country. These areas are shown in Figure 2.5.

As Figure 2.5 indicates, most of these 'assisted areas' were in the north and west of the country. Another factor Keeble had put into his analysis, however, was labour availability, calculated on the basis of levels of unemployment. The hypothesis was that firms were decentralizing in search of reserves of labour, and probably cheaper labour since wages were likely to be lower in areas with high unemployment (1976, pp. 71–4, 102). However, the map of unemployment in the mid-'60s looked very like the map of government-assisted areas; and indeed the level of unemployment was an important element in the designation of assisted areas. This meant that these two factors were hard to disentangle. In the light of his statistical results, Keeble concluded that regional policy had been the more significant influence.

Two other variables were also found to be important. There was a significant negative relationship between the scale of manufacturing activity in an area at the beginning of the period and subsequent manufacturing growth. This was interpreted as indicating the influence of 'substantial agglomeration diseconomies' together, perhaps, with regional policy controls and planning constraints in the largest industrial centres (ibid., p. 114). **Agglomeration diseconomies** are the financial burdens (diseconomies) imposed by location in a major urban area (agglomeration). In this case, these were interpreted mainly as the high cost of land and premises, which could affect companies through the high housing and travel costs (and therefore possibly wages) for their workers (pp. 74–8), and the relative congestion and age of building in cities. For these reasons, it was argued, the previous relative advantages of an urban location (including agglomeration economies) were by 1966 being outweighed by the disadvantages. As Keeble pointed out, this factor was important not only in interregional decentralization but also in intraregional shifts from big cities.

The final variable identified as important was 'residential preference': manufacturing was shifting to more 'environmentally attractive' areas of the country.

In a similar analysis for the first half of the 1970s, Keeble (1980) showed that the relative importance of these factors had changed. By this time the most important factor was agglomeration diseconomies. Both residential preferences and government policy had dropped out of the picture. This was interpreted in the light of the worsening of the general economic situation. In relation to residential preferences it was argued that 'it does seem that

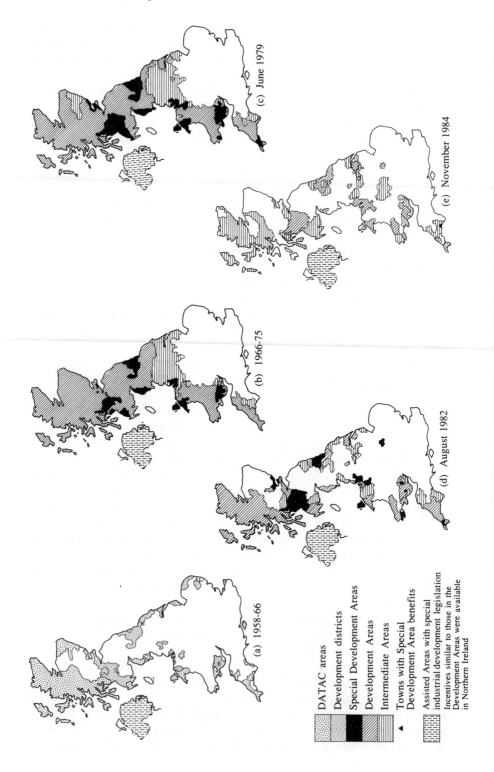

(a) 1958-66

(b) 1966-75

(c) June 1979

(d) August 1982

(e) November 1984

DATAC areas

Development districts

Special Development Areas

Development Areas

Intermediate Areas

Towns with Special
Development Area benefits

Assisted Areas with special
industrial development legislation
Incentives similar to those in the
Development Areas were available
in Northern Ireland

under conditions of national manufacturing decline, variations in residential attractiveness . . . have not exerted any obvious influence on manufacturing location trends at the county level, in sharp contrast to trends during the 1960s' (p. 957).

A final variable, the economic activity rate among women, was also examined. Keeble (1980) had included this variable as a proxy for 'the restructuring hypothesis', by which he meant the argument that the real reason for decentralization was that manufacturing industry was under pressure to cut costs and had changed location in a search for cheaper, 'green' labour. Areas where there had previously been little opportunity for women to have waged work (the coalfields of the old peripheral regions were the classic example) would provide such a reserve of labour and would therefore be attractive to manufacturing industry. Although there was 'a relatively high negative correlation' (Keeble, 1980, p. 958) between female activity rate and manufacturing change, however, once again there was a problem of disentangling variables. Most of the areas with low female activity rates also had low densities of manufacturing employment. Thus the effect of the former got lost in the more widespread effect of the latter. Keeble concluded that agglomeration diseconomies were the most important cause of manufacturing decentralization in the 1970s.

2.4.2 'Restructuring'

Keeble's methods and conclusions were disputed by others. One level of criticism concerned the nature of the explanatory variables themselves (for instance, Sayer, 1982). It was pointed out that it was hardly surprising there was a significant negative relationship between existing levels and subsequent change since 'decentralization', i.e. movement away from existing areas, was precisely what was to be explained. This had been interpreted as reflecting 'agglomeration diseconomies', but, it was argued, this was an assumption not an outcome of the analysis; and anyway 'agglomeration diseconomies' was very much a catch-all term. Other criticisms concerned the impossibility of disentangling the effects of different variables. This meant that the effect of factors (for example, female activity rate) which might be extremely important in particular instances could be lost simply

(opposite) Figure 2.5   The geography of UK regional policy, 1958–84: Special Development, Development and Intermediate Areas[1]

[1] *These different types of Assisted Areas were eligible for different levels of regional grant aid, mainly in the form of financial incentives for new investment: Special Development Areas had the highest priority, then Development Areas, and Intermediate Areas lowest.*

Source: Keeble, 1976, pp. 227, 228; Martin, 1986, p. 273

because of the impact of much more general variables (such as low density of manufacturing employment).

There is also another and much more fundamental level of critique and debate. This came primarily from those who had adopted what Keeble called the **restructuring** hypothesis (section 2.4.1). The 'restructuring school' argued that it was not possible to provide an explanation in terms of location factors alone; what was needed was to set these factors within the wider context of the restructuring of industry (Massey, 1979; Sayer, 1982). Chapter 1 made clear that British manufacturing was coming under increasing international competition and that its weaknesses were being exposed. The restructuring school argued that to understand what was happening to the geography of British manufacturing at this time it was necessary to analyse this situation. They argued that decentralization could not be divorced from the increasing pressures which industry was facing, nor indeed from deindustrialization itself: that while location factors might indicate why movement took place from area A to area B rather than from area Y to area Z (though the technical arguments above disputed even that), they gave no help in explaining why there was movement in the first place. If in the 1960s firms *had* responded to regional policy assistance, for instance, it was necessary to know why at that time they had *needed* that assistance.

This restructuring approach argued that it was necessary to look at what was happening within industry itself and in the wider economy. It was pointed out that from the early '60s onwards some parts of British manufacturing had been facing increased economic difficulties, in particular because of heightened international competition, which firms had been adopting strategies to counter. The restructuring school argued that decentralization had been an element in these strategies. It had been one way of making firms more competitive. To understand this, however, it was necessary to analyse how firms responded to these pressures and, in particular, to examine the changing requirements of production.

Moreover, from such analysis it was clear that in fact companies had responded in a whole range of different ways to the pressures upon them, and indeed that the nature of those pressures varied between industries and between firms. For some firms the most urgent necessity was simply to reduce immediate labour costs, and decentralization for them was a straightforward way of finding cheaper labour. Such firms were likely to have particular characteristics: they were probably relatively labour-intensive, so labour was an important part of their costs; or they might be located in an area where labour costs were rising particularly fast, or where labour availability was a problem. In all these cases regional incentives might be important, but only in the context of a need to reduce costs and an ability to move, rather than as the initial motivation, and as part of a bundle of considerations rather than as a separable 'factor'.

Even then, though, firms would have to balance the advantages of a central location against those of decentralization: some clothing firms, for instance, could not leave London because of their need to be near the fashion market. Other companies, in sectors where the opportunities for technological change were greater, met the increasing competition by introducing more automation into their production processes. In such cases again regional policy aid might be important: the grants were sometimes significant subsidies to the updating of technology, for instance. But often, too, the technological change shifted the companies' labour requirements. This might mean that a firm was 'released' from ties to traditional, skilled (and often well-unionized) labour; the technical change freed it to seek out cheaper and less well-organized labour elsewhere. In such a case, technical change, regional policy, the desire to undercut union strength, and a search for cheaper labour are inextricably interrelated. It is impossible to distinguish them as 'separate factors'. Moreover all of them have to be set against the background of the changing pressures on industry deriving from wider changes in the national and international economy.

By examining decentralization in this way, the restructuring school argued, the role of regional policy was seen to be more complex. In some cases it might have been irrelevant because companies would have decentralized anyway; in others it might have enabled decentralization or, in combination with other factors encouraged it; in some cases it might indeed have been the single most important immediate consideration. But, whatever the case, in order to assess the effectiveness of regional policy it was necessary to examine it in relation to the context in which it was operating.

Finally, the restructuring school conceptualizes industry more clearly as capitalist. Industry's motivation is to make a profit, and a company's 'geographical behaviour' is part of trying to attain that aim: changing location could be a way of staying profitable.

Activity 2.2

The two approaches disagree about how to explain the decentralization in the 1960s and early '70s. In particular, they have very different assessments of the importance of:

- regional policy
- labour availability.

What were these different assessments, and why did they differ?

It will help in attacking this major issue to follow a sequence of steps:

(a) Which factor did the location-factor approach think was most important in the 1960s?

(b) Why? (Note: in order to answer this type of question it is necessary to look at what was counted as explanation by this school, i.e. what led them to believe this?)

(c) What led this school to believe that labour availability was less important than other factors in both the 1960s and the early '70s? (Hint: What is meant by labour availability? Do you think adequate measures were used?)

(d)   Why does the restructuring school argue that location factors alone cannot explain decentralization?

(e)   Within the overall context of increasing pressures upon manufacturing industry, both regional policy and labour availability could be significant to firms to contrasting degrees and in different combinations. Why? Give two examples.

The debate over regional decentralization in the 1960s and '70s thus raised many crucial issues about the nature of explanation in the social sciences. The two schools came to different conclusions because they asked different kinds of questions and had different views as to what counted as an explanation, and of how an explanation should be evaluated.

The location-factor school argued that regional policy was the most important cause of decentralization in the '60s because it was the factor most significantly correlated with change in manufacturing employment, that is, it matched the pattern of relative manufacturing growth most closely. In contrast, the restructuring school argued that this matching of hypothesized causes and effects, and especially when the causes were restricted to geographical location factors, was inadequate. First, it failed to take account of the fact that British industry at the time was undergoing traumatic upheavals and that the impact of this upon firms had to be recognized if the *need* to decentralize in the first place was to be understood. Second, the restructuring might take many different forms. Some firms might simply move to cheaper labour; others might use the opportunity to update their production processes thus making them less dependent on traditionally skilled labour forces; others again might simply respond to the lure of regional incentives. The point, according to the restructuring school, is that the relative importance of these factors, and perhaps even more importantly the way they combined together, would depend on the characteristics of each case. Thus, trying to find the best 'fit' between factors and outcomes was not very illuminating; what was necessary was to investigate combinations of causes at a more detailed and qualitative level.

2.4.3   Urban decline

These debates over the nature of theory and the nature of explanation were not, of course, confined to this issue of decentralization. Very similar debates arose in the discussion of urban decline. As we saw in section 2.3 the processes of decentralization took place not only from central regions to the regions of the north and west, but also within regions from large towns and conurbations to small towns and more rural areas. Unlike the interregional decentralization, which seemed to come to an end in the mid-'70s, this process seemed set to continue, at least in relative terms. The debate over how to explain this industrial decline of cities raised many of the same questions about the nature of explanation as have just been discussed. What was at issue was the future of cities themselves.

A dominant characteristic of the location-factor school is its focus on the particular features of areas in order to explain their relative fortunes. Thus, to explain what was happening to cities it was necessary to look at the characteristics of cities. More specifically, if cities were losing jobs, there must be something wrong with them. In the long debate over urban decline this school has put forward various factors: that population decentralization has left behind, in the inner cities especially, a disproportionate number of the unskilled and the 'hard-to-employ'; that physical dereliction and social problems make cities unattractive to new investment; and that local councils and planning authorities have been obstructive and unhelpful to the private sector. It is these negative characteristics which, it has been argued, lie behind the problems of urban decline.

The restructuring school replies with many of the same points as in the decentralization debate. While certainly not denying the potential influence of certain characteristics of cities (though they would dispute some, and point to others as being more effects than causes of urban decline), they argue that these factors have to be considered in the light of what is happening to industry itself. Not only the characteristics of cities but also the requirements of industry need to be taken into account, and both are changing. For the restructuring school the loss of manufacturing jobs in the economy as a whole explains many of the problems of urban areas. The fact that urban areas were hit early and particularly hard by this loss is then explained by conditions which operate within this broader context: for example, that cities tended to have the older and thus often less profitable parts of individual industries; or that they suffered from decentralization to cheaper and less organized workers. The general shape of the argument is that of a context of deindustrialization in which cities are hit harder as companies struggle to maintain profitability. In that struggle capital's antagonistic relation with labour, its need to cheapen wages and undermine labour organization, was probably a particularly important component.

However, as in debate over most issues, not all the protagonists fall easily into one camp or the other. There are indeed more than two camps. One influential argument about urban decline has been put forward by Fothergill and Gudgin and their associates. Their argument begins from a position very similar to that of the restructuring school: that the loss of manufacturing jobs in urban areas is in part the result of national shifts, from manufacturing to services, and towards higher unemployment. In those shifts, however, as everyone agrees, the cities have lost out particularly badly. The question is why? Again Fothergill and Gudgin's argument shares much with that of the restructuring school: 'The geography of employment growth and decline is in our view determined by the interaction of national economic trends and the characteristics of localities. Trends in the national economy confront firms with pressures they cannot easily resist' (*Fothergill, Gudgin, Kitson and Monk*, 1986). They also argue, as would the restructuring school, that while most firms face these pressures, the nature and extent of the pressure will vary.

At this point, however, the approaches diverge. *Fothergill, Gudgin, Kitson and Monk* (1986) argue that one locational characteristic above all has been responsible for the relative decline of cities, and that is the problem of availability of land. They argue that long-term technological changes mean that manufacturing needs more space per worker, and also often larger plots, and that this both puts cities at a disadvantage in relation to other areas and means that, even if all available urban land were used for manufacturing, there would still be a decline in employment.

There are three main ways in which this explanation differs from that of the restructuring school.

1   All the emphasis is put on one factor – the availability of land. Factors such as the availability and characteristics of labour are seen as having been important at certain periods 'until the early 1970s' (ibid.), but not as being fundamental. Here we have a hint that what divides the theorists is not only their answers but the time-frame of their questions.

2   *Fothergill* et al. are indeed looking at a much longer time-span. The increasing space-per-employee needed by manufacturing is a long-term trend. The industrial decline of the cities in comparison with other areas is thus not a product of any crisis or restructuring in the UK economy but a result of a continuous long-term change. Their data do bear out a long-term relative decline in urban manufacturing (ibid., Table 2). In other words, the argument is that there has not, in terms of this particular shift, been a sharp break in the recent period.

In reply, the restructuring school, while agreeing that it is important to distinguish long-term and short-term changes, might argue that within any long-term decentralization there have been periods of crucial importance. The same data also show that London and the conurbations fared more badly between the mid-'60s and early '70s than either earlier or later and that, as *Fothergill* et al. agree, labour questions seem to have been particularly important during this period. Something crucially different was happening, beyond any long-term trend.

3   However, the two schools conceptualize things differently. For *Fothergill* et al. issues of labour are technical questions of availability. Land problems are seen to arise from the technically necessary modernization of manufacturing industry. They do relate this to the capitalist character of industry, and to the market economy, but the restructuring school would argue that the implication of this is that it is important to specify the particular capitalist nature of industry. Thus its replacement of labour by machines is not only a 'technical' necessity but part of the drive towards making profits. There is little indication of the social organization of production in *Fothergill* et al.'s explanation: no recognition, for instance, that 'labour availability' is not just a technical question, but that the search for

cheaper labour and the desire to escape and undermine well-unionized workers is a reflection of the long antagonistic struggle between capital and labour.

2.4.4 Debate

In assessing these different explanations, and approaches to explanation, it is important to be clear about the nature of the differences between them. We shall mention just four of them here.

First, they adopt different methodologies. The location-factor approach focused on large numerical data sets and on finding statistically significant relationships between variables. Their search was for empirical regularity. The restructuring approach tended to focus more on detailed investigation of what had been happening in a small number of cases, in a particular industry perhaps. The latter pointed out that, while there was a general process of restructuring, the way it worked out in practice was different from case to case and that therefore it was pointless to search for highly regular patterns. The first approach replied that this was all very well but then how could we ever assess the importance of one variable against another in the overall changes? The restructuring school answered that you could not do that anyway, because the importance of a variable precisely depended on the wider context in which it was operating, but the most important contextual reason was probably manufacturing industry's need to cut costs in face of newly increasing competition. And so the debate continued.

That discussion in turn reflected a second difference. The first school of thought tended to examine data on outcomes in order to find an explanation. The second school, in contrast, focused on the processes of change. The latter argued, as seen above, that a given 'cause' may result in a variety of outcomes, depending on the circumstances in which it is operating. Regional policy, for instance, had different effects in different situations. They also argued that apparently similar outcomes can in fact be the product of a variety of different causes. Not all moves to the regions would result from the same 'factor'. This relates back to the discussion of issues of conceptualization in section 2.2.

Thirdly, it is not only that the approaches give different 'answers', it is also that they are asking different questions. For the first approach, the question was why did that specific geographical change take place? For the second approach this could only be answered by asking another, deeper, question: why did geographical change take place at that period at all? *Fothergill* et al. argued that the whole time-frame of the question needed to be longer. The nature of the 'causes' identified by the different approaches, in other words, reflected very clearly the way the enquiry was framed in the first place.

Fourthly, the approaches differ, at least implicitly, in how they view one of the central concerns of this and related Open Texts: the geographical organization of society. At first sight 'geography' is most important in the location-factor approach, since both its question and its answer are explicitly geographical: 'why this particular geographical shift?' . . . 'because of these geographical factors'. The restructuring approach, in contrast, moves away from the specifically geographical question and answer and examines the wider social changes (in this case in industry) and their relation *to* geography. In fact, however, this approach also sees geography as important, though in a different way. For the second approach, two things were significant: that a major change in British industry (the fact that it was experiencing increasing competitive difficulties) was in turn being reflected in geographical changes, and that these geographical changes (for instance, the decentralization in an effort to cut costs) were themselves one way in which British industry was seeking to combat the growing pressures upon it.

Summary of sections 2.3 and 2.4

- At the same time that there has been a shift in the size and importance of manufacturing within the economy as a whole, there has also been a transformation in the geography of manufacturing within the country.
- From the mid-'60s to the mid-'70s there was some tendency towards increasing regional equality in terms of unemployment numbers; since the mid-'70s this process has been reversed. Regional inequality began to increase again, although along different lines.
- These changes are the combined result of a number of different processes, including differential decline, decentralization and the spatial concentration of growing sectors of manufacturing.
- At the more local level there has also been a marked shift away from major urban areas towards areas which previously had been less industrialized.
- All this again raises issues of the definition of deindustrialization and of its relationship to wider international restructuring.
- There is a major debate about the explanation of these geographical shifts. Behind this debate lies the deeper issue of the relationship between geographical change and national manufacturing change.

2.5   Explaining the changes: uneven development

It is this relationship – between geographical change and economic change – that we are now going to investigate further. So far we have established that major changes have been going on both in the UK economy as a whole and in its geography. We have also looked at some of the processes which have contributed to these shifts and at debates over their explanation. But such shifts are not unique to this period. And what this section will do is stand back from the particularity of today (though continuing to use it as an example) and ask why economies develop such geographical variation and why their geographies are subject to change. A key concept in understanding such major shifts, and relating them to wider economic change, is **uneven development**.

Uneven development is a concept which can be used in a variety of contexts. Writers often refer to uneven development between sectors, for example, or between firms within a sector. In this and related Open Texts we shall use the term to refer specifically to uneven *geographical* development, and the focus will be on uneven development within a national economy. In fact, uneven development at international and intranational levels are closely associated (*Thrift*, 1986).

2.5.1 Changing patterns

Superficially, there is little disagreement between theoretical approaches over the fact that capitalist economies develop unevenly over space. It would be hard to dispute the generality of the existence of geographical inequality, within countries, in levels of development of industry, or levels of unemployment, and the unequal social conditions which these imply. However, the explanation of such differences varies greatly between theoretical traditions.

Theoretical approaches based on *neo-classical* economics certainly agree that inequalities may develop between regions within a country. Early development is likely to be uneven because of differentiation in initial conditions. However, this theoretical approach would argue, such inequalities are in principle temporary. This is because the inequalities will themselves give rise to counter-processes (equilibrating mechanisms) which will lead to an eventual evening-out, as the process of development shifts towards the previously less developed areas. It is recognized that in practice 'equality in equilibrium' is most unlikely to be reached, since well before such processes could have fully played themselves out other changes may well have disrupted the system in other ways. The historical process is therefore likely to be more like a shifting see-saw as the balance of development switches between different regions. Nonetheless there is an underlying tendency towards equalization.

There is certainly historical evidence from the economic geography of the UK which, at first sight at least, might lend credence to this view. Over the long historical period since the Industrial Revolution, the focus of industrial development has shifted a number of times. Moreover, Keeble argued (see section 2.4) that the shifts in the 1970s were due precisely to the counter-processes which can be sparked off by the concentration of development in a particular area. He argued that agglomeration disconomies were the prime explanation for the decentralization. These processes could also be seen as

embodying tendencies towards regional equality. The decentralization towards the old industrial periphery marked a shift of jobs back to regions
which since the 1930s had had dramatically higher unemployment rates than
elsewhere.

A *Marxist* interpretation of uneven development would also recognize
that the development of a region is likely to set off mechanisms which
eventually halt or restrain the process. For Marxists, too, as an area becomes
developed it can acquire characteristics which make it less attractive to
capitalist production. Some of these characteristics would be not unlike
those of a neo-classical analysis: old buildings, congestion, high land prices,
high wages. Marxists, however, would lay more stress on factors such as the
development of a well-unionized workforce and the frequent need for
industry to hold down wages. They would, moreover, analyse these factors
as reflecting the capitalist social organization of production. Industry is
constantly roaming the world seeking out more profitable conditions of
production, and one important element in that search might be a cheap and
unmilitant labour force. Thus the development of an area can eventually
produce its own counter-tendencies not just because of congestion, or
because the buildings and infrastructure are ageing, but also because of the
rising living standards (and therefore cost) and better organization of
labour. Thus, the decentralization of industry to the peripheral regions was a
classic example of its seeking out a green and vulnerable labour force (the
women of these areas), a necessity forced on industry by competition.
Moreover, in contrast to the neo-classical school, Marxists have often
emphasized that before any countervailing tendencies set in, the processes
of growth in one region and decline elsewhere may for long periods become
self-reinforcing.

From this theoretical perspective there is no underlying tendency towards
equality. It is more that industry opens up and exploits certain areas (or
rather the people of those areas), subsequently – when it runs into the costs
of such development or encounters resistance – to abandon them to unemployment and decay. Even where the costs derive simply from physical age
(of plant and buildings, for instance, as in today's inner cities perhaps) it is
cheaper, from the point of view of the individual company, to abandon that
area in favour of a 'greenfield site'.

The neo-classical assumption of an underlying tendency towards equality
is, however, most hotly disputed by a school of thought which would argue,
by contrast, that the very fact of uneven development at any one time creates
further processes which make that inequality hard to counter. Instead of a
see-saw process as different regions take over the running, a vicious circle
sets in – a process of *cumulative causation* – by which the places which
initially take the lead generate, by that very fact, all kinds of other advantages which make their position unassailable. (For these regions the process
is a virtuous circle.) Such advantages might include the concentration of
people and therefore of a large market for consumer goods and services, the
development of the area as the nodal point of the transport system, or the

generation of a community of skilled workers and technical know-how. The combination of such characteristics with the operation of local *multiplier effects* will, it is argued, generate the self-reinforcing growth spiral, further improving the position of the initially advantaged region. Demand will increase, for inputs, for labour and for consumer goods; investment will therefore be encouraged and this in turn will hasten the processes of technical change and productivity increase. (The elements of these which would reduce costs – such as the better transport system, the cheaper access to all kinds of services and so forth – are elements of agglomeration economies.) By contrast, regions which lose out in the early development will see even their initial potential undermined relative to the growth-regions. Unemployment and low wages will mean low local buying power, infrastructure of all kinds will remain relatively undeveloped, and low rates of investment will hold back technical progress thus further disadvantaging the region. These divergent internal growth mechanisms will be reinforced by the nature of the interaction between the regions. The expanding region will attract capital for investment and workers will migrate from the less advantaged areas. Thus the inequalities between the regions are further increased.

The evidence discussed above might seem immediately to refute this theory. Yet section 2.3 also pointed out that geographical inequality had been increasing again, especially since the late 1970s. Moreover, throughout all these swings, London has retained a peculiar importance within the national economy as a whole. How is that to be explained? With such potentially conflicting evidence, how are we to judge between approaches?

2.5.2   Underlying relations

In order to proceed further with this debate, it is necessary to look more deeply at the form of the arguments. One point on which all the above theories agree, although they would put different degrees of explicit emphasis upon it, is that 'space is socially produced'. That is to say, characteristics of places, which give rise to the equilibrating tendencies of neo-classical theory or the reinforcing tendencies of cumulative causation, or which propel capital's restless search for profit described by Marxism, are characteristics produced by society itself; indeed they are products of the very industrial system which subsequently reacts to them.

Yet once we accept this, it is also evident that the notion of 'level of development' goes beyond simply the numerical extent of employment and unemployment. London, to take the most obvious example, is dominant within the UK economy, not only because it is the biggest agglomeration of physical development, nor because it is the largest concentration of employment, nor even because on average and in spite of the poverty within it, it is rich. It is so because of the *function* of much of its economic activity within the economy as a whole. It is a centre of *control*. It is the location of central government, of the headquarters of many major firms, and it is, as will be seen in Chapter 3, the overwhelmingly dominant centre of banking and finance; it is the home of 'the City'. So whatever the numerical distribution of jobs or of unemployment, the tentacles of control over those jobs, and over the functioning of the economy as a whole, in the main lead back – if they stay within Britain at all – to London.

We have been discussing uneven development. But the question now arises: the uneven development of what? It is clear that what is at issue here is more than geographical inequalities in the pattern of employment and unemployment, even in their broader social implications. Those things are important enough in themselves, but they are also expressive of inequalities at a deeper level. What is at issue is the nature of the relations between the economic activity in different regions. It is in the nature of these relations, as well as in the quantity and quality of employment, that the inequality between regions may be rooted.

Thus, as we saw earlier, much economic activity in other regions of the country is subordinated to functions performed in London. This raises the issue of how we are to interpret the decentralization of jobs which took place between the mid-'60s and the mid-'70s. Did it really lead to greater 'equality' between regions? It certainly did, if only temporarily, in terms of levels of unemployment. But what about in terms of economic relations? Where whole firms moved out, especially where these were dynamic and growing firms – which they often were – the answer is again probably positive. This situation was most characteristic, as we noted in section 2.3, of the less urbanized regions of the south of the country.

In the case of the regions of the north and west, however, the situation was different. Here, many of the new jobs were in branch plants, the controlling headquarters of which remained in the central regions of the country. In terms of such companies, therefore, the economic activity in the central region was dominant and that in the peripheral region was subordinate. In turn this difference may affect the stability of the employment, and the likelihood that it will generate further growth in the region concerned. Branch plants in regions far from head office may be more vulnerable to closure, while the more routine production work which is carried out in them may be more vulnerable to automation than the work done centrally. Indeed quite a proportion of the branch plants which were established in the peripheral regions in the 1960s and '70s have now closed; their spin-off effects were small and the unemployment in those regions, as we have seen, has risen sharply again. 'Uneven development' relates to far more than numbers of jobs and levels of unemployment.

One way this can be conceptualized is in terms of the different roles, or sets of functions, which the economic activities of a region play in the wider national, and international, economy. Different regions – or the people and economic activities within them – play different roles within the overall division of labour. Indeed, what the geography of employment and unemployment reflects is precisely the geography of the division of labour in society. The division of labour in society is the basis, it is argued, for a **spatial division of labour** (Massey, 1984).

The degree to which that spatial division of labour is one of regional inequality (uneven development) will reflect:

(a) the degree to which the division of labour in society is itself unequal; and

(b) the way those inequalities are organized over space.

Thus, the fact that in the UK parts of the City control parts of manufacturing industry, and that within firms (and also between them) there are hierarchical divisions of labour, between levels of management, for instance, or between management and the shop-floor, or between professional/scientific workers and manual workers, or between sectors, means that there is inequality structured into the division of labour.

It is also the case that in the UK this division of labour is quite highly structured over space. Managerial and control functions, and the relatively highly-paid jobs that go with them, are highly concentrated into the south and east of the country. There are other aspects of the division of labour within industry which also have a spatial form. In recent years, one of the fastest-growing groups in manufacturing, in proportional terms, has been scientific and technical workers. Technical workers with an academic qualification are tending to replace the engineers of former years. Moreover, while the engineers tended to work on or near the shop-floor, today's scientific and technical professionals are just as likely to be located far from actual production. In many cases they are in high-status, semi-rural locations. And increasingly they have been clustering into the outer South East. In contrast to these concentrations of managerial, professional and technical workers in the south and east, in the regions of 'the north' workers in direct production (whether in manufacturing or services) tend to form a higher proportion of the total population.

There is thus a broad spatial division of labour within which control functions are concentrated in London, scientific and technical functions concentrated in the south and east, and production, while it occurs throughout the country, is a higher proportion of economic activity in the regions of the north and west.

2.5.3 Change over time

If uneven development has its foundation in the unequal division of labour in society, then over time regional inequality will change, not only in its geographical pattern, but also in its nature, as the division of labour in society changes. To give one obvious example: for decades earlier in this century the major differences in economic activity between regions in this country were based on sectors of production. It was a spatial division of labour based on specialization by sector: engineering goods and cars in the West Midlands; textiles, clothing and engineering in the North West; coal and steel in the central lowlands of Scotland and the valleys of South Wales, and so on. To a much greater degree than today, though even then it varied greatly between regions, these industries were also owned locally. The managers and the technicians (then engineers) were more likely to be locally based. In this situation one of the most important dimensions of uneven development was the inequality which resulted from differences between sectors and in particular from the economic fortunes of different sectors. If a sector collapsed it would be likely to take 'its region' with it. The classic British 'regional problem' of the coalfields in the 1930s resulted from the collapse of the coal industry (partly as a result of the collapse of the UK's position within an earlier international division of labour) which had been so central to the economic structure of a number of areas of the country. At a wider level, as we saw earlier, the West Midlands has suffered heavily in more recent years because of its specialization in manufacturing.

That sectoral spatial division of labour is no longer dominant in the UK. It began to break down in the post-war years and during that period, too, the concentration of control functions in London also began to increase. Since the 1960s there has been a marked convergence of regional economic structures in terms of their mix of manufacturing industries and, as was seen in section 2.3, in the balance between manufacturing and services. Judging by the problems caused by regional specialization when an area's specialism went into decline, this shift might have been expected to lessen the degree of uneven development. And yet, in fact:

> ... broad convergence in industrial structure does not imply convergence in economic prospects. Within services as well as manufacturing, the south is increasing its role as the 'core' of the space economy, through its concentration of corporate headquarters, R and D activities, availability of venture capital and so on. In contrast, the north has a concentration of lower paid employees working in branch plants whose prospects (e.g. adoption of new technology) are determined elsewhere. The earlier distinctiveness of numerous regional industrial structures has been replaced by a north/south distinction in corporate and occupational structures. (Goddard and Combes, 1987, pp. 15–17)

In other words, far from having lessened, uneven development has changed its nature as the geography of the division of labour in society, and the dimensions of that division of labour itself, have evolved. The argument is that there is a new spatial division of labour (Massey, 1984).

Moreover these different forms of uneven development are constructed one upon the other. At any one time, the new and growing (or even merely relocating) parts of an economy will be selecting their locations from a highly complex geography. They will be responding to the conditions produced by earlier phases of uneven development and building on the inheritance of previous geographies of earlier divisions of labour and their associated structures of dominance and subordination. The geography (the existing form of uneven development) faced by the sunrise sectors of today is the inheritance of centuries, and in particular of the two centuries since the Industrial Revolution.

But it is not just the geography which changes. So do the locational requirements of industry, as was seen in section 2.4. The requirements of the sectors which are expanding today bear little resemblance to the requirements of the industries of the last century, or indeed to the industry of only a few decades ago. What they do have in common is that in all cases industry will be looking for the location where it can make the best profit. It will, in that sense, be *using* the existing form of uneven development to its maximum advantage. Thus the industry which decentralized from central region to periphery in the 1960s and '70s was using locational change, within the context of existing forms of uneven development, to improve its competitive position. It was the legacy of the previous form of uneven development based in the sectoral spatial division of labour (high levels of unemployment from previously dominant sectors which had overwhelmingly employed men) which provided the conditions (regional policy grants, a 'green', female labour force anxious for paid employment) which attracted in this new form of economic activity and laid down a new form of uneven development. In that sense the production and reproduction of uneven development is not just a reflection of changes in the wider economy and its division of labour, it is, as was pointed out in section 2.4, integral to those changes.

2.6   A historical turning-point?

Earlier sections of this chapter have indicated the existence of recent, major changes within manufacturing in the UK economy, in the geography of manufacturing and in uneven development more widely (for uneven development cannot be considered only in relation to manufacturing – and later chapters will add to this wider picture). It is also argued that a new spatial division of labour is being established.

However, a number of theories argue that the changes are even bigger than this: that we are at a major historical turning-point in the nature of the UK economy and in its urban and regional geography. The different schools would characterize that turning-point, and the mechanisms which give rise to it, in different ways, however. We shall look at two of these schools here, both of which were introduced in Chapter 1: the regulationist school and long-wave theories. (World-system theories are less relevant here because, as was pointed out in Chapter 1, they pay little attention to the internal structure of national economies.) In their original formulation these two schools were both more concerned, if not exclusively so, with macroeconomic and in some cases social historical development. It has taken subsequent theoretical work by others to relate them to geography. It should also be stressed that it is perfectly possible to have reservations about, or even to reject, both these schools, and yet to accept that there has indeed been a major shift in the economy and geography of the UK since the mid-1960s!

2.6.1   Regulationist theories

For regulationist theories the history of capitalist development has been a series of phases each dominated by a different combination of regime of accumulation and mode of regulation. There is a strong notion of system, and each historical phase is brought to an end by internal changes within that system, perhaps by the exhaustion of the regime of accumulation or by the stifling of accumulation by the mode of regulation of society. At the core of this system is the changing social organization of production itself, the changing *labour process*. The hypothesis is that we have now reached the end of the particular combination known as *Fordism* and are embarking on an as yet embryonic and relatively unknown period, but one which has already been given a name – *neo-Fordism*.

Fordism, according to this approach, was characterized by mass production, mass consumption, state intervention into the management of the economy, collective bargaining, indeed the whole ideology of collectivism, as opposed, for instance, to individualism and the provision of certain services through the welfare state (see *Martin*, 1988).

It has been argued that the mass production element of Fordism was never as strongly developed in the UK as in, for instance, the United States. This lesser development made it less strong, and – it is argued – accounts for industry's earlier collapse beginning in the 1960s. The particularly high rate of loss of manufacturing jobs in the UK and the consequent problems for inner cities and manufacturing regions would therefore on this reading be in part due to the relatively fragile development of Fordism, which means that certain manufacturing industries had remained relatively backward and therefore less competitive.

This immediately raises a problem for regulationist theories. Their argument depends on a notion of society as a system which is dominated by particular forms of social and economic organization. Even while the system remains capitalist it may at different phases be dominated by differently organized social and economic structures. But what does 'dominated' mean? If Fordism in production did not develop very fully in the UK, can it really be said to have 'dominated' the economy and society? Certainly a form of production does not have to be *numerically* dominant (to be present in a majority of factories, for instance) for it to be the most important in terms of influence on the economy as a whole. But the theorists do not specify precisely *how* important Fordism was, nor how its hypothesized dominance was established. We shall take up this issue in detail in Chapter 4.

At a wider level, in relation to society as a whole, it might equally be questioned how dominant collectivism and state provision have ever been in the US. The characteristics of 'Fordism' mentioned above seem sometimes more an amalgam of features of different societies (mass production in the US, collectivism in the UK and Europe) than a precise analysis of any one society. This is a real problem with concepts as broad (indeed some would say elastic) as those of Fordism and neo-Fordism.

But Fordism – it is argued – *was* established in the UK and, moreover, it had its own geography. The dominance of mass production meant that this was a system characterized by large plants. Consumer goods industries were the linchpin, and these were overwhelmingly located in the West Midlands and in and around Greater London. It was here that were found the richest markets. The northern industrial regions, in contrast, were dominated by the older sectors which had been the basis of earlier expansion. These sectors, it is argued, mainly produced intermediate goods, that is inputs, such as machinery, which were sold to other sectors. These sectors had long been in decline – reflecting the decline of the UK as a world economic power – so the people of these regions did not have the buying power to attract the new consumer goods industries.

Further, the post-war boom at the height of Fordism led to an increased demand for labour. In the UK new workers were found amongst women who were increasingly drawn into paid work, and also through migration both from Commonwealth countries and from the now declining northern regions to the midlands and south.

The *pattern* of uneven development was thus between growth in the South East and West Midlands of England and decline in much of the rest of the country. The *form* of uneven development, it is argued, was based on sectoral specialization: different regions specialized in different groups of industries. Here again it is possible to question the regulationists on their interpretation of the facts. As we saw in section 2.5, the sectoral spatial division of labour was already beginning to break down in the UK during the post-war years when Fordism is supposed to have been at its height.

In the end, it is argued, Fordism collapsed under its own weight. The accretion of gradual changes led to a crisis and to the necessity for structural change. Mass production led to rigidities and difficulties in changing product and design. The fragmentation of tasks which went along with Fordism reached technical, social and political limits. Technically, it meant problems of co-ordination within production; socially, the sheer boredom of a minutely divided labour process, or technical division of labour, showed signs of countering its technical possibilities of increasing productivity; and, more widely, the collective bargaining by workers in large factories began to put pressure on profits. Moreover, imbalances arose within the economy as a whole, in particular between consumption goods and capital goods. The mass production labour processes proved difficult to extend to certain consumption sectors, and in particular to the services (such as health) which were provided collectively through the welfare state. This meant that it was impossible sufficiently to cheapen the production of that most vital product of all – the labour force itself. And this in turn made it difficult to maintain profits in the economy as a whole. It also meant, precisely because such services were in large measure provided publicly, that private investment and accumulation were being squeezed, so the regulationists argue, by an expanding state sector.

One response to this decline in the dynamism of Fordism was the geographical decentralization of production in search of cheaper labour. This took place both to the Third World (Chapter 1) and to more rural and peripheral regions of the UK (sections 2.3 and 2.4). There seems at this point to be disagreement among the regulationists, with some hypothesizing that the decentralization within Britain was the beginning of a new phase of (neo-Fordist) accumulation (Aglietta, 1979; Dunford, Geddes and Perrons, 1981), while others (*Martin*, 1988; Marshall, 1987) clearly see it as an attempt to use geographical restructuring to prolong the life of Fordism. In general, given that the decentralization was based on a Fordist fragmentation of the labour process, and that the plants which were decentralized were often precisely of the mass production variety, the second interpretation seems more tenable. What is clear, however, is that decentralization ushered in a new form of uneven development.

Fordism, however, is now being replaced by neo-Fordism. New technologies mean that high productivity is now possible with small-batch production. The emphasis is on flexibility – in terms of response to the market and in terms of the labour force. This emerging kind of organization within production is sometimes called *flexible specialization*. More widely within society, it is argued, competitive individualism challenges collectivism; the provision of services through the state is abandoned in favour of privatization so expanding again the sphere of potential profit-making. The decline of collectivism, and of large plants, and the increasing demand for a 'flexible' workforce pose immense threats to trade unionism.

All this in turn, though as yet embryonic, may have major geographical implications. Cuts in the public sector eat away at one of the few parts of the economy with a relatively even geographical distribution, especially local services (Massey, 1984). The new 'geography of flexible accumulation' focuses economic growth, and particularly growth in higher-status employment, far away from the old industries, the old collectivisms, the ideological as well as the physical inheritance of Fordism. The competitive individualism of the growth regions of the country, and the retreat of the collectivist ideologies of 'the north' are thus an essential part of the emergence of neo-Fordism in its current form. And in its current form it would seem to be leading, at both regional and local level, to an increasingly unequal national geography (*Martin*, 1988).

2.6.2   Long-wave theories

Another approach to conceptualizing the simultaneous changes in the economy and geography of the UK has been made using variants of the theory of long waves. As was seen in Chapter 1, the main debate here has revolved around how to explain the long waves. As we shall see, a similar debate is taking place amongst those who are trying to link long waves to theories of geographical change. Here, too, there are debates over what mechanisms underlie the long cycles and to what extent their causes are internal to the capitalist system or derive from external factors.

But there is also, at this intranational level, another debate. It was pointed out in Chapter 1 that geography was not integral to the theory of long waves, apart from the descriptive fact that different countries have taken the lead in successive cycles. In the use of the theories to analyse developments *within* the UK, however, there have been attempts to link long waves to the changing nature and pattern of uneven development. Perhaps the best-known attempt to make such a link has been by Peter Hall. As Figure 2.6 indicates, he argues that the first Kondratiev wave was dominated by Lancashire, Shropshire and the Black Country, the second by South Wales and

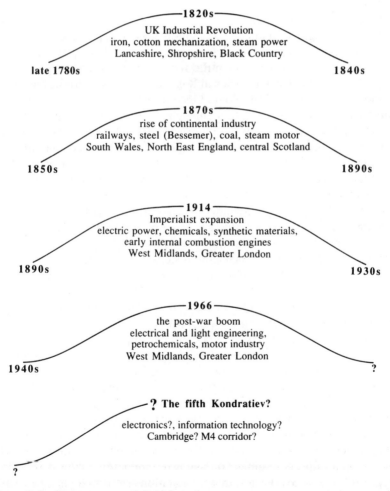

Figure 2.6 *Long waves and British regions*

the North East, and the third and fourth waves by the West Midlands and Greater London (*Hall*, 1985). The fifth wave, the one which it is hypothe-sized is starting now, seems likely to be based in the non-industrial parts of the south and east of England, especially the M4 corridor and around Cambridge. The question is: why has this happened?

Hall takes a Schumpeterian view of long waves and translates it into a geographical context. That is to say, his explanation of long waves lies in technological change which results from the bunching of innovations made by entrepreneurs. Hall argues that this bunching is not just historical, but also geographical. 'Economic success', he writes, 'lies with the country and the region and the city that innovate, that keep one step ahead of the action' (*Hall*, 1985). Such bunches of innovations will initially produce strong growth in the regions of origin, a growth which will, as the product range matures, spread out to other regions. But by this time the profit level will be falling and the impetus will be dying away. The new industries, in their turn, will become sunset sectors.

Why, then, might such bunching of innovatory entrepreneurship occur in particular regions? Hall argues that for the fifth Kondratiev one of the key elements is the presence of scientific research: the initial trigger for the development of the new industries of this long wave – electronics, informa-tion technology and biotechnology. Once triggered, however, a process of cumulative causation sets in. Companies cluster together anxious not to miss out on the latest developments and the growing pool of scientifically-skilled labour. Hall talks of 'intellectual "external economies"' and compares this clustering with 'the traditional industrial quarter in the inner areas of the great Victorian cities'. Here the external economies were of a different form and the location, of course, is today no longer in the inner city. In part, and reinforcing the locational attributes of Cambridge and the 'M4 corridor' which were mentioned above, this is because of the social choices of the elite workforce. In comparison with the 'new' areas, regions of older develop-ment, especially inner cities, have huge disadvantages. The only possibilities for such areas might lie in attracting to them (through government policy) low-paid jobs demanding minimal skills. The only exception, Hall argues, is if a new entrepreneurial tradition could be created in the inner city.

There is much here that chimes well with the empirical evidence in earlier sections. The concentration of new sectors, the apparently hopeless derelic-tion of inner cities, the mind-numbing and badly-paid work in the branch plants which are a more important component in the economies of the regions of 'the north'. But what of its adequacy as an explanation? Clearly, it suffers from the charge of an unexplained psychologism which can be levelled at all Schumpeterian versions of long-wave theory (see Chapter 1). Indeed, for Hall, places themselves almost become the actors – 'regions which innovate'. On the other hand, he does try to give a social context and explanation for the geographical bunching of innovations in his descriptions of regional differences. Part of that explanation seems to lie in an essential inequality between people in different places, between the 'hard-to-employ' of inner cities and the sparkling entrepreneurs of Cambridge and the M4 corridor, for instance. But this, too, seems questionable. The location of the entrepreneurship of the fifth Kondratiev actually seems determined by publicly funded research, and most of the scientific and professional work-force actually *moved in* to the areas. Once there, and finding them nice places in which to live, the areas' dynamism was ensured by the social preferences of this elite.

Hall's theory is sectoral. Different industries grow and decline; sunrise and sunset. It is also very cyclical: the M4 today is very like the industrial district of the nineteenth century. In that sense it is quite a deterministic theory. It leaves little room for influence or manoeuvre. Indeed Hall's own policy-prescription is very much to 'go with it', to follow and facilitate the developments which will, anyway and ineluctably, take place.

Other authors have tried to use the theory of long waves in ways that escape from these characteristics, which they see as problematical. Freeman (1987) and Rothwell (1982) embed their conceptions of the technological change between waves in a broader confluence of social factors. Rothwell (1982), who also points to regional variations in the production of innova-tions, explains it not in terms of different local levels of entrepreneurship but in terms of the regional bias of R&D expenditure towards the South East, the older and more traditional technology structure of some northern re-gions, the unequal availability of venture capital between regions and the local planning environment for small firms. His analysis, therefore, opens the possibility of policy intervention to alter the geography of innovation. It might be possible to relocate government research establishments and to target high-technology, public-sector purchasing to create more demand for innovations in older regions, for example.

Marshall (1987) follows Mandel (1975) in relating long waves to major shifts in the wider economy, and especially to movements in the rate of profit, but goes beyond Mandel in trying to make the theory less determinis-tic. He does this by making the labour process, and the shift from Fordism to neo-Fordism, more central to his analysis and by bringing in social and political forces at every stage. The greater focus on labour process also leads away from a primarily sectoral basis of analysis. The new technology of the fifth wave affects the process of production as much as the kinds of products which are produced, and the new labour processes can be applied to older industries as well as new. This directly challenges the notion of a hard distinction between sunrise industries and sunset industries with the latter doomed inevitably to decline. And that in turn means that the options for regional development, too, may be more open. In many ways this brings Marshall closer to the regulationist school and indeed he explicitly incorpo-rates aspects of their analysis in his approach. He is, however, critical of the regulationist approach, at least as applied by Dunford and Perrons, for not really incorporating uneven development as part of their explanation. This is a main aim of Marshall's work. He argues that it is not just that the long waves each have a different pattern but that regional differentiation, and regional political and social movements, are crucial to the shape of long waves themselves. Thus:

> These evolving patterns of uneven development are not simply reflections or outcomes of the long waves in the national economy. They *are* the process of national economic change and development. At different times, and in different ways, the spatial divisions in economic organization have played a role in the national patterns of short-term fluctuations characteristic of the successive historical periods. The succession of leading industrial regions have (sic) provided the basis for regional social and political movements which have, at critical moments, contested and to varying degrees determined the ensuing course of national and sometimes international economic development. The key factor in the overall course of British economic development has been the particular, even unique, class character of British capitalism in the division between industrial and finance capital which has itself entailed a spatial division between the industrial provinces and the metropolitan hub of finance and commerce. (Marshall, 1987, p. 228)

This more complex approach to long waves leads also to a more complex view of uneven development. The changing regional pattern of industrial development has entailed more than shifts between sectors. The focus on the labour process and on the division of labour allows other forms of uneven development to be picked up. Thus, while inter-sectoral divisions were indeed dominant in the wave up to the inter-war depression, the latest phase of Fordist restructuring has involved the establishment of 'a new *intra*-sectoral spatial division between regions specializing in different sub-sectors within the same industry, such as research and development, component manufacture and final assembly' (ibid., p. 228). Although it might be pointed out that the new spatial division of labour can produce divisions within regions as well as between them, in general this approach accords with the argument in section 2.5 that uneven development changes in its form as well as in its pattern between different historical periods.

It is on the basis of this that the latest – fifth – long wave is emerging. Like the regulationist school, however, this view of long waves would stress that the fifth wave is as yet only embryonic and its form is still to be determined. Indeed, even its strength in the UK is as yet in question. The UK economy, in the international realm of uneven development, is not leading this upswing. Cambridge, England and the M4 corridor are subordinate to Cambridge, Massachusetts and Silicon Valley in California and to other centres such as those in Japan. Moreover, whatever its strength, its form within the UK, including its geography, will depend on social and political developments. Thus it is pointed out that support for microelectronics has been biased towards the south of the country, and it is argued that emphasis on a division between sunrise and sunset, on finance at the expense of manufacturing, on entrepreneurship and new firms as opposed to restructuring existing industries, will all encourage the confinement of the fifth wave of economic growth to a few small areas of the country.

Activity 2.3

(a)   How would you assess, first, long-wave theories and, secondly, the regulationist approach in relation to:

  (i)   their characters as theories;
          (You could look at the following:

  • Are they asking the same questions?

  • What assumptions do they make about society?

  • What aspects of economy and society does each approach prioritize?

  • What about their relation to evidence?)

  (ii)   their application at international level (see Chapter 1);

  (iii)   their application to the UK.

(Note: answers to these may overlap – (ii) and (iii) may be used as illustrations of (i), for instance. And can you refute or respond to some of the criticisms?)

(b)   What differences are there in the implications for the future economic geography of the UK between long-wave and regulationist theories?

(c)   How would you characterize uneven development? (You might refer to the ways in which industry can be organized over space; to patterns and forms of uneven development; to how it changes over time.)

2.6.3   Debate

In their 'pure' forms the regulationist and long-wave schools are very different. The regulationist school has a more developed notion of society as a total system and of contradictions arising within that system, leading to periods of disruption and the emergence of new phases of accumulation. In contrast the long-wave school focuses more precisely on technology, though it is notable that much of the debate within that school has been about what causes technological change and how that change should be seen as part of a wider system. These concepts of 'system' are important and themselves subject to debate. They will be examined further in the next chapter. But they raise again the issue of how one assesses the importance of different forms of organization within an economy and society, and especially in what sense, and when, it is possible to say that a particular form of organization dominates a system. This is both a conceptual issue and one of data. As we have seen, there are real questions about how to use in a really precise way some of the very general concepts of the regulationist school.

  Parallel to this contrast is another, that while the long-wave school tends to focus on production the regulationists see the wider social and political structures of society as being necessary to the maintenance of particular regimes of production. While the long-wavists might point to effects of changes in production on wider society, they are less likely than the regulationists to see the cause-and-effect relation going the other way.

There are other contrasts, too. The long-wave school tends to conduct analysis in terms of sectors, whilst the regulationists would focus on changes in the labour process which, while undoubtedly being associated with the growth of new sectors, may also transform existing ones. The long-wave school tends to see historical phases more cyclically, and to encounter repetitions and similarities between cycles. For the regulationists history, to use a delightful phrase of Aglietta's, is 'innovatory': there is no cyclical repetition but a succession of phases which only emerge and come to an end as a result of their own characteristics and particular historical circumstances. It is in that sense a much more open-ended notion of time.

For this reason the regulationist school appears less 'deterministic' than long-wave theories. Yet within each school, and perhaps particularly among those using a long-wave framework, there is debate about the degree to which in spite of all the observable regularities the shape of the future is mouldable, is ours to create.

In fact, in most of the applications of these theories to UK geography, they are used as broad, interpretative frameworks rather than as precise specifications. Indeed in a number of cases there is explicit meshing of the two approaches. In all cases, however, what is at issue is the integration of the historical periodization of British society with changes in its geography. What they confirm is the complex notion of uneven development outlined in the last section, and how the changing geography of the UK since the mid-'60s has been part and parcel of its wider transformation.

Summary of sections 2.5 and 2.6

- There is little disagreement between theories that economic development within capitalist societies such as the UK tends to take place unevenly, but different theories would set that unevenness in contrasting contexts: of long-term equilibrium, increasing polarization or shifting patterns of continuing inequality.

- But uneven development can be argued to be about more than patterns. It also concerns the relations between economic activities in different regions. Such relations both define the form of inequality between places at any one time and also help set the scene for the next form of uneven development.

- Uneven development can change in both its pattern and its form over time.

- Such changes may be associated with equally structural changes in the wider economy and society.

- Both regulationist and long-wave theorists argue that such a double transformation – of economy and geography – is currently under way in the UK.

- Although there are common concerns shared by the two theories, and indeed attempts to draw on both of them, there are also differences in terms of, for instance, the way in which they characterize society, or the part of it they are dealing with, the degree to which they focus on production and technology, whether their focus is on sectors or wider processes, and in relation to evidence (both in terms of whether their balance is towards description or explanation and in terms of their interpretation of evidence).

Further reading

Probably still the standard work on deindustrialization is *Deindustrialization* edited by F. Blackaby (Aldershot, Gower/National Institute of Economic and Social Research, Economic Policy Papers 2; 1979). This is a collection of papers from an early seminar held to discuss, and to try to define and explain, deindustrialization. It is quite technical, and probably difficult for people without some background in economics.

A more recent collection, which reflects some of the same debates and also considers their implications for the economic geography of the UK is *The Geography of De-Industrialisation* edited by Ron Martin and Bob Rowthorn (London and Basingstoke, Macmillan; 1986). This contains a wide selection of accessible articles which span not just the decline of manufacturing but also the geography of the growth of new manufacturing sectors and of services.

The Anatomy of Job Loss: The How, Where and Why of Employment Decline, by Doreen Massey and Richard Meegan (London, Methuen; 1982), is a study of job loss in a range of manufacturing sectors. It argues that in order to understand the geography of employment decline it is necessary to understand the changes going on in production itself.

Turning again to the growing sectors of the economy, there is *Western Sunrise: The Genesis and Growth of Britain's Major High Tech Corridor*, by P. Hall, M. Breheny, R. McQuaid and D. Hart (Hemel Hempstead, Unwin Hyman; 1987), which examines the factors behind the growth of high-tech in the M4 corridor, points to the importance of government policy, and expresses reservations about the size of the high-tech contribution to employment growth. In methodological contrast, Andrew Sayer and Kevin Morgan in *Microcircuits of Capital: The Electronics Industry and Uneven Development* (Cambridge, Polity Press; 1988) take a restructuring approach in examining the geography of the microelectronics industry at international, national and regional levels.

One aspect of the regional geography of job loss and job change which it has not been possible to examine in the chapter is the contrasting ways in which different regions of the UK relate to the international division of labour. There are a number of articles which analyse this important aspect of explaining a region's economic fortunes. The West Midlands is examined in *Jobs Crisis and the Multinationals: the Case of the West Midlands* by F. Gaffikin and A. Nickson (Birmingham, Birmingham Trade Union Group for World Development, 1984) and the North West of England in 'North West England 1971–77: a study in industrial decline and economic restructuring' by P. Lloyd and D. Reeve (*Regional Studies*, 1982, Vol. 16, No. 5, pp. 345–60). This latter article also deals with a number of other issues discussed in this chapter, including the evidence of change in the mid-'60s, the difference between cities in their manufacturing/service balance, the difference between rural areas in the north and south, and the geographical centralization of control.

More general overviews, and interpretations of recent changes in the economic geography of the UK are provided in: *Unequal Growth*, by Steve Fothergill and Graham Gudgin (London, Heinemann Educational; 1982), which focuses on the urban-rural shift in manufacturing; *Spatial Divisions of Labour: Social Structures and the Geography of Production* by Doreen Massey (London and Basingstoke, Macmillan; 1984) which argues for a spatial divisions of labour approach to uneven development; and *Long Waves of Regional Development* by Michael Marshall (London and Basingstoke, Macmillan; 1987) which uses a long-wave perspective, but draws also on aspects of the regulationist approach, in an analysis of the last century-and-a-half of uneven development in the UK. It includes a good explanation and discussion of long-wave theories.

3 Towards a post-industrial economy?

John Allen

Contents

3.1	**Introduction**	92
3.2	**Services: changes in the economy**	94
3.2.1	Service industries	96
3.2.2	Service occupations	101
Summary of section 3.2		103
3.3	**Post-industrial services**	103
3.3.1	The Fisher/Clark thesis	104
3.3.2	From industrialism to post-industrialism	105
Summary of section 3.3		107
3.4	**The new service economy**	108
3.4.1	The self-service economy	109
3.4.2	Waves of innovation and economic restructuring	111
Summary of section 3.4		113
3.5	**Enduring capitalism**	113
3.5.1	Services in late capitalism	114
3.5.2	The logic of capitalist industrialization	117
Summary of section 3.5		119
3.6	**Continuity and change**	120
3.6.1	Structural change and system change	120
3.6.2	Services and economic change	122
3.7	**Services: an uneven geography**	124
3.7.1	Geographical questions	125
3.7.2	A post-industrial south?	127
Summary of section 3.7		134
Further reading		135

3.1   Introduction

Much of the previous chapter was taken up with the question of what kind of economy is emerging in the UK. Since the first signs of a contraction in the employment base of manufacturing in the 1960s, the question of what is happening to manufacturing in the UK has rapidly become one of central importance. Deindustrialization, on whatever basis it is assessed, has prompted discussion over whether we are now in the midst of a period of major structural change, whether the UK economy is at some kind of turning-point. So far, the discussion of this turning-point and the debate over the direction of change has been conducted mainly in terms of what kind of manufacturing sector is likely to emerge out of the economic down-turn. There is, however, another version of what is happening to the UK economy, one which looks towards services rather than manufacturing as the basis upon which the economy will be re-established. According to this version, the turn towards services – the shift in the balance of employment from manufacturing to services – is the direction in which all the major industrial economies are moving and in itself need not be seen as a problem. The general shift in economic activity from manufacturing to services is taken as an indication of the emergence of a new type of economy, a **post-industrial economy**, in which services and not manufacturing is dominant.

The view that the major industrial nations are in a period of transition – at the end of a long period of industrialism and entering a new phase of post-industrialism – pre-dates the onset of deindustrialization and the debates around the issue. The term 'post-industrialism' is attributed to Daniel Bell following the publication of his influential text, *The Coming of Post-Industrial Society* (1973), and has its roots in an altogether different period – the relatively settled period of economic growth in the 1950s and early 1960s. Against the backdrop of apparent economic stability and increasing affluence the idea that the major industrial nations were at some kind of break-point held considerable appeal. These nations were about to turn their back on an era of smoke-stacked factories, heavy machinery and blue-collar work, and embrace a new world of services, with its professions, white-collar employees and new office developments. This view of economic change did not go unchallenged at that time, however (Kumar, 1978), but the events of the early 1980s have led to a renewal of interest in the post-industrial thesis. With the collapse of manufacturing employment in the UK and the elevation of services to the position of the major – and in many areas of the country the sole – source of employment, the term 'post-industrial' has gained a wider currency. More than this, the recent changes in the economy have brought into question the received notion of manufacturing as the 'motor' of economic growth and created an upsurge of interest around the role of services in the economy. One interpretation is that Britain is in the process of adjusting to the post-industrial transition.

The idea that Britain is moving towards a service economy, that the foundations of a post-industrial economy are under construction, is the focus of this chapter. This focus on services shifts our attention to a different aspect of the *social division of labour* from that discussed in the previous chapter, namely the separate firms and industries that make up the service sector. In short, we remain with the division between sectors of the economy – between manufacturing and service industries – and between enterprises in the economy – between service companies and institutions. However, before we can start to examine the significance of services in the economy, it is necessary to have some idea of what is meant by the term 'services'. As we shall see in section 3.2, this is a more difficult exercise than it would appear. Like the term 'deindustrialization', the term 'services' is open to a number of interpretations and it is important to be aware of some of the different uses of the term before turning to the question of whether Britain is or is not a service economy.

Following that, we shall look at three different theoretical accounts of the growth of the service sector in Britain. In working through the accounts particular emphasis has been placed upon the nature of the theoretical arguments involved. As in the two previous chapters and indeed throughout this text, we wish to make explicit how theories *construct* their explanations. In this sense we will be looking at the practice of 'theorizing' as much as at what the theories actually have to say. In exploring this issue it is useful to watch out for two aspects of theoretical interpretation. The first is the *kinds of evidence* that the theories appeal to in support of their views. Although the three theories are engaged in a debate over the role of services in the economy and whether or not this represents the arrival of post-industrialism, they are discerning in their use of evidence and the points on which they engage one another. The three theories are also selective in another way, in the *concepts* that they choose to prioritize over others. The attachment of importance to some and not other concepts within a particular theory is generally a reflection of certain underlying assumptions held by a theory about how society as a whole is organized and how it changes. This point should be familiar to you from the discussion of long-wave, world-system and regulationist theories in Chapters 1 and 2. I repeat it here, as in sections 3.3 to 3.5 we will be looking at three different theories, each of which takes a different starting-point to the debate over the service economy, which in turn influences their conceptual framework and what counts as valid kinds of evidence.

Another continuing theme that we will be addressing in this chapter is the issue of *structural change*. The initial focus will be upon the notion of structural change that is employed in post-industrial arguments, which, it should be noted, is taken to represent not merely a change in the *direction* of the economy, but a shift from one type of economic *system* to another. This view of economic change is not shared by the other two theoretical accounts, whose views are set out in sections 3.4 and 3.5. To enable an explicit comparison of the different conceptions of economic change held by the three theories, the substance of each is summarized in section 3.6.

Finally, in section 3.7 we turn our attention to another dimension of economic change, that of *uneven development*, and look at the ways in which the expansion of the service sector is also reshaping the map of employment by creating new lines of division and inequality between regions. Once again, the focus is upon the theoretical interpretations of the form and pattern of uneven development that are beginning to emerge. In this sense, there is a direct parallel to the debate in Chapter 2 over the uneven impact of deindustrialization. There is, however, one significant difference. In comparison with the debate over deindustrialization, the debate on the uneven development of service sector growth is less advanced; the theoretical divisions are less clear-cut. Nevertheless, an attempt has been made to identify the theoretical differences that are emerging.

First, however, there is a more pressing issue which has to be addressed, namely, what are services?

3.2   Services: changes in the economy

In attempting to answer this question, I was tempted to follow the *Economist* and define **services** as: 'anything sold in trade that could not be dropped on your foot'. Despite the rather flippant tone of the statement, it does convey what many people regard as the main characteristic of services – the absence of a physical or material form. Thus it is commonly held that services are economic activities whose output is not a physical product. Associated with this view is the general contention that services are consumed at the time they are produced, and therefore they cannot be stored, transported or resold. This conception of services has its attractions, not least of which is that it appears to distinguish the output of services from that of manufacturing. Whereas the output of manufacturing production takes a discrete, material form, the output of service production is regarded as, in some sense, intangible, as a non-material product. The difficulty with this conception of services, however, is that, on closer inspection, it admits too many exceptions.

It may be true for many services which are involved mainly with the transmission of information such as financial, legal and educational services, but for other services such as catering and food preparation, film production or computer services, I am not so sure. Nor is the case of information-based services so clear-cut, as most involve some form of tangible documentation, for example, off-the-shelf insurance policies, legal briefs, or even this text! If we were to extend this line of reasoning, we would also have to consider the materiality of services such as hairdressing, advertising and repairs which, arguably, take a tangible form and benefit their customers for a period of time after production. True, a haircut cannot be stored, transported or resold, but the example of advertising and repairs is open to debate. We could take other examples, but I think these are sufficient to indicate some of the difficulties that are involved when a deceptively simple question is posed such as 'what are services?'

Activity 3.1

As a brief aside, the issue raised here is principally one of perception, or rather one of *representation*, where certain products are represented as and connected with a material form and others are not. The term representation is used here as it suggests that ideas are *constructed* rather than simply reflected upon or passively received. There are usually reasons why some ideas take hold and persist while others fail to do so. It may be argued that, in general, the output of services is less material than manufacturing. This is true. But the issue of tangibility goes further than this: it is evaluative; it says something about service products and service jobs. As you read through the rest of section 3.2, bear in mind the following two questions.

(a) Are service jobs 'real jobs'? Many are occupied by women on a part-time basis. Is this significant?

(b) Do services create 'real wealth'? The overseas earning capacity of banking and insurance are referred to as 'invisible exports'. Why should this be the case?

These questions take us beyond the scope of this chapter, but they are raised again in Chapter 6. We shall continue by looking at the role history has played in forming a definition of services.

In part, the absence of a clear definition of services can be traced to the treatment that services received in past economic literature. Earlier studies of services in the 1930s and 1940s which were concerned with the long-term trajectory of industrial economies tended to define services in a negative rather than a positive manner – that is, by what they were *not*. Thus services were not agricultural, extractive or manufacturing activities. The remainder, a diverse assortment of economic activities which included trade, transport, telecommunications, finance, research, health, education, recreation, personal services and public administration, collectively have come to represent the service sector. Classifying services in this way, as some kind of residual category, has, as indicated above, left its problems. The search for characteristics which are common to all services has floundered and attempts to treat the services as a homogeneous group have been plagued by the differences between services, in the kinds of labour involved, the type of work performed and the nature of the product.

One way around the intractable problem of defining the term 'services' has been proposed by Gershuny and Miles (1983). Sidestepping the question of definition, they distinguish between four different uses of the term 'services'.

1   *Service industries* comprise the service sector. They are defined as firms or enterprises whose final output is in some sense non-material, irrespective of the types of occupation that make up a firm's labour force. The indifference to occupational type is a key aspect of this definition. Both manual and non-manual occupations make up the labour force in service industries. In 1981, for example, just under half of the male labour force and around a third of the female labour force in service industries were in manual, 'blue-collar' occupations. (We will return to the implications of referring to services *as* industries.)

2   *Service occupations* are not restricted to the service industries, nor, as indicated above, do they constitute the total workforce of service industries. Service occupations are present in *all* sectors of the economy, in manufacturing and agriculture as well as in the service sector, and refer to workers such as clerks, sales staff, cleaners, maintenance workers, accountants, lawyers and health workers who are not directly employed in the production of material products.

3   *Service products* are also distinct from service industries. Service firms produce service products, but manufacturing firms also produce them and may sell them in connection with their goods. An example would be where the sale of a good also includes a maintenance contract or an information service.

4   *Service functions* are a less familiar aspect of service activity. The term is used by Gershuny and Miles to draw attention to the fact that all products, whether material or immaterial, involve people in some kind of service activity. This activity is not restricted to the wage economy; it includes people using goods to 'service' themselves, for example in the way that people use washing-machines to 'service' their own laundry needs. The significance of this term will become clearer in section 3.4, where the arguments of Gershuny and Miles are discussed in some detail.

For the remainder of this section we shall develop the distinction between service industries and service occupations as it provides a useful starting-point to consider some of the major post-war trends in service employment. In the absence of a precise definition of services, the distinction enables us to disentangle the growth and contraction of service employment across a range of service industries from the separate but related growth of service employment in the economy as a whole.

3.2.1   Service industries

At some point in the mid-1960s employment in the service industries exceeded the sum total of employment in the manufacturing, agricultural and extractive industries in Britain. This can be seen from Figure 3.1 which

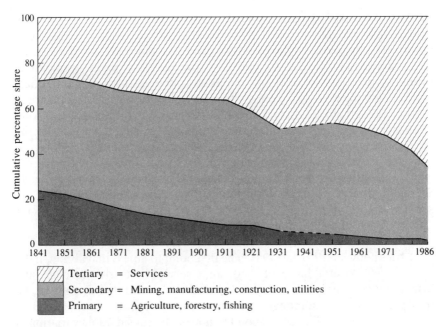

Tertiary   = Services
Secondary = Mining, manufacturing, construction, utilities
Primary   = Agriculture, forestry, fishing

Figure 3.1   Sectoral shares of employment, 1841–1986
Source: Based on Robertson, Briggs and Goodchild, 1982; Rowthorn, 1986, p. 4;
updated with Department of Employment data

provides a long-term comparison of changes in the share of employment in
the three main sectors of the economy – the primary, the secondary and the
tertiary (or service) sector. Two trends are useful to note. First, that the
appearance of the service sector, as noted in Chapter 2, is not a recent
feature of the British economy. Although the actual industries within the
sector may have changed over time, for example with the decline in the
numbers of domestic servants since the turn of the century, the sector itself
has been an important source of jobs since the mid-nineteenth century. The
proportion of service sector jobs within the economy as a whole, however,
has risen over time.

Second, that since the 1960s the share of service sector employment has
risen considerably while the share of employment in the manufacturing
sector has fallen. In the previous chapter you may recall that job loss in
manufacturing started in the mid-1960s. Since that date the number of jobs
in the service sector has risen by over three million. By 1981 the service
sector accounted for 61 per cent of total employment, and by the mid-1980s
this figure had risen to 65 per cent.

On the basis of these figures, there has clearly been some kind of shift in
the axis of the economy from manufacturing to services. But what kind of
shift is involved? There has certainly been a shift in the sectoral pattern of
employment, but has there been a parallel shift in labour from manufacturing to services? This is less clear. Looking at the figures for manufacturing

job loss alongside the figures for employment gain in the services, it may appear that the labour shed from manufacturing industries has been absorbed by the service industries. This cannot be inferred from the sectoral trends shown in Figure 3.1. Among those who have lost jobs in the manufacturing sector, some are unemployed, as indicated in Chapter 2, and others will have left the waged economy, either through retirement or the failure to register as unemployed. In fact, Figure 3.1 tells us very little about what kind of changes are involved in the shift from manufacturing to services or the type of economy that may be emerging. There are a number of points to consider. First, what is the nature of the expansion in the service sector – which industries are growing and what kind of jobs are being created? Secondly, what is the nature of the links between the manufacturing and the service sectors and, thirdly, how should we think about service sector output? Each of these points will be discussed briefly in turn.

Table 3.1 sets out the pattern of employment change in the service industries between 1959 and 1981. The first point to note is that although the service sector overall has expanded, some service industries have actually lost jobs over this period. These losses are concentrated mainly in the transport industries, although the numbers employed in personal services have also declined. The second point to note is the considerable variation in the rate of employment change among those industries that have grown since the 1960s. The fastest growth rates have occurred in the welfare, health and education services, together with the financial and business services. Not far behind in employment growth are the leisure and recreational services, the hotel and catering industry, private motoring services, and the post and telecommunications industry. In comparison with these industries, retail trade and public administration have experienced limited job growth. What is not evident from this table, however, is the pace of employment change in the different industries throughout this period. For example, the public sector services (the bottom three categories in Table 3.1), grew rapidly in the 1960s and early 1970s and accounted for over half the total increase in service jobs in this period. Subsequently, with the cuts in public expenditure, there has been a decline in the overall growth of public service jobs. By the late 1970s and early 1980s the major source of growth in service employment was in the private sector (*Martin*, 1988).

Activity 3.2

Despite the decline in the growth rate of public service employment since the late 1970s, the public service sector still accounts for a significant proportion of total employment in the service industries. And so, too, do the transport and distributive industries, notwithstanding the job losses in the former industry. Examine the figures in the second column of Table 3.1 and then attempt the following activity:

(a) Add up the total employment in public services in 1981, that is, the

Table 3.1   Employment change in the service industries, 1959–1981, Great Britain

	Employment (000s) 1959	Employment (000s) 1981	Change (000s) 1959–81	Percentage change
Public passenger transport (roads and railways)	705	393	−312	−44.3
Goods transport and storage (road haulage, warehousing, wholesale distribution)	1030	1269	+239	+23.2
Sea and air transport	317	218	−99	−31.3
Private motoring services (garages)	339	482	+143	+42.2
Retail distribution	1844	1846	+2	+0.1
Post and telecommunications	334	430	+96	+28.7
Financial services (insurance, banking, finance)	458	779	+321	+70.0
Other business services (property, advertising, business services, unallocated central offices, law, accountancy, research and development, other business related professions)	464	1070	+606	+130.7
Leisure and recreation services (including broadcasting and gambling)	238	334	+96	+40.2
Hotels and catering	665	928	+263	+39.6
Other personal services (hairdressing, laundries, dry cleaning, shoe repairers, private domestic services[1])	268	157	−111	−41.3
Public administration (central and local government)[2]	1255	1400	+145	+11.6
Health and education	1616	3124	+1508	+99.3
Welfare services (social services, voluntary organizations, religious organizations)	259	675	+416	+160.6
All service industries (thousands)	9797	13105	+3308	+33.8
Share of total employment (percentage)	44.79	61.48		

[1] Private domestic service is not included in figures based on Department of Employment sources

[2] Population Census figures for this group include the armed forces. They are not included in Department of Employment figures

Source: Buck, 1985

last three categories. Now work out what percentage they represent of all service sector employment.

(b)   Add up the total employment in all the transport and distributive industries, the top six categories. Work out the percentage of total service sector employment that they represent.

(c)   The two figures should add up to around 75 per cent. Together, then, the public services and the transport and distributive industries make up the bulk of service sector employment. But these services are not among those that are experiencing the highest growth rates in the 1980s. The profile of the service industries is shifting.

Concealed within the figures for employment change within the service industries, there is another kind of employment change taking place. In the 1970s alone, over one million part-time jobs were created in the service industries. In 1984 almost 90 per cent of the 4.9 million part-time workers in Britain were in the service sector, and the overwhelming majority of those jobs were occupied by women (Robinson, 1985). Even though full-time workers still account for the majority of service sector jobs, the growth of part-time jobs does raise a number of questions about what type of 'service-based' economy is emerging in the UK.

A further employment trend which is central to any account of service sector expansion is the rise in the number of jobs transferred from manufacturing to service industries as the former 'contract out' services to lower costs. Since the mid-1970s the recessionary shake-out in manufacturing has led to the externalization of various corporate services, previously provided 'in-house'. Precise figures for this trend are difficult to obtain, but one estimate suggests that around 300 000 jobs may have been added to the service sector in the first half of the 1980s (Rajan, 1987). These are not new jobs as such, but rather jobs that have been reclassified as service sector jobs. They represent a shift in the **social division of labour** related to changes in the organization of manufacturing production. Any preoccupation with the growth of employment in service industries may therefore divert our attention away from the wider changes within the economy as a whole which are actively reshaping the boundaries between manufacturing and service industries.

Finally, there is the issue of service sector output. From the discussion of manufacturing output in Chapter 2, it should be apparent that a growth in employment is not the same as a growth in output. Employment and output represent the different ways of measuring the progress of an economy. The UK economy may be a service-based economy in employment terms, but this does not give us an accurate picture of the output of service industries, that is, the productivity of the service sector. Indeed, the relatively slow growth of productivity in many industries is one of the principal reasons for the increase in service sector jobs. At the national level, however, the service industries have accounted for over half the economy's total output since the late 1960s (Barras, 1984). On this evidence, then, it would appear that the UK *is* a service economy.

Such figures, however, should be approached with caution. First, the growth of services in total output is a relative growth, relative that is to manufacturing. As the output of the latter declined significantly in the late 1970s and early 1980s, so the *relative* share of service output in the economy rose. The balance of output between the sectors thus has shifted, but what this does not tell us is whether services are now the 'engine' of growth within the economy. This is a separate issue and will be pursued in Chapter 6. Secondly, there is the difficulty, discussed earlier, of identifying service output. Many services, it was noted, have a degree of intangibility and their quality is often an important aspect of their delivery. Typically, a doctor alters the state of a patient's health, the teacher shapes a pupil's knowledge, and a hairdresser changes the physical appearance of a customer. How, then, is the output of such activities to be measured? In the absence of 'hard' data, such as the volume of goods produced (the measure of output in manufacturing) or the volume of sales (as with retailing) or the tonnage per mile/kilometre (as with goods transport), a proxy measure is sought. A proxy is a substitute measure which is used to gauge output. The most frequently used proxy is employment data. This is adopted as a measure of output in industries such as advertising and a range of personal services, and it is also used as a proxy for output in the public sector, with services such as education, defence, the fire service and public administration. This practice, as I suspect you have realized, has its limitations. For employment data, as noted above, are not a particularly accurate indication of output. You may recall the phenomenon of 'jobless growth' in the manufacturing sector discussed in the previous chapter. Within services, the shift in retail banking from personal service to automatic cash dispensers is a similar example of 'jobless growth' (Rajan, 1987). We should be careful, then, not to confuse the level of employment with the level of output in the service industries.

3.2.2 Service occupations

To recap, the reason for distinguishing between service industries and service occupations was to show employment change within service industries separate from employment change within the service occupations, which are present in all sectors of the economy. Cleaners and security staff, for example, are employed in manufacturing industry, clerks and accountants are employed in the mining industry, and so forth. Service employment is thus not restricted to the service industries. A service worker, following Gershuny and Miles, 'is anyone who engages in work where immediate output is typically either non-material or ephemeral' (1983, p. 47). Thus 'blue-collar' workers such as transport workers may be considered as service

workers, which implies that service employment is not confined solely to
those who wear a white collar.

Turning to the profile of occupational change in Britain, Figure 3.2
indicates that the majority of the working population in the 1960s, around
two-thirds of the labour force, was employed in service occupations. Since
then the number of service workers in the economy has continued to rise,
particularly in the white-collar occupations – the 'administrative, professional and technical' group and the 'clerical' group. Among the other service
occupations – security, cleaning, catering, sales and transport – the pattern
of development is less regular, with no significant changes over the period.
For the remaining group, workers in manual non-service occupations, those
who are directly involved in material production, the pattern is one of
decline.

Two aspects of this profile deserve brief attention. The first is the apparent trend towards the 'professionalization' of labour – indicated by the
growth in the number of administrative, professional and technical workers
in the occupational structure. The second aspect is the relative stability in
the proportion of transport workers over the two decades, despite, as we
know from Figure 3.1, the job losses that have occurred in the transport
service industries since the 1960s. How is this explained? It has something to

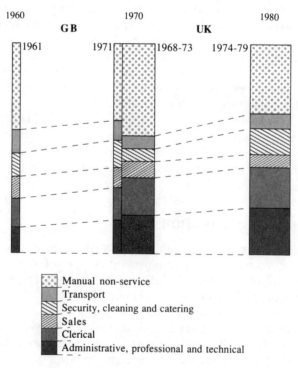

Figure 3.2   Changing occupational profiles of employment
Source: Adapted from Gershuny and Miles, 1983

do with the distinction between service industries and service occupations. Although the number of workers in the transport industries may have declined, it does not follow that the number of transport workers in the wider economy has also fallen or fallen to the same extent. Transport workers are employed in all sectors of the economy, for example in manufacturing firms who operate vehicle fleets. Transport workers, therefore, do not have to be employed in the service industries to produce service products. The same point also applies to white-collar workers in manufacturing, who by the early 1980s made up around one-third of the total workforce in the manufacturing sector. Service occupations, then, are *what people do* as opposed to the industry which employs them. In section 3.4, in particular, we shall see the theoretical significance of drawing this distinction.

Summary of section 3.2

• Problems of definition have obstructed the analysis of services. A clearer view exists of what services are not than of any positive identification of their characteristics.

• In the absence of a precise definition of services, a distinction was drawn between four different uses of the term 'services'. Two of those uses – service industries and service occupations – provided the framework for a discussion of service employment trends in post-war Britain.

• *Service industries* account for the majority of employment in the economy, but the rate of growth varies between industries and some industries are contracting in employment terms. Much of the recent growth in service sector employment has been in private services. Part of this growth is attributable to jobs transferred from manufacturing to service industries as the former externalize services previously provided 'in-house'.

• *Service occupations* have increased since the 1960s, whilst those occupations directly involved in goods production have declined. White-collar workers represent an increasing proportion of the labour force, and within this category there is an apparent trend towards the 'professionalization' of labour. At the same time it should be borne in mind that much of the recent growth in employment in the service industries has been in part-time work.

3.3 Post-industrial services

So far we have restricted our attention to some of the main empirical trends behind the shift in the structure of the economy from manufacturing to services. The shift is apparent in employment terms: all the available evidence indicates that service employment is the major source of jobs in the UK economy. Any kind of evidence, however, requires interpretation. Why has service employment risen rapidly in the post-war period? And what significance should we attach to this development? Does such a trend signify the arrival of a post-industrial economy? It depends. It depends upon how such a change is theorized and this, in turn, is related to different theoretical accounts of how the economy changes and how it is organized. In this section we look at the arguments of Daniel Bell (1973, 1980) which remain the clearest and most influential account of the changes involved in the transition from industrialism to post-industrialism. First, however, we turn to a view of economic change which pre-dates Bell's analysis and which underpins most accounts of the break from an industrial to a post-industrial economy.

3.3.1   The Fisher/Clark thesis

Any description of the service sector has to take into account the legacy of what has become known as the Fisher/Clark thesis or the 'three-sector' model of economic growth. According to this view, which was first developed in the 1930s, economic progress is marked by the successive growth and decline of the three sectors of the economy. In the long term, employment in the economy would gradually shift from the primary sector through the secondary (manufacturing) sector and then to the tertiary (or service) sector. The trajectory along which all economies, as they industrialized, would inevitably pass was asserted on the basis of two pieces of 'evidence'.

First, as economies grow, rising productivity levels made possible by technological advances allow workers to pass into the next sector. Thus, just as the industrial revolution in the last century led to the mass movement of workers from the primary to the expanding manufacturing sector, so in the late twentieth century rising productivity in the latter will lead to a shift of labour from manufacturing into the new 'lead' sector, the service industries. Secondly, as national incomes rise, the increase in demand generated will be channelled first into the secondary sector and then into the tertiary sector, in accordance with Engel's Law. Engel, an oft-cited figure among post-industrial writers, was a Prussian statistician who in the early nineteenth century pointed to the tendency, as societies become richer, for consumers to spend proportionately less of any increase in their income on staple foods. By extrapolation it is concluded that today's rising income levels generate increased demand for services compared with manufactured goods. Taken together, the two trends are offered as an explanation of the growth of a service sector which provides the majority of jobs and, in turn, fulfils rising consumer demands.

Leaving the question of demand to one side for the moment, there are two rather different points about this account which should be raised briefly. One concerns the inevitability of the historical progression through the sectors. As noted earlier, in relation to Figure 3.1, the service industries have been an important provider of jobs in the UK economy since the last century. This had led some observers, notably Robertson, Briggs and Good-child (1982), to cast doubt upon the idea of a simple linear progression through the sectors. They conclude that the available evidence points to employment in the long run shifting out of the primary sector into *both* the manufacturing and the service sectors. Nor does this national trend appear to be atypical. Similar trends are evident in the economies of Japan, Canada and the United States which indicate that labour has shifted out of the primary sector into the service sector prior to or in parallel with the expansion of the manufacturing sector (Singelmann, 1978).

The second point concerns the specific connection that is drawn between an increasingly dynamic manufacturing sector and the growth of the service sector. For the 1950s and early 1960s in Britain there is some evidence to support such a contention, but, with the onset of manufacturing recession and the fluctuation in productivity levels and output, the connection is questionable. If, however, the growing number of jobs within the service industries is viewed as a consequence of rising productivity levels within manufacturing, then the labour released should have been reabsorbed by the service sector. This does not appear to be the case. As noted earlier, most of the newly created jobs in the service sector are occupied by women on a part-time basis, whereas most of the labour expelled from manufacturing has been in full-time jobs occupied by men.

There is, then, some doubt about the validity of a linear model of economic change that proposes a sequence of labour shifts through the sectors. There is no doubt, however, that since the 1960s the majority of the labour force in the UK is no longer engaged in agriculture or manufacturing. The majority is engaged in the service sector. The question, here, is whether this development represents a structural shift from an industrial to a post-industrial economy.

3.3.2 From industrialism to post-industrialism

The post-industrial view of the economy described by Bell and other writers focuses upon the primacy of services and the movement away from manufacturing production as the main activity of western economies. It recognizes three phases of economic development which are not unlike those proposed by Fisher and Clark: a pre-industrial, an industrial and a post-industrial phase. Within each phase certain service activities are present. In pre-industrial economies personal domestic service is one of the major categories of employment. In an industrial economy, the growing services are those that support manufacturing, such as transport, distribution and banking. In a post-industrial economy a different kind of service economy is emphasized. These are referred to by Bell (1980) as the human and professional services: human services include health, education and social welfare, together with a range of personal services, primarily cultural and recreational; whereas professional services include research, development and other information-related activities.

Two other distinctive features of post-industrialism are connected with the rise of a service economy. The first is the shift to white-collar occupations, illustrated by the displacement of manual work by non-manual work. Within the white-collar category particular importance is attached to the professional, scientific and technical occupations. These groups are considered to represent the key occupations in a post-industrial economy. They are the custodians of scientific and technical knowledge that, according to Bell, is shaping the direction of post-industrial change. 'Industrial society' for Bell represents 'the co-ordination of machines and men for the production of goods. Post-industrial society is organized around knowledge, for the purpose of social control and the directing of innovation and change; and this in turn gives rise to new social relationships and new structures' (1973, p. 20).

The second feature is the shift in demand from material commodities to (immaterial) services mentioned in section 3.3.1. Bell, like Fisher and Clark before him, cites Engel's Law in support of this shift in demand. As the incomes of an increasingly productive workforce rise and people's basic material needs are progressively met, their needs expand first for consumer durables and then for luxury items – immaterial services, such as education, health, leisure and the arts. And as these new demands are generated, the structure of the labour force shifts from the production of material goods to immaterial services to meet them. Production and employment, therefore, are increasingly concentrated in the area of services, orchestrated by the key professional groups. Bell, however, offers no direct evidence to substantiate the claim that there has been a shift in demand to services. Instead he infers from another piece of evidence, the growth in service employment, that there has been a simultaneous growth in the provision of final (immaterial) services to consumers. This link, as we shall see in the next section, has been contested (Gershuny, 1978).

The type of evidence appealed to by Bell in support of his argument is revealing. Ample evidence is provided to show that the structure of the labour force in post-war United States has shifted towards service employment. From the figures provided in section 3.2 a similar shift can be discerned in post-war Britain. If we restrict our attention to broad employment trends – the growth of employment in the service industries, the increase in white-collar occupations and the rise of professional workers – then Britain, too, has a majority of its labour force in service employment. But what importance should we attach to these broad employment trends? Are employment figures alone sufficient to infer that the economy has shifted from a goods to a service economy, that the economy has moved from an industrial stage to a post-industrial stage. What about the question of output?

Bell, as noted above, takes the figures for service growth as an indication of growth in the production of final services. In part, this failure to interrogate the issue of output is a reflection of Bell's conception of how societies change and how they are organized. He argues that societies are organized around what he refers to as certain 'axial structures'. In industrial society, a goods-based economy, the 'axial structure' is 'economizing – a way of allocating resources according to the principles of least cost, substitutability, optimization, maximization, and the like' for economic growth (1973, p. 12). In post-industrial society a new 'axial structure' has emerged which is reshaping the economic and social structure, that of 'theoretical knowledge'. In this context knowledge and information are the strategic resource, the transforming agent behind innovations in the management and organization of the economy. In choosing to prioritize this characteristic, Bell draws attention to the occupational groups that he considers are in possession of this knowledge – the professional and technical groups. The changing pattern of employment therefore – the shift from blue-collar to white-collar occupations and the pre-eminence of professional and technical groups within the latter category – is not merely a general feature of post-industrialism, it is one of central significance. The importance that Bell attaches to employment changes in the occupational structure, therefore, is not a random preference; it stems from his theoretical view of how societies change and which groups are the catalysts of change.

Two further general observations can be made about the view of economic change that is held by Bell and other post-industrial writers. The significance of both points will become clearer in section 3.6.

One is its association with the rather questionable linear model of economic change proposed by Fisher and Clark. Thus the latest post-industrial sequence is identified by a series of tendencies which collectively represent a new phase of economic development. The second concerns the nature of the break between a post-industrial era and a new post-industrial order. Clearly post-industrial writers locate the dynamic of this new economic phase within the latest post-industrial sequence; it is an internal characteristic. In that sense the development of a post-industrial economy is *unconnected* to the forces which shaped industrial society. The changes, therefore, add up to a different kind of economic system. The changes do not preserve an existing set of economic structures; they represent an altogether different type of economy. The United States is considered to have entered this phase sometime in the 1950s; in Britain's case the date is less clear – either in the mid-1960s or in the 1980s depending upon which aspects of service growth are emphasized.

Summary of section 3.3

- The asserted transformation of the economy from an industrial to a service-based post-industrial economy rests upon a linear model of economic change that was first proposed by Fisher and Clark in the 1930s. In this long-term view the weight of employment moves from the primary sector to the secondary sector and then to the tertiary or service sector. The inevitability of this historical progression through the sectors does not, however, fit with the examples of the UK, Japan, Canada and the United States.

- Although the Fisher/Clark thesis does not entail the post-industrial argument, the two accounts offer a similar explanation for shifts in patterns of demand. For Bell, as incomes rise, people's horizons expand beyond material goods and new demands develop for immaterial (luxury) services. In turn, this shift in demand is translated into a boost in the number of service workers.

- This shift in demand is assumed rather than demonstrated by Bell. Considerable evidence, however, is provided by Bell to show that a shift in the US occupational structure – from blue- to white-collar work – has taken place in the post-war period. Similar evidence exists for Britain (section 3.2). On the basis of this evidence which, it is assumed, is a reflection of the increased demand for services, the post-industrial transition is asserted.

- Finally, Bell draws specific attention to the growth of professional and technical workers and identifies them as the key occupations around which the structure of post-industrial society is organized.

3.4   The new service economy

One of the most trenchant critiques of the post-industrial thesis is Gershuny's *After Industrial Society?* (1978). In this text Gershuny takes to task a number of post-industrial themes, but he reserves particular attention to those writers, such as Bell, who take the emergence of a service-based economy as an indication of post-industrialism. The focus of his critique reflects, understandably, his own choice of questions rather than that of Bell. The two authors share a common concern with the sectoral pattern of employment change, but whereas Bell develops his arguments around the centrality of 'theoretical knowledge', Gershuny pursues the related strand of 'post-industrial needs' and how they are met. Part of Gershuny's overall argument is to undermine the emphasis placed by post-industrial writers on the emergence of a formal service economy. In its place he wants to emphasize the growth of a 'self-service economy' – a type of 'do-it-yourself' economy which enables people to 'service' themselves by substituting goods for services. Thus washing-machines replace laundry services, cars replace public transport services and so forth.

The 'self-service economy' thesis is only one aspect of Gershuny's work, albeit a central aspect. In subsequent works, in particular *The New Service Economy* (1983, written with Miles), he links this aspect to a view of economic change that you have met before in Chapters 1 and 2: Kondratiev's long waves of economic expansion and contraction. More accurately, he wants to explain the emergence of 'self-servicing' in terms of the *technolo-gical* changes in the post-war period which have made it possible for people to 'service' themselves. For example, the technological innovations that have led to the cheap, mass production of cars, a mass broadcasting net-work, a regular domestic electricity supply and the like. The point, as we shall see in section 3.4.2, owes more to Schumpeter's notion of technical innovations 'bunching' together at certain times, than to Kondratiev's account of economic development. First, however, we look at how Ger-shuny explains the apparent shift to a 'self-service economy' and the growth of service employment in post-war Britain.

3.4.1 The self-service economy

There is no disagreement between Gershuny and post-industrial writers that service employment is a general feature of advanced economies. The evi-dence shown in Figures 3.1, 3.2 and Table 3.1 is not in dispute. The disagreement arises over *why* service employment has grown substantially in the post-war period. For Bell, and others, service employment has grown in response to the rise in demand for services, which stems from the develop-ment of a new category of 'post-industrial needs'. The logic of the argument is straightforward and thus appealing: from the growth in peoples' income and the satisfaction of material needs, to the development of new demands for services, through to an increase in the number of service-workers re-quired to provide the services. Gershuny disputes this explanatory logic and offers an alternative account of the post-war growth of service employment.

At its simplest, the account runs something like this. True, people's consumption needs have risen in the post-war period. But it is wrong to assume that these needs can only be met by the provision of services. Needs can be satisfied by either manufactured goods or services, and the manner in which they are satisfied changes over time. Transport needs, for example, can be met by public transport, taxi or by private motor car; entertainment needs by theatre, cinema or by television, and so on. The *same* service function therefore can be performed in a number of different ways. Slower labour productivity growth in the service industries owing to the labour-intensive nature of many personal services has, however, led to a situation whereby the price of services rises faster than that of manufactured goods. Households thus tend to substitute goods for services (for example, washing-machines, cars, videos, vacuum-cleaners etc.) and use their own labour to 'service' themselves. This is the trend towards a self-service economy, based upon the ownership and use of material commodities. The trend, therefore, is away from the consumption of services and towards the purchase of goods. Why, then, is there also a trend towards service employ-ment? The answer, which is the *reverse* of post-industrial views, is that service workers do not only provide services to consumers; they are also concerned with the manufacture of goods. A large proportion of the growing number of workers in service industries *and* in service occupations contribute to the production of material commodities. And the increased demand for many of these commodities can be traced to the emergence of a self-service economy.

There are two points worth pulling out from this summary. One is Gershuny's focus upon the *connections* between the manufacturing and the service sectors. The emphasis is not upon a 'goods economy' or a 'service economy', but upon the *relationship* between sectors and how employment changes in the different sectors are inextricably linked. This is a broader and more complex view of how an economy works and changes than is generally found in post-industrial accounts. In particular it prioritizes the concept of the *division of labour* to show how much of the growth in service employment can be attributed to three separate but related trends, *which together stem from the increased production of manufactured goods*. The first is the growth of employment in *service occupations* (managers, technicians and other professional staff) whose labour is required to increase the efficiency of manufacturing production. This is the shift towards 'white-collar' work noted by Bell and others. The second is the growth of specialized *service industries* as manufacturing firms 'subcontract' services to 'producer' service firms. This is another familiar trend, namely the redistribution of jobs between sectors. And finally, an unfamiliar trend, one that is connected to the rise of the self-service economy: the growth of employment in what Gershuny and Miles refer to as 'intermediate consumer services', that is, the services required by households to 'service' themselves. Television repair services, garage services and DIY stores are the most frequently quoted examples. It is less important to remember the detail of these trends than it is to recall that Gershuny attributes these shifts in the division of labour, particularly the first two trends, primarily to *changes in the technological and organizational structure of production within industries*.

The second point can be stated fairly briefly and concerns the interpretation of Engel's Law by post-industrial writers. Gershuny, in rejecting the identity between the growth in service employment and the increase in demand for services, is also questioning the post-industrial assumption that Engel's Law is applicable to services. Rather he wants to assert that changing technology has also altered patterns of consumption. People have been able to 'service' themselves by substituting goods for services only because of *technical and organizational changes* in the way goods have been produced and delivered, and in the development of new products. For example, if you compare the production and delivery of The Open University's educational materials with the labour-intensive delivery of education displayed in conventional universities you can gauge the relevance of this point.

Central, then, to this view of service employment change and the rise of a self-service economy is the role of technological and organizational change. And behind this particular aspect of economic change, according to Gershuny and Miles, lies the driving force that accounts for this pattern of change, the *social innovations* that have shaped economic development in

Britain over the last thirty years. Before turning to this issue, it is worth noting briefly how the same piece of empirical evidence – the growth of service employment – is open to a quite different theoretical interpretation from that of the post-industrial argument. The conceptual distinctions drawn by Gershuny and Miles between service industries, service occupations and service functions, and their focus upon the *relationship* between different sectors of the economy, provide the basis for a different explanation of the shifts in the division of labour that have taken place over the post-war period. The direction of their enquiry, the particular questions they ask, also influences the kinds of issues that they address. What is and what is not drawn into focus can be gleaned from the following activity.

Activity 3.3

Can you think of any service activities that may have escaped, at least up to now, the goods-substitution effect? The trends indicated in Table 3.1 are a useful place to start.

(a)   Examine the figures for employment growth in the hotel and catering industry or in leisure and recreational services. To what extent has there been a substitution of goods for services in, say, sports activities or in the hotel trade?

(b)   Is the argument for a self-service economy equally applicable to private and public services? What substitution, for example, has occurred within the health or welfare services?

3.4.2   Waves of innovation and economic restructuring

According to Gershuny and Miles the emergence of a self-service economy is connected to the availability of a range of new products in the post-war period and the availability of infrastructural systems which enable people to use the products to 'service' themselves. The new products and the infrastructure are integrally related. Without a road infrastructure the scope for the development of private transport is limited; without a national electricity grid the market for washing-machines, vacuum-cleaners and televisions is restricted. And so on.

In post-war Britain the infrastructure for these markets was laid in the 1950s and the next thirty years witnessed a rapid growth in the ownership of cars and domestic equipment. New industries developed to meet the growth in demand for the new products, and innovations, for example in car assembly techniques and in the use of plastics in the chemical industry, made possible the development of new, cheaper products. This was the post-war boom. It also laid down a distinctive post-war sectoral division of labour which rested upon what Gershuny and others have referred to as 'heartland technologies'. It is not important here to dwell upon the detail of these technologies, only to note that they are held to have a limited life and that by the 1980s they were considered to have exhausted their potential (Freeman *et al.*, 1982).

The relevant aspect of this view of technological change to note here is that it is not viewed as a continuous, linear process, but rather one that is marked by breaks. The technology that launched the post-war boom is seen to have run its course. This view draws upon Schumpeter's arguments that technical innovations do not appear continuously but in 'clusters' of activity – new products opening up new markets and new industries – followed by long periods of consolidation of previous technical advances. For the manufacturing industries, the 1950s' *wave of innovation* is seen as all but over, with little scope for the development of new products with existing infrastructure. Of the new products that have emerged, few as yet appear to have any significant potential for job generation.

It would also seem to follow that if, as Gershuny argues, the majority of service workers are involved in the production of goods and not services then they too are at a break-point. This is less clear, but it is apparent that Gershuny thinks that the 1980s heralds a new wave of innovation, based upon the heartland technologies of microprocessors and telecommunications systems, which will give rise to a new series of products and, in turn, new ways for people to 'service' themselves. This would appear to be a reference to the onset of the fifth Kondratiev wave discussed in Chapter 2. The loose scenario is one of the 'wired city' followed by a bundle of innovations in domestic, educational, health and recreational technologies which create the potential markets for remote health-care packs, remote learning facilities, remote shopping and the like. This is a scenario which, interestingly, is not far removed from revised post-industrial sketches which look towards knowledge-based information technology (or IT) products as the lynch-pin of an 'information economy' (Miles, 1985).

Here, then, we see the beginnings of an engagement between two relatively distinct theories, an overlapping area of concern which has led some post-industrial writers to adjust their focus of enquiry. Yet despite this example of theoretical renegotiation, there are still major differences in the respective accounts of economic change. The first difference concerns their conceptions of change. Whereas post-industrial theorists hold onto a linear model of cumulative change, the socio-technical approach of Gershuny and Miles isolates *critical, disruptive periods* of technical change which have radical consequences for the structure of the economy. In these brief, critical periods of restructuring some industries and some markets will disappear as new clusters of innovations open up new markets and reshape patterns of industry and work. The second difference is one of timing. Post-industrial Britain was hailed in the 1960s and encompasses the growth of an information economy as one of its 'realized' projections. From a socio-technical viewpoint the period 1950–1980 represents the wave of innovation that produced the post-war boom. Thus we are now into a critical phase of restructuring which is deemed to have far-reaching consequences for the economy and people's lifestyles. And the third difference is over the nature of the service economy. Despite some convergence, post-industrial writers still emphasize the growth of a formal service economy, whereas the emphasis, for Gershuny and Miles in particular, is squarely on new developments in the self-service economy.

Summary of section 3.4

• Gershuny's disagreement with Bell is not about the fact of service employment growth, but over why it has grown. Gershuny disputes the logic of Bell's argument. The growth of service employment is not taken as an indication of the growth in the demand for services. On the contrary, the rise in service workers is taken as an indication of the increased demand for goods as households substitute goods for services. As the technical and organizational structure of production changes within industries, an increased number of service workers are required to maintain goods production both in the manufacturing *and* the service industries – to meet the demands of a growing self-service economy.

• According to Gershuny, the self-service economy arose out of a wave of technological innovation in the post-war period which led to the development of a range of new products and a supportive infrastructure that enabled people to 'service themselves'. This period is now considered to be at an end. The economy has entered a critical phase of restructuring which is likely to result in a new 'bundle' of technological innovations which, in turn, will provide new ways for people to engage in self-service activities.

• The notion of a post-industrial Britain, therefore, is misconceived. The flaw attributed to Bell's argument is that he interpreted the growth of service employment as a sign of an emergent service economy, rather than as an indication of a growing goods-based, self-service economy.

3.5 Enduring capitalism

Critiques of a post-industrial service economy have not been restricted to technological reappraisals. Another type of critique, broader in scope than the previous explanation, operates with a different line of questioning. It takes its starting-point from Marxism and analyses the growth of the service sector in the context of changing capitalist social relations in the post-war period. Mandel's work, *Late Capitalism* (1975), has probably been the most influential text within this tradition, although more recent accounts, also rooted in a Marxist tradition, diverge from his analysis. This is to be

expected, not only because the shape of the economy is constantly changing, but also because there are different strands of thought and interpretation within Marxism.

Notwithstanding such differences, this type of approach is characterized
by its rejection of the post-industrial view that the decline of manufacturing
is synonymous with the decline of industrialism. Just as capitalism is not re-
ducible to smoke-stacked factories, so, it is argued, industrialism is not
wholly about the manufacture of goods, assembly-line technology or particular forms of employment or investment. The fact that banking, insurance, hotels and catering, wholesale and retail distribution are referred to
as service *industries* is offered as a sharp reminder of the point. The corollary of which is that the shift in employment to the service industries is not
linked to some new organizing 'knowledge' principle; rather it is related to
the same processes which led to the earlier formation of manufacturing industry – the *accumulation of capital* and the search for profitable investments.

The stress of this approach, then, is upon the shifts in the pattern of
capital investment which have taken place in order to maintain the process
of capital accumulation. In common with the socio-technical approach, the
Marxist view recognizes the disruption of *structural changes* in the economy, but goes on to argue that such changes preserve the dominance of a
wider *system* of capitalist social relations. The notion of a continuous yet
changing capitalist economy will be picked up later. First, however, we will
take a closer look at how Marxist writers, in particular Mandel, account for
the expansion of the service sector in the post-war period.

3.5.1 Services in late capitalism

From Mandel's point of view, post-industrial theorists are guilty of a kind
of wish fulfilment. In observing the growth of service employment and the
expansion of the service industries they readily pronounce the end of industrial capitalism and the rise of post-industrial economic structures, as if
the one development inevitably led to the other. This may be a valid criticism of the more popular versions of the post-industrial thesis. As a criticism
of Bell's ideas, however, it is too general. Bell, for example, is ambiguous
about the demise of capitalism: his major pronouncements refer to the end
of industrialism, the end of factory-based goods production rather than to
the end of capitalism. In fact, Bell has very little to say about capitalism as
an economic system. And this neglect is the major point of difference between Mandel's account and post-industrial accounts of the rise of a
service-based economy.

According to Mandel the post-industrial account fails to consider the ways
in which capital reshapes the economy and its employment structures to
satisfy profitability. To focus upon the growth of service employment and
the shift to white-collar occupations is to ignore the underlying economic

processes that are responsible for such changes. Equally, to concentrate, as Gershuny has done, upon technological innovations as the catalyst of economic change is seen to miss the economic processes that guide the direction of technical change – the processes that influence which new technologies are developed and which new services are marketed. Neither of these changes would be considered unimportant or trivial by Mandel, but their very occurrence remains to be explained and this requires an assessment of the relative profitability of different economic activities.

On this account the service industries have expanded in the post-war period because of their relative profitability. Services represent a viable alternative source of profitable investment to manufacturing at a time when returns on investment in the latter are declining. This movement of capital into the service sector is seen by Mandel as part of the 'logic' of 'late capitalism' – the post-war phase of capitalist development. To maintain the value of their investments, capitalist enterprises have diverted excess capital into the service industries, into wholesale and retail outlets, hotels, rental services, leisure centres and the like, whilst simultaneously replacing labour-intensive services with material goods that enable consumers to 'service' themselves.

Thus the movement of capital into services involves two related trends. One is the familiar trend towards a self-service economy, with the substitution of goods for services made possible by technical innovation. In this instance, however, the driving force is not technology *per se*, but the profits realized through the standardization of goods and their lower cost in comparison with the equivalent labour-intensive service. The second trend primarily involves what Mandel refers to as 'the industrialization of the sphere of reproduction', that is, the increased frequency by which the consumer needs of people are met by privately organized and supplied services. The privatization of health care and education are part of this trend, and so too is the creation of new markets for recreational and leisure activities, the 'commodification' of culture, and the general spread of conditions of employment, similar to those in manufacturing industries, to service occupations. According to the regulationist school, one of the theories that figured prominently in Chapters 1 and 2, it is precisely these domestic service markets that were developed from the early 1980s because, unlike manufacturing markets, they are largely sheltered from foreign competition. This particular point is debatable, as we shall see below. Nonetheless, the growth of these markets can be seen as one kind of response to the decline of the mass commodity markets that are considered central to the Fordist regime of accumulation.

Two points are important to note about this second trend. One is the shift in employment that follows the shift in investment to the service sector. By the mid-1980s, for example, one million people were employed in the hotels and catering industry in Britain, a rise of over 300 000 since the early 1970s (Damcsick, 1986). The second point is related to long-term developments within capitalist economies and is one that did not figure in the two previous accounts: the importance of the *organizational structure* of service capital. Following the movement of capital into the service sector, this approach draws attention to the increasing *concentration* of ownership that has occurred within the service industries once an area has been 'opened up' for investment. This is coupled with a trend towards *diversification* as the large, multinational companies which have entered the service sector spread their investments across a range of products and services to minimize the risks of specialized investment. British American Tobacco (BAT), for example, is best known for its prominent position in the tobacco industry. This is, however, only one 'arm' of its corporate interests. BAT industries also has a financial arm, which includes Eagle Star, the insurance company, and Allied Dunbar (formerly Hambro Life); a retail arm in the form of the Argos Group, the catalogue showrooms business; and a paper arm in the Wiggins Teape Group. From this vantage point, there is little sense in referring to some of these services as 'post-industrial' as they are clearly owned by enterprises which span a range of manufacturing *and* service industries.

It should be remembered, however, that these consumer-orientated service industries are not the major concern of post-industrial arguments. Bell, for example, stressed the role of knowledge and information as the motivating force behind the expansion of the service occupations. The type of services that could be included here refer to almost all the activities dealing with research, development, management, administration and marketing. None of these activities, however, would be considered by Mandel to represent a break from industrial production. On the contrary, the development of these service occupations would be taken as evidence of the increasing specialization and complexity of industrial production in 'late capitalism', within both the manufacturing and the service sector. This state of affairs has arisen because companies have increasingly had to restructure their activities in order to trade within increasingly competitive and differentiated markets. One consequence of this restructuring is that more people have become employed in the development, design, management, promotion and servicing of products; that is, those occupations which embody the knowledge and information skills identified by post-industrial theorists.

Far from representing a new economic era these changes in employment are explained by Marxist writers as yet a further extension of the *technical division of labour*. And if companies 'buy in' these services rather than provide them themselves, this gives rise to a further development in the *social division of labour* as new firms and industries expand to provide these services. From this viewpoint the growth of service industries is primarily a spin-off from manufacturing production and amounts to new developments within broader economic structures which remain geared to profit-orientated production (Walker, 1985). In effect, it is seen as part of the restructuring of Britain's industrial base, as both manufacturing and service firms reorganize production to reduce costs by externalizing service activities peripheral to their main lines of business.

Notice, incidentally, that the concept of the division of labour also occupied a prominent position in the socio-technical approach and it performed a similar explanatory role, namely to highlight the interdependence of manufacturing and service sector employment. In that approach the shifts in the division of labour are attributed to technological changes and are drawn upon to support the argument for a self-service economy and the increased demand for material goods. Within a Marxist approach the shift in the division of labour is attributed to a different set of causes. Although it acknowledges the importance of technical change and the effects of changes in demand patterns, the changes in the division of labour and the growth of employment within the service industries are traced to the shift of capital from less to more profitable activities.

This type of explanation, then, in comparison with the two previous accounts, raises a different set of questions about the nature of services in the economy which range from the organizational and ownership structure of services to the changing patterns of capital investment and accumulation. The direction of the enquiry is different again and so too is the scope of the explanation. It is not necessarily any broader in scope than the other two accounts, but its focus upon capitalist social relations as opposed to technological changes or employment trends provides a different conceptual prism, as it were, through which the shifts in the division of labour are interpreted.

3.5.2 The logic of capitalist industrialization

A distinguishing characteristic of Mandel's explanation of the post-war expansion of the service sector is his insistence upon locating this trend within the *historical development* of capitalism as an economic system. His reasons for insisting upon a long-term view are two-fold. First, Mandel wishes to stress that service industries are *not* a post-war feature of capitalist economies. Industrialization in the seventeenth and eighteenth centuries would not have occurred, or would not have occurred so rapidly, had there not been an expansion of those services – banking, insurance, transport and trade – which enabled manufacturing production and sales to proceed with limited interruption and for goods to be distributed and exchanged. The second and related reason for adopting a long-term perspective is the emphasis that it accords to the *continuous* features of a capitalist economy, in particular to the competitive nature of capitalist production which compels private enterprises to accumulate or risk collapse. Thus the switch in investment to services, the entry of multinational companies into hitherto undeveloped markets, such as contract cleaning and catering, are all seen as an extension of the same economic 'logic' which led to the development of an industrialized, manufacturing economy in the last century.

Whether these new developments are interpreted, as Mandel argues, as the result of a diversion of excess capital into services to avert a fall in the average rate of profit or, as in the regulationist view, as a response to the crisis of Fordism and the search for new markets, the logic behind them is the same – the need to secure profitable investments.

Clearly, the emphasis that is placed upon locating service sector development within a long-term, historical perspective is designed to undermine post-industrial arguments and bring into question the validity of a primary focus upon post-war developments. It is not that history is simply called up in support of Mandel's viewpoint; rather it is the interpretation of history that is at issue. As we have seen, post-industrial arguments rest upon Fisher/ Clark's linear model of economic development and on the explicit recognition that different services are associated with the pre-industrial, industrial and post-industrial phases of development. This view of history assumes that each phase is separate and unconnected, each with its own dynamic of change, whereas Mandel emphasizes a process of capitalization which, over time, has incorporated agriculture, manufacturing *and* services into the realm of industrialized, commodity production. As capitalism has developed, commodity production has become more widespread which, in turn, has led to a deepening of the social division of labour.

The expansion of the service industries in the post-war period is one example of such an extension of the social division of labour. The separation of a number of specialist services, such as advertising, marketing, legal services and accountancy, from their previous position within the manufacturing sector also has a number of historical parallels: for example, the separation of heavy industrial goods production from consumer goods production into separate firms and industries in the nineteenth century, or the more recent spin-off of the food processing industry from agricultural production.

What is distinctive about the expansion of the service industries is, first, the redistribution of employment from the manufacturing to the service sector that has occurred and, secondly, the industrialization of services that has taken place – the increased automation of service delivery, the standardization of products and the growth of part-time and casual labour within the service industries. Fast food outlets and 'industrial' cleaning are two examples that are often cited. This latter observation is interesting in itself, for it contains a quite different assessment of service work from the rather positive evaluation of service jobs offered by post-industrial theorists. Indeed it is a characteristic of Marxist approaches that they tend to emphasize the *similarities* between manufacturing and service work rather than – as post-industrialists do – the differences between the two. Once again the different emphases stem from the different starting-points of the two approaches and the different aspects of service sector development which they choose to focus upon.

The tendency to see similarities between manufacturing and service work where others see differences, to see the industrialization of service work where others see its professionalization, emphasizes the continuity of a capitalist system of social relations which has the capacity to alter economic structures. The shift in the structure of the economy from manufacturing to services, therefore, does not amount to a shift in the fundamental character of capitalism. 'Manufacture', according to Clarke and Critcher, 'is not the essential feature of capitalism; the economic logic of profitability and the private ownership of capital are essential – and they are unchanged by the growth of the service sector or the export of industrial (manufacturing) production to developing countries' (1985, p. 197).

The 'logic of profitability' in this context does not imply some kind of progressive historical logic, that is, one which leads inevitably towards the development of a service economy. If it were such a logic, then it would share with the post-industrial view a gradual, linear notion of economic change. In fact the conception of economic change which underpins the logic of profitability is one that is closer to the socio-technical approach, in as far as the drive for profitability *constantly* involves structural change and hence periods of economic dislocation. The dislocation between the loss of full-time, male jobs in manufacturing and the growth of part-time, female work in the service sector is an example of such a change, and so too are the periodic waves of technological innovation as new ways of producing com-modities are introduced. What distinguishes Mandel's interpretation of economic change from either of the two explanations, however, is the importance that he attaches to the idea of a capitalist *system* of economic relations which governs the direction of *structural* economic change. From Mandel's viewpoint the change from a manufacturing to a service-based economy in post-war Britain represents a structural change *within* the capi-talist system.

Summary of section 3.5

- According to Mandel the growth of the service industries in the post-war period represents a shift in the pattern of capital investment from less to more profitable activities. Once 'opened up' for investment, the profitability of services is calculated in the same way as manufactured goods. The 'industrialization of the sphere of reproduction' is an extension of this drive for profitability and reaches its climax under 'late capitalism'.

- The growth of service occupations within both the manufacturing and the service industries is traced to developments in the technical and social division of labour. Although technological and organizational changes are behind those developments, the underlying cause is attributed to the ne-cessity of capitalist enterprises to reorganize production to maintain a com-petitive advantage.

- The view that the economy has moved beyond an industrial era is misplaced. Whereas post-industrial arguments identify a break between the present era from that of industrialism, Marxist writers emphasize the con-tinuous features of a capitalist system and tend to identify similarities between manufacturing and service work. (This is not to imply that Marxists play down the distinction between services and manufacturing. On the issue of output some Marxists hold the view that services are less productive than manufacturing. We will return to the significance of this point in Chapter 6.)

3.6   Continuity and change

So far we have worked through three different explanations of why the UK economy in the post-war period has shifted its base from manufacturing to services. In support of its particular viewpoint, each explanation angled the focus of its account to emphasize certain aspects of service sector growth and appealed to different kinds of evidence. The three explanations also diverged substantively over the *type* of economic changes that have taken place. In one sense the root of these differences can be traced to different assumptions about what an economy is. This theme will also be picked up in Chapter 6. In this section I want to draw your attention to the different *conceptions* of economic change held by the three theories. Let me begin by disentangling some of the varieties of economic change that occur in a modern economy.

3.6.1   Structural change and system change

Any economy is constantly changing. As some people enter the labour force for the first time, others are about to exit on retirement, or sooner. People change jobs or leave one employer to work for another. Companies change hands, but remain producers of computer software, distributors of retail goods, or providers of accountancy services, or whatever. None of these changes represents a change in economic structure. None, that is, unless there is a significant shift in the number of workers or companies in one or more directions – to the service sector, to high-tech industries and so forth. If the number of workers moving from manufacturing to services is roughly balanced by those moving in the other direction, either in a literal sense or through the processes of new recruitment or retirement, then no sectoral structures have been altered.

This is not to imply that structural changes in the economy are rare. They are not. You have encountered a number of post-war structural changes in this chapter and in the two previous chapters: for example, the emerging dominance of multinational corporations, the shift in employment from manufacturing to service industries, the change in the balance of white- and blue-collar occupations, the shift to part-time employment and so on. These are all kinds of structural change. They are structural economic changes and not merely changes in the occupants of the different roles that workers or companies perform in the structures of the economy. But there is more to structural change than this. If we consider each of these structural changes in isolation from each other, then we lose any sense of *periods* of structural change. In Chapter 1, for instance, the 1970s and 1980s was referred to as a period of upheaval, a period in which changes have occurred on several fronts, altering the general direction of change within the economy. What happened in one sector of the economy had an impact upon other parts of the economy and, in turn, these changes affected the overall direction of change. For example, in both Chapters 1 and 2, the regulationist account of the breakdown of Fordism and the rise of neo-Fordism referred to a wide range of structural changes in the process of production, in the mode of consumption, in state regulation and in the regulation of international finance. The shift from Fordism to neo-Fordism, therefore, represents a fundamental change to the ways in which the economy has previously been organized.

As you know, this is only one interpretation of this period of structural change, but it does convey the idea of such periods as historical turning-points, as moments of major structural transformation. The shift to a post-industrial economy can also be seen as such a turning-point. Before we examine how the three explanations conceptualize this declared turning-point, there is a further distinction to introduce, that between periods of structural change and periods of system change.

This distinction is hard to pin down. Whereas there is more or less of a consensus among the three theoretical approaches over what amounts to a structural change, there is considerable variation in the use of the term 'system'. To describe something as forming a system is to refer to a particular combination of structures or processes, whether they be economic, political or social relations, as relatively coherent in some way. You may recall the 'strong' version of coherence evident in world-system theory in Chapter 1, where the world economy was conceived as more than the sum of national economies; an overarching dynamic is attributed to the world economy. The kind of relative coherence referred to above is a rather different notion, one which lays stress upon the compatibility of structures and processes, on how they combine with one another. The actual combination is not pre-ordained in some kind of directed way; the combination is an historical product which changes over time. The intellectual stress here is upon identifying systems which operate *as if they were* a coherent set of processes or structures. The distinction between systems and structures is a rather abstract one and is best understood through examples. As we compare and contrast the three different accounts of economic change, the point to bear in mind is that theoretical approaches disagree over what amounts to an economic system, its temporal span and geographical extent. The disagreement is primarily one of *substance* – what structures and processes are identified – which, collectively, add up to something like a coherent economic system.

3.6.2   Services and economic change

The fundamental point to note is that each explanation operates with some notion of an economic system. In post-industrial theories the concept of an economic system which is in use is a rather shadowy, ill-defined notion and greater emphasis is placed upon a series of structural changes which, together, add up to the arrival of a new economic era, a post-industrial era. Thus we are informed of a shift in the sectoral structure of the economy from goods to services, a change in the occupational structure from blue- to white-collar occupations, and so forth. Despite this emphasis upon structural change, it is apparent that the central claim of post-industrial theory is that the new economic features represent something like a 'system shift'. Industrialism is basically a pre-1945 affair of factories, machines, material goods and cloth-capped workers. Post-industrialism is the world of services, office workers and information.

The notion of a turning-point is apparent, but the period is more than one of major substantial transformation: it is a period of transition between two qualitatively different types of economic system. In post-industrial accounts the economy evolves in distinct stages, with the most developed economies, those that are service-based, setting out the path of development that other economies are destined to follow. In the post-war period the United States acts as the role model with Britain following in its footsteps. The deterministic view of historical change which underpins post-industrial arguments is clearly evident.

The socio-technical approach operates with a more restricted notion of system. In this approach the concept of a socio-technical system refers to a distinctive combination of innovations which rest upon certain 'heartland technologies' which, in turn, are applied across a range of industries and their products. The application of these technologies and the creation of new markets is made possible by the existence of an appropriate material infrastructure, and the willingness of people to alter their lifestyles to take advantage of the new ways in which their needs can be met. Thus, the latter social innovations are integral to the successful adoption and diffusion of the technological innovations. From this standpoint the emergence of a self-service economy is the product of social innovations in the 1950s and 1960s which provided the demand for a range of new products which, in turn, led to the growth of certain consumer industries in the post-war period. This period of growth, it is claimed, is now over. The socio-technical system upon which it rests is stagnating, and the makings of a new socio-technical system based upon new heartland technologies, primarily that of microprocessors, is with us. A 'system shift' is recognized; one that will lead to new ways for people to 'service' themselves.

In contrast to the post-industrial account, then, the turning-point does not mark the end of industrialism: it signals the passing of a particular combination of technical and social structures, and the patterns of work and industry associated with them. The conception of economic change is also different. There is no 'march' through successive stages of economic development. Rather, the continuity of industrialism is punctuated by sharp bursts of technological change as a new cluster of innovations take effect, followed by long periods of consolidation as industries adopt the new technological practices. As with long-wave theories there is a regularity in the pattern of change, although what emerges in each successive 'system' is not pre-determined; it is shaped as much by political choices as it is by technological developments.

The third approach, Mandel's account of service sector growth, operates with yet another notion of economic system, one that has been shaped by the framework of its enquiry. Because it starts with the idea of capitalism as a broad, historical economic system, it views the structural changes identified by the post-industrialists as amounting to no more or less than that – a series of structural changes. Collectively, these structural changes are not taken to represent a shift from one type of economic system to another. Rather they are taken to represent a series of developments within a system of production that is marked by irregular and disruptive periods as industries and occupations contract and expand, appear and disappear, in line with the movement of capital from less to more profitable activities.

According to this view, post-industrial theorists are guilty of two misconceptions: one of foreshortening the history of industrialism and the other of foreclosing the geography of industrialism. (On the former misconception, see Kumar, 1978.) On the first count, Mandel argues that the expansion of the service sector does not supplant an industrial economy; there is no turning-point of the kind envisaged by post-industrialists. The growth of the service sector is an extension of the process of industrialization and commodity production that reaches back into the eighteenth and nineteenth centuries. On the second count, post-industrialists are accused of ethnocentrism, that is, they consider economic change from the vantage point of the advanced economic nations. In particular, they fail to include in their accounts any connection between the post-war global relocation of manufacturing industry to the newly industrializing countries and less economically developed nations *and* the decline of manufacturing and the growth of service industries in the advanced economies. In part the latter growth represents the development of internationally competitive service industries, primarily financial and business services, which derive economic benefits from 'servicing' global manufacturing production. In other words, the post-industrial sketch of a new economic era is considered to be based upon a kind of geographical myopia, a narrow vision of the links between changes in the advanced economies and changes elsewhere. Here lies a crucial difference between the post-industrial and the Marxist concepts of an economic system.

3.7   Services: an uneven geography

So far, we have restricted our attention to broad changes in the national economy. In one sense this national focus was chosen for us. Each of the different theories we have examined pitches its explanation at this level of enquiry. They ask questions about how and why the economy has shifted over time and about the overall pace of change. Answers to these questions, however, do not exhaust our understanding of economic change. There is another dimension of change to consider, that of geography.

As with the pattern of manufacturing job loss, the growth of service employment in post-war Britain has not occurred evenly across the country. In recent years, southern parts of the country have experienced rapid service sector growth, whereas some northern areas have witnessed a limited expansion or even an erosion of their service base. The pace of change has varied between regions, and so too has the impact of change. Uneven geographical development is not an accidental or arbitrary feature of economic change; it is, as you have seen from Chapter 2, part and parcel of the processes of economic change. Over time the uneven growth and decline of different sectors of the economy have shaped and reshaped an uneven pattern of economic development. As the structure of the economy has changed, so too has the uneven geography of industry and employment.

A sharp illustration of this process of uneven development was given in the previous chapter. In the first half of the 1980s it was those regions in the 'south' of the country – the South East, South West and East Anglia – least affected by manufacturing job loss that also gained the most jobs from the expansion of the service sector. This growing divide between north and south has led some commentators to describe Britain as a 'dual' economy – with a 'deindustrialized' north and west and a 'post-industrial' south and east (Marshall, Damesick and Wood, 1987).

The trends are clear, but before examining them more closely it is also important to recall that the geography of service sector growth is less uneven than that of manufacturing decline. The difference is, in part, attributable to the more even distribution of public sector jobs throughout the country. There is a different geography at work here, a different set of processes operating from those of the market. Yet with the most recent expansion of service jobs occurring in the private sector and concentrated in the southern half of the country, it is common to find areas outside of the 'south' where the public sector is the dominant employer. If the constraints on government expenditure continue, areas with a high proportion of public service jobs such as Northern Ireland, Scotland, Wales and the North and North West regions are likely to feel the greatest impact.

The trend should not be overstated, as there are patterns within this shift that require further investigation. Nonetheless, it is possible to see how the map of service jobs is being reshaped. In this context, it is important to bear in mind that the uneven development of the service sector is more than a question of job numbers in different regions. It is also a question of the different types of service *industry* that are located in different areas and the geographical variation in the types of service *occupation*. There is a qualitative as well as a quantitative dimension to service jobs. By 1981 all regions had 50 per cent or more of their total employment in the service sector. But not all regions were characterized by the same industrial profile or occupational structure. The research and development industry, for example, is concentrated in the southern regions, as are many business services (Gillespie and Green, 1987). Banking is concentrated in London, reflecting its historical role as a national and international financial centre. Indeed, all the service industries shown in Table 3.1 are, with varying degrees, unevenly distributed across the regions.

3.7.1 Geographical questions

We will address the geographies of some of these industries shortly and also some of the more stark variations in the spatial unevenness of occupational groups such as professional service workers. None of these patterns, however, nor the ways in which they are changing, are seriously in dispute. There is a broad degree of consensus among geographers about the uneven pattern of service employment. Where disagreement has arisen is over the reasons behind this uneven pattern, over the causal processes that have shaped it and directed its development.

Unlike the debate that you encountered over the geography of manufacturing decline, the geographical debate over service employment growth has been less intense and in consequence its parameters are less well defined. One significant reason for this state of affairs is that, until recently, the study of services within urban and regional geography has been a relatively neglected subject in comparison with manufacturing. Broadly speaking, a manufacturing-centred view of the economy has influenced the directions of research. However, with the demise of Britain's manufacturing base, the important role of the service industries as a generator of jobs has been thrust to the fore. Within a relatively short period of time the outlines of a debate have emerged and, perhaps not surprisingly, the *terms* of the debate have been influenced by the three theoretical accounts of national economic change that we addressed earlier. The key word here is influenced. Neither of the geographical approaches we are about to examine is a direct application of, say, post-industrial theory or the logic of capitalist industrialization to the changing geography of service employment. The debate over the emergence of a service-based economy in the United Kingdom started in the 1970s and continues to evolve. The debate over the geography of service change, as indicated, is just beginning and the two approaches have used the earlier debate to pose specific *geographical* questions.

One approach, for example, which may be referred to as a 'market-based' approach (*Daniels*, 1986; Marshall, Damesick and Wood, 1987), starts by asking questions about what kinds of *demand* exist for services in the economy. The thrust of this approach is to identify which kinds of demand are related to which types of service industry and then proceed to chart their locational differences and spatial pattern. On this basis, two types of service industry have been identified – *producer services* and *consumer services*. Greater attention has been paid to the geography of producer services, as they are held to be the main contributor to spatial variations in service employment. This group of industries includes services such as banking, insurance, advertising, market research, professional and scientific services, and research and development, which meet the demand for intermediate services from manufacturing and other service industries in national and international markets. Consumer services, as the term implies, meet the demand for final services from households, and exhibit a more even geography in relation to the distribution of the population and their purchasing power. In choosing to prioritize the importance of demand characteristics, this approach emphasizes one of the main features of post-industrial arguments. The emphasis, however, has been adapted to explain a related but different subject matter. Nor is the emphasis upon markets taken to be the sole criterion of service location. This approach also stresses the need to understand service location in the context of how technological and organizational changes within service firms have altered the geography of *supply*, with some industries serving peripheral markets from more central locations (Marshall, 1985; *Wood*, 1986). Here, we see the influence of ideas that are embedded in the socio-technical approach.

The second approach has its roots in a Marxist account of economic change. Some of its characteristics will be familiar to you from section 3.5 and also from the restructuring approach outlined in the previous chapter, where it was presented as one of the ways of understanding the geography of manufacturing job loss. Recently this approach has been extended and adapted to the changing geography of service employment (*Allen*, 1988; Buck, 1985; Massey, 1984; Urry, 1987). Although there are different strands to this approach, its central focus is upon the changing organization of production within the service industries and the extent to which these changes are a product of wider, structural changes in the British economy. It asks a different set of questions about developments in the division of labour within both manufacturing and service production which, in turn, leads it to examine variations in the spatial organization of production and how different service industries use space. In doing so, this approach also considers changes in the technological and organizational structure of industries and their spatial implications. Unlike the first approach, however, this position argues that such changes cannot fully be understood unless the capitalist organization of the economy is recognized. In this account it is the drive for profitability, the production for profit, that lies behind the spatial reorganization of the service industries.

The theoretical traditions that inform the two positions should now be evident. What remains is to explore the main direction of the arguments. To do this, we shall take the crucial issue raised at the beginning of this section: the uneven development of service employment that is widening the divide between north and south. In particular we shall look at the spatial concentration of services in the south, and their close proximity to London despite the trends towards decentralization. Before doing so, you should note that the mode of presentation is different from the preceding sections, in that the two positions are contrasted directly in order to highlight the different ways they approach the issue.

3.7.2   A post-industrial south?

Figure 3.3 reveals as much as it conceals. A quick glance reveals the dominant position that the South East has occupied throughout the post-war period, reflecting the size of its working population. In 1981, 38 per cent of *all* service sector employment was located in the South East and within that region the majority was concentrated in Greater London. On this evidence, any talk of a north-south divide in services would be better expressed as the South East versus the rest of the regions. What this regional picture does not reveal, however, are the recent trends in service sector growth which in fact are contributing to the north-south employment divide. Nor does it reveal the recent decentralization of private service employment from London to the South East and the adjoining regions or, for that matter, the wider decentralization of public service jobs from London which took place in the 1960s and early 1970s.

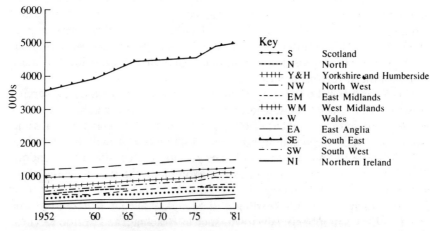

Figure 3.3   Regional employment change in services, 1952–1981
Source: Hudson and Williams, 1986, Figure 2.1F, p. 57

The key period of spatial change for the service sector was in the late 1970s, a decade or so later than the first signs of manufacturing decline in Britain. And the major process at work was a shift away from the public sector services towards the private sector. The late 1960s and the first half of the 1970s was a period of strong service employment growth across the country, attributable largely to the expansion of the public sector, in particular to health and education services. By the end of the 1970s the pattern had altered significantly. Figure 3.4 gives you an idea of the regional impact.

Activity 3.4

Examine the regional differences in employment change between public and private services for the period 1976–81.

(a) For public services, the overall national trend is one of decline. Which regions have experienced a decline in public services below that of the national average (−1.5 per cent)?

(b) For private services, the national trend is the reverse. Which regions have experienced a growth rate in private service jobs above the national average (7.0 per cent)?

(c) How has Greater London fared in both private and public services in relation to the national average?

With the exception of the East and West Midlands, none of the regions outside of the south in the latter half of the 1970s experienced a growth rate in private services above the national average (the figure for the West Midlands was just slightly above the national average). Indeed, aside from Scotland and Wales, this situation was compounded by the relative deterioration of their public service base. By the mid-1980s the 'service gap' between north and south had widened. Between 1979 and 1986 some two-thirds of the 860 000 jobs created in the service industries were located in the three southern regions (*Martin*, 1988).

The second trend to note is the dispersed geography of the new service growth in the south. As elsewhere, much of the expansion in service sector employment in the southern regions has occurred in free-standing cities and large towns. To a large extent, however, employment growth in these areas is attributable to the decentralization of private service jobs from London. Moves by larger service companies, for example in the insurance industry, have also generated local employment growth. Old industrial towns around London, such as Luton, Reading and Slough, have benefited from this trend, as have a number of new towns such as Bracknell and Milton Keynes, and so too have major provincial cities further afield such as Bristol, Ipswich and Cambridge. The result is a deconcentration of service employment in

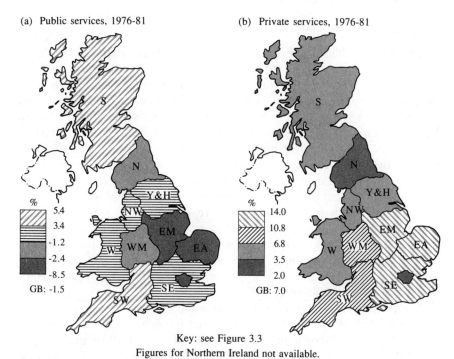

(a) Public services, 1976-81

(b) Private services, 1976-81

Key: see Figure 3.3

Figures for Northern Ireland not available.

Figure 3.4 Regional percentage employment change in public and private services, Britain, 1976–81

Source: Damesick, 1986, Figure 2a and 2b, p. 220

the 'south' away from the capital city and, interestingly, one which is parallel to the growth of high-tech industries along the M4 corridor and around the M25 and M11 motorways. In fact, service employment is numerically more important in these areas than the high-tech developments. There is, however, an important difference between the two patterns of growth. Whereas the high-tech activities are to be found in the smaller towns and 'rural' areas, the new 'service centres', as noted, are located in the cities and larger towns. An exception to this pattern is the research and development industries which have also tended to locate in small, non-industrialized towns (Howells, 1984; Gillespie and Green, 1987). Having said that, it is still important to bear in mind that London, despite its employment decline in some service industries, still dominates the south. London's role as a 'world city', as a major centre of international finance and commerce, its buoyant consumer-orientated services and its significantly higher proportion of service workers, put it into a different, higher category of 'service cities'.

The main question, of course, is how is this changing pattern of uneven development to be explained? Let us begin with the growth of service employment and its geographical concentration in the large towns and cities of the south and then move onto the issue of job decentralization.

The 'market-based' approach

From a 'market-based' approach the first issue is best understood by disentangling the range of factors that have encouraged the *demand* for private services and identifying the ways in which service companies have reorganized to *supply* the new markets. Much of the work done has focused upon the producer service category as these services are seen to hold the key to future patterns of service growth at both the national and sub-national level. In much the same way as the high-tech industries in the southern regions are seen as the way forward for Britain's manufacturing sector, so producer services in the cities are taken as the pivot of national service sector growth. Part of the argument here rests upon the predication that information-based services, of which producer services are considered a prime example, represent the leading edge of the economy. And with the existing over-representation of these activities in the southern half of the country, particularly in London and the South East, it has been suggested that this advantage will further reinforce the uneven geography of service employment (Hepworth, Green and Gillespie, 1987).

In effect, what is being suggested here is the growth of urban agglomeration economies in the south. You have met the term 'agglomeration economy' before in relation to the 'deindustrialization' of the old manufacturing areas. You may recall that it was Keeble (1980) who concluded that agglomeration *diseconomies* were the most significant reason for manufacturing decentralization in the 1970s. Here, in respect of services, it is the positive advantages of agglomeration that are at issue and which, in part, account for the different factors behind the demand for producer services in southern Britain in the 1980s.

At the risk of losing some of the subtlety of the argument, three factors have been identified which reinforce a southern service bias. The first two factors are related. One is the demand that stems from the existing location of service activities. The type of activities indicated are the location of corporate headquarters, particularly in the South East; the growth of financial and business services in southern provincial cities such as Bristol and Cambridge, and the expansion of consumer service markets, such as theatres, restaurants and retail stores, generated by the growth of high-income occupations. The second factor encouraging the demand for producer services is the growth of service export markets. The obvious examples are banking, insurance, aviation and shipping, but accountancy, advertising and legal services are also important international markets, for London-based service firms in particular (Daniels, Leyshon and Thrift, 1986). Putting both aspects of demand together there are signs that in Marshall's view indicate 'a trend towards a "dual" economy in the United Kingdom in which those regions least affected by job loss in manufacturing also benefit from agglomerative tendencies in the service activities' (1985, p. 1165). Finally this view is lent support by the relative health of manufacturing industry in the south compared with the north which has also stimulated the demand for specialist, private services ranging from business services to contract cleaning and catering services. Much of this growth stems from manufacturing firms 'externalizing' services peripheral to their core activities and which are now increasingly provided by service firms from central, provincial locations.

The growth of producer service agglomerations in southern Britain should, however, be seen in the context of the decentralization of service employment from London and by implication the internal reorganization of the larger producer service companies since the mid-1970s. If the success of London has created diseconomies for some producer services, such as the insurance industry, the provincial towns and cities offered a number of advantages from cheaper land costs and lower office rents to reduced labour costs. Other producer services, in particular a number of larger companies within the business service sector, have reorganized their activities to enter new markets in provincial, urban locations either by developing existing sites or by setting up new outlets. There are other factors listed by this approach, for example the impact of technological change upon producer service location, which is also seen to influence the growth of urban service agglomerations in the southern regions. Indeed, it would appear that this approach *consists* of a list of changing demand and supply factors and this makes its presentation and evaluation all the more difficult. Nonetheless, it does prioritize the role of markets and, as we have seen, it is the markets for producer services – manufacturing, other service industries and export – and the locations from which they are served that create agglomerative tendencies in the large towns and cities of the south. And London, despite dispersal trends, remains the most significant location for the supply of and demand for producer services.

The 'production-based' approach

From the point of view of the 'production-based' approach, many of the factors listed above, including the emphases upon agglomeration economies, are not contested. The analysis is not considered in any way to be factually incorrect; it is rather that its emphasis is misplaced. Changes in the pattern of demand for private services and changes in the ways in which that demand is met are seen to occur without acknowledging the basis upon which different industries establish production in different regions. According to this view, the ways in which different private services use space reflect the *calculation* of profitability that has been made. Sometimes the calculation may be reflected in a decision to relocate routine clerical work from London to a provincial city to reduce labour and organizational costs. Many of the larger insurance companies, for example, have adopted this strategy. In other services such as accountancy, the major firms, through a process of acquisition and merger, operate a system of branch offices which mirrors a geographical pattern of profitability. Similarly, in the private services that run alongside public services, such as private health care and private education, their geography is skewed towards prosperous areas in the southern region.

This is not simply a markets versus profits opposition; rather it is argued that the different *structures* of service industries, whether they are dominated by large or small firms, whether they are characterized by a high or low degree of labour organization, or whether they face domestic or foreign competition, or both, all influence the types of profit calculation that are made. In this sense the growth of private services in the cities and larger towns of the south reflects a variety of locational strategies that have been adopted by service firms to maintain or increase their competitive position. In contrast, in the public sector where locational decisions are mediated by political rather than financial considerations, a different geography, as we have seen, is evident. The requirements of location are different and so too are the relations of control.

The issue of control is a crucial aspect of this approach. A central reason for London and the South East's dominance of the service sector, it is argued, is not the agglomerative pull that it exerts on private service companies, nor the concentration of information-based activities, but the *control functions* that reside in the headquarters of the major service organizations located in or near the capital city. Across a wide range of service activities from banking, insurance, advertising and accountancy to the hotel trade, retail and the cultural and entertainments industry, the majority are controlled from London and the South East. Much of the service activities in other regions, in the branch networks of business organizations, in the clerical 'back offices' of insurance companies, and in the multiple outlets of the consumer-orientated industries, is governed from the South East. Smaller firms and self-employment are more significant in the service industries than manufacturing, but in employment terms they are overshadowed by the increasing domination of the different service industries by national and international service companies.

There is a further strand to this argument. A corollary of the trend towards the increasing concentration of ownership and diverse organizational structure of service firms appears to be a widening of the division of labour. In the south, however, perhaps contrary to expectations, this has not produced a sharp *spatial* division of labour between, on the one hand, professional workers in one part of the south and clerical and manual services elsewhere. It is certainly the case that professional service workers are over-represented in London and the South East, but so too are clerical and manual service workers. The same is true for the larger provincial cities in the south. The pattern varies from industry to industry, but what is apparent in the service-dominated labour markets in these areas is the increasing *polarization* of the employment structure between well-paid, full-time, 'career' professional and administrative jobs and lower-grade, frequently part-time, routinized service jobs (*Allen*, 1988; Boddy *et al.*, 1986; Damesick, 1986). And this leads to a further point. For it is those groups at the top end of this unequal occupational structure that have, within limits, the ability to choose where they live and work, and this has generally favoured areas around or in the southern towns and cities. Locations which are attractive to key staff precisely because, in contrast to many northern cities, they are relatively unscathed by previous manufacturing development. The availability of particular kinds of skilled service labour is thus seen as another contributing factor to the uneven development of the service sector.

Pulling out the differences

In broad terms the difference between the two approaches can be gleaned from the different ways in which they characterize the process of uneven development and, more generally, economic change. Within a 'market-based' approach, there is an underlying emphasis upon the discontinuity of economic development which has taken a definite geographical form. In short, it would appear that a past era of industrialism in the north and west has given way to a southern-based professional service economy. The description of the latter as a 'post-industrial' space economy merely serves to reinforce this interpretation. Elements of a cumulative causation model of uneven development are also at work here, with the agglomerative trends in southern town and cities widening the gap between north and south, buttressed by the continuing domination of London and the South East.

In contrast, the process of uneven development within the 'production-based' approach is not seen as the product of 'groups' of services responding to demand factors and reorganizing their supply accordingly; rather, the reorganization that is at issue is the reorganization of the relations of production over space to satisfy profitability. This accords with the notion of uneven development outlined in section 2.6 in the previous chapter. Different types of service industry with different locational requirements use space to improve their position in a competitive national and international economy. In doing so, they lay down a new form of uneven development, by investing in new locations where the appropriate range of skills is available or developing existing locations to meet the changing requirements of service production. Many of these locations are in the south precisely because the existing pattern of uneven development provided the conditions, in particular the appropriate labour sources, currently required by labour-intensive service industries. As further shifts in the technological basis of service production occur and as the larger service companies organize their production on an international basis, it is also likely that a different set of labour requirements will come to the fore and with it the possibility of a new form of uneven development.

The exception, here, is the role of London. Whilst the fortunes of the regions and the cities within them have fluctuated, London has retained its significance as the locus of power – as the site of private corporate control and of state control. For the second approach, there is also a further dimension to the continued importance of London, that of the City. In this case the City is not seen as the embodiment of one of the most significant, perhaps *the* most significant, producer service – financial services – but as the site of finance capital which operates with a series of interests that sets it apart from capital employed in the service or manufacturing industries (Harris, 1985). Its success is not measured in output terms, nor are its activities unravelled by tracing patterns of demand; its productive activity, as it were, is measured by the amount of financial assets under its *control*. And its ability to manipulate financial assets, stocks and shares, securities, bonds, loans and deposits, gives the City its central, controlling role in the economy. The City does indeed provide a range of monetary services and in that sense it is part of the service sector, but its spatial significance, as was noted in the previous chapter, extends beyond its locational boundaries. According to this view the City has not only contributed towards the concentration of service development in London and the South East, it has also played a significant role in the overall restructuring of the UK economy in the post-war period.

Summary of section 3.7

• Since the mid-1970s the uneven development of service sector expansion has reinforced the gap between north and south. A major contributing factor has been the shift away from public sector services towards the private sector. Within the south, London remains the major centre of service employment. Much of the recent expansion of service employment, however, has taken place in free-standing cities and large towns within the southern regions, and much of this growth is attributable to the decentralization of service jobs from London.

• Two different explanations of the changing pattern of uneven development were examined. The following table acts as a summary of the main differences between the two approaches.

	'Market-based' approach	*'Production-based' approach*
Starting-point	Demand and supply for services.	Changing organization of production within a capitalist economy.
Key concepts	Markets, producer services, consumer services, agglomeration economies, technical and organizational change.	Profit calculation, spatial division of labour, organizational structure (of firms), control functions.
Focus	The kinds of demand that exist for services in the economy and how the geography of supply has altered to meet them.	The conditions under which different service industries have established production in different regions – how they use space.

Further reading

Krishan Kumar's *Prophecy and Progress* (Harmondsworth, Penguin Books; 1978) remains the most accessible critique of the claims of post-industrial writers. Written from a sociological viewpoint, the book is a model of how to evaluate theoretical positions. A review of the more recent writings which loosely fall under the post-industrial heading is Boris Frankel's *The Post Industrial Utopians* (Cambridge, Polity Press; 1987).

Books on services and the service economy are beginning to appear, but there is no comprehensive text available as yet. Pascal Petit's *Slow Growth and the Service Economy* (London, Frances Pinter; 1986) is an interesting book which draws upon regulationist views. And – if you can seek it out – *Growth and Technical Change in the UK Service Sector* by Richard Barras (London, The Technical Change Centre; 1984) is a detailed account of the economic performance of the service sector since the 1970s. On the employment side, Amin Rajan's *Services: A Third Industrial Revolution?* (London, Butterworths; 1987) outlines the trends and prospects for job growth in the service industries.

If, like me, you are still unsure what services actually are, most books and articles on services devote some attention to questions of definition and conceptualization. Richard Walker's article, 'Is there a service economy? The changing capitalist division of labour', in *Science and Society* (Vol. 47, No. 1, pp. 42–83) is a useful way into the conceptual issues.

Finally, the literature on the changing geography of services, as indicated in the chapter, is less developed than it is for manufacturing. A cross-section of the different explanations of the pattern of service growth is given in the accompanying Reader to this text (Massey, D. and Allen, J. (eds) (1988)).

4 A crisis of mass production?

Richard Meegan

Contents

4.1	**Introduction**	137
4.2	**The rise, triumph and decline of Fordism**	139
4.2.1	Fordism and the labour process	139
4.2.2	Explaining the rise and decline of Fordism: some theoretical issues	145
4.2.3	Defining Fordism	152
4.3	**Crisis resolution: neo-Fordism and flexible specialization?**	163
4.3.1	Neo-Fordism and flexible specialization	163
4.3.2	Flexible production technologies and the changing labour process	164
4.3.3	Neo-Fordism: the evidence	170
4.4	**The geography of Fordism, neo-Fordism and flexible specialization**	174
4.4.1	The geography of Fordism and neo-Fordism: the debate	174
4.4.2	Fordism and neo-Fordism and the UK's changing economic geography	177
	Summary of section 4.4	181
	Answers to Activities	182
	Further reading	182

4.1   Introduction

As Chapter 1 demonstrated, there is no shortage of theories which purport to explain the dramatic downturn in international economic growth in the years since the mid-1970s. The relative scale of this decline is vividly illustrated in Figure 4.1. This figure charts the rates of growth of gross domestic product (GDP) and trade (with exports as a proxy) for the advanced capitalist countries since early industrialization in the first half of the eighteenth century. Compare the growth rates in the different periods shown. The spectacular growth of the years between 1950 and 1973 stands out in particularly sharp relief. But note also the scale of the decline in the years since 1973. This decline has been such that, in the most recent period shown (1979–1985), growth rates in both GDP and exports are substantially below those of what is often referred to as the 'second industrial revolution' (Hobsbawm, 1968; World Bank, 1987) almost a century earlier.

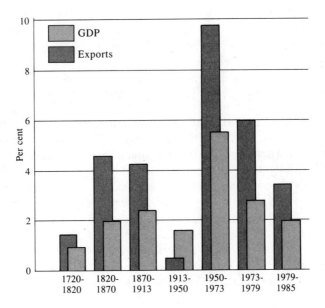

Figure 4.1   Historical trends in the growth of real GDP and exports in selected countries, 1720–1985

Accurate historical data for world exports and GDP are difficult to obtain, so the chart shows average growth rates for six major industrial countries: France, Germany, Italy, Japan, the United Kingdom and the United States. For exports, the growth rate for 1720–1820 includes only France and the United Kingdom; the average for 1820–70 includes France, Germany, the United Kingdom and the United States. The GDP growth rates have the same coverage, except that the first period is 1700–1820 instead of 1720–1820, and the US is excluded from both the first and second periods.

Source: World Bank, 1987

Indeed, the average growth rate of GDP in the 1980s only just matches tnat of the period between 1820 and 1870, when the global market first emerged. And growth rates of exports when this global market was being established actually exceeded those registered in the first half of the current decade.

In this chapter we shall look at the explanations put forward for this dramatic reversal in economic growth by two schools of thought that are currently receiving much academic and political attention. The first of these has already been introduced in Chapter 1 and briefly discussed in Chapter 2 – that is the 'regulationist school' based mainly around the work of French Marxists including Michel Aglietta, Robert Boyer, Alain Lipietz and Christian Palloix. The second is developing around the avowedly non-Marxist theorizing of two North American writers, Michael Piore and Charles Sabel, and inspired in particular by their book *The Second Industrial Divide* which was published in 1984. In many respects, as we shall see in the discussion that follows, the work of these authors and their supporters in the fields of industrial sociology and industrial and labour market economics fits in with what has been called the 'institutional tradition'. (This term was first coined in the inter-war period to refer to a school of American economists, most notably Thorstein Veblen, who criticized what is now called neo-classical economics using a conceptual framework that incorporated socio-cultural institutional forms.)

While these two 'schools' differ substantially in the concepts that they use and in their broad explanatory frameworks – differences which we will explore in the next section – both contend that the key to understanding the shift from 'boom' to 'stagnation' in western economic growth lies in the rise and decline of a particular form or 'regime' of economic organization and regulation. The form in question is that of mass production and the institutional and regulatory framework (or mode of regulation) built around it which together combine to make up 'Fordism'. In these theories it was Fordism on which the 'golden age' of western capitalism was built in the two decades following the ending of the Second World War – and it is the breakdown of Fordism which explains the subsequent decline or crisis. Moreover, both theories share some similarities in their conceptualization of the era that they see as succeeding Fordism, variously referred to as 'neo-Fordism', 'post-Fordism' and 'flexible specialization or accumulation'.

At the heart of both theories is the division of labour within production. This is what is known as the technical division of labour. Its emphasis on the division of labour in the workplace marks it out from the broader social division of labour discussed in the previous chapter. In the next section we will define it more carefully in the context of a discussion of another key concept in the Fordist/neo-Fordist debate, namely that of the labour process (which refers to the way in which labour is organized and controlled within production). A brief historical discussion of the Fordist labour process sets the scene for a comparison in section 4.2.2 of the different ways in which the institutionalists and regulationists conceptualize the development of the Fordist era. In section 4.2.3 the discussion shifts to the difficulties involved in identifying Fordism empirically. The emphasis in both theories on manufacturing, and their prioritization of sectors within it, are discussed and the difficulties of relating the variety of actual production and labour processes to the notion of Fordism are explored. Section 4.3.1 focuses on the similarities and differences in the two theories' views of the solution to the crisis of Fordism – neo-Fordism for the regulationists and flexible specialization for the institutionalists. Sections 4.3.2 examines the main features of the so-called new flexible production technologies and the changing patterns of consumption that are associated with them, while section 4.3.3 looks at some of the evidence for this new production regime. Section 4.4 concludes with a discussion of the geography of the different production regimes, examining some of the main strands of the debate in this area in section 4.4.1 and seeing how these relate to recent changes in the UK's economic geography in section 4.4.2.

4.2   The rise, triumph and decline of Fordism

4.2.1   Fordism and the labour process

An important feature of the 'Fordism debate' is its combination of analysis of both what is going on in production and the way in which consumption is brought into balance with the goods produced. On the production side Fordism concentrates in particular on the organization and control of labour. This is the labour process aspect of Fordism and it is important to understand its meaning.

Bowles and Edwards define a **labour process** as the application of human labour '. . . in the transformation of our natural surroundings with the intention of producing something useful (or thought to be useful)' (1985, p. 37). For the regulationists the key words in this definition are those in the brackets. In their Marxist conceptualization of the labour process it is the capitalist who decides what is to be produced and 'usefulness' is measured by considerations of profitability. Capitalists buy workers' capacity for labour or 'labour power' at a value below that which the workers' labour adds to the commodities that they are set to produce. By dint of their ownership of the means of production, capitalists are able to appropriate the difference between the cost of the labour power they purchase and the market value added to the commodities by the extra 'unpaid' labour that they can extract from their workers. The cost of labour power is set at a price/wage determined by labour market conditions and the price of commodities that workers need to buy in order to survive and 'reproduce themselves' (a conventional standard of living). In addition to wage costs the capitalist also has to meet the costs of the means of production used up in production, but the difference between these costs and the market value added to the commodities by unpaid labour – or surplus value – reverts to the capitalists (or is 'realized') when the commodities are sold. The labour process is thus the source of this surplus value.

The regulationists and institutionalists agree that the labour process of Fordism is structured around the organizational and technological innovations of two key figures in the history of capitalist production, both North American engineers working at the turn of the century – Frederick Taylor and Henry Ford. It was Taylor, obsessed with the separation of mental and manual labour, the fragmentation and deskilling of work tasks and the assertion of managerial control in the workplace, who came up with a set of self-professed 'principles of **scientific management**'. Hill identifies three key features of these principles:

> Taylor's scheme involved first the systematic analysis of the process of production and then its fragmentation by means of a greatly increased division of labour. Individual jobs were to be simplified to the performance of a single task wherever possible. The skill requirements of jobs were to be minimized by reducing operations to their component parts, many of which could then be undertaken by unskilled labour. The performance of jobs was to be carried out by workers, but all the elements of work planning which were traditionally done by workers were to be taken over by management, thus separating planning from doing. In this way, work tasks could be simplified, standardized and de-skilled. This in turn would increase efficiency and profitability: less skilled and therefore cheaper labour could be employed; labour productivity would increase once workers specialized on one endlessly repeated task; managers would have greater control of production costs ...
>
> The second aspect of scientific management concerned the re-integration of the production process which had been fragmented by the increased division of labour: this was now to be co-ordinated and controlled by management. The principle of task control was that *managers* should plan and direct the organization of production, which was an attack on the discretion employed by foremen as well as the delegation of control to labour. Managers were to be the new masters of the workplace ...
>
> The third element, which was the development of an efficient cost-accounting system based on the systematic time and motion analysis of operations and the setting of standard times, for the first time provided the information necessary for managers to monitor the effectiveness of work. (Hill, 1981, pp. 25, 26; emphasis in original)

This breaking down of production into specialized activities and the organization of the workforce around this specialization is what we referred to in section 4.1 as the **technical division of labour**.

The impact of Taylor's management principles on the labour process was greatly amplified when they were applied in the organization of production around the assembly lines pioneered by Henry Ford in his River Rouge car plant in Detroit just before the onset of the First World War. The 'Taylorist' division of labour and fragmentation of skills were intensified by a system of mass production in which the pace of work was mechanically controlled. Taylor provided the organizational principles for increased managerial control over the labour process; Ford provided the technology – the mechanized assembly line.

Extract 1 is a description, by a recent biographer of Henry Ford, of the introduction of the first such line in Ford's magneto department in 1913. Note the highly structured technical division of labour and the increases in productivity as the moving line was progressively mechanized by the production managers. You might also care to judge the euphoric tone of the final sentence of the extract in the light of the following anecdote, recounted by a Swiss car factory superintendent to the US Federal Trade Commission in 1916:

> There applied for work at this factory one day a man who represented himself to be a skilled erector of automobiles. The plant needed such a man, hired the applicant, and assigned to him the assembly of an automobile. It soon became apparent that this employee did not even know where or how to commence the assembly. The superintendent said to him:
>
> 'We thought you were a skilled erector of automobiles.'
>
> 'I thought I was', replied the new employee.
>
> 'Where did you work?'
>
> 'At the plant of Ford Motor Co.'
>
> 'What did you do?'
>
> 'I screwed on nut No. 58.'
>
> (quoted in Gartman, 1979, p. 203)

Extract 1

The introduction of the mechanized assembly line at Ford

Workers lined up side by side, facing the flywheels designed by Spider Huff. These flywheels rested on waist-high metal shelving along which the components could be slid, and below the shelf each man had a bin containing just one or two simple components.

Until this date the magneto assemblers had worked at benches with a complete range of magnets, bolts, and clamps, each of them fitting together some thirty-five to forty complete flywheel magneto assemblies in the course of a nine-hour day. Now they were each assigned just one or two of the twenty-nine different operations that went into the assembly – a magnet to place, a couple of nuts to start or tighten before they pushed the assembly down to their neighbour – and immediately their production time fell quite noticeably. With the old system it had taken at least fifteen minutes to produce one magneto. Now the assembly time was thirteen minutes ten seconds.

When the waist-level shelving was replaced by a rather more elevated, motorized conveyor belt which set the pace for the line, production time fell still more; and when further analysis refined the division of tasks along the belt, the average assembly time per magneto fell to seven minutes, and then to five. Through the introduction of continuous movement, it had become possible for one man to do the work which had previously occupied three or four – nor was there any longer the need for the worker to be especially skilled. Any manual labourer could do the job.

The first moving assembly: the magneto line, Highland Park, 1913.

Soon another conveyor belt was carrying engines along, and their crankshafts and pistons were fitted as they moved. The making of transmissions was similarly analysed and its component stages strung out along a moving belt. Suddenly, in the summer of 1913, the production managers at Highland Park had a problem. These new continuously moving assembly systems were producing so much that they were threatening to flood the final chassis assembly – the conclusion of the whole production process generally thought of when people refer to 'the' assembly line.

Stopwatches went into action. An analysis of production at Highland Park that August showed 250 assemblers and 80 parts carriers working nine hours each per day for twenty-six days to complete 6,182 chassis and motors – an average of twelve and a half man-hours per chassis. As an experiment, a crude moving line was set up, with a rope running 250 feet down the factory from one chassis to a winch which hauled the rope in slowly across the floor. As the chassis moved, a team of six assemblers kept pace with it, picking up parts as they needed them from strategic dumps along the way – and lo and behold, the average number of man-hours needed to complete a chassis using this method fell to five hours and fifty minutes.

Eliminating the trotting escort, and repositioning the assembly workers in stationary positions along a moving line that had been raised to just above waist height cut production times even more dramatically. Work was analysed still more thoroughly and subdivided accordingly.

'The man who places a part does not fasten it,' said Henry Ford. 'The man who puts in a bolt does not put on the nut; the man who puts on the nut does not tighten it.' Average chassis assembly time fell to ninety-three minutes.

The lesson was obvious. Within months Highland Park was a buzzing network of belts, assembly lines, and subassemblies: a dashboard assembly line, a front-axle assembly line, a body-and-top assembly line. The entire place was whirled up into a vast, intricate, and never-ending mechanical ballet.

Highland Park, 1913: one day's output.

'Every piece of work in the shops moves,' exulted Henry Ford; 'it may move on hooks, on overhead chains ... it may travel on a moving platform, or it may go by gravity, but the point is that there is no lifting or trucking. ... No workman has anything to do with moving or lifting anything.' Let the conveyor do the walking. 'Save ten steps a day for each of 12,000 employees, and you will have saved fifty miles of wasted motion and mis-spent energy.'

Ford output figures rose dramatically. Highland Park's 1911–12 production of 78,440 Model T's had been achieved with a work force of 6,867. The following year production more than doubled, and the work force more than doubled as well. But when, in 1913–14, production nearly doubled yet again, the number of workers needed to manufacture this dramatically increased number of cars did not increase. This was the year in which the moving assembly line was introduced, and thanks to its efficiencies, the size of the work force at Highland Park actually fell, from 14,336 workers to 12,880. In his drive to produce the people's car, Henry Ford had turned a giant key that admitted him to a magical new world.

Source: Lacey, 1986, pp. 144–6

The English car-worker, reminiscing for the BBC television programme *All Our Working Lives* about his experience of night-shift working, might also be expected to have something to say about just how 'magical' the 'new world' was for the people who worked in it:

> 'My wife always insisted that I had my breakfast before I went to bed. And I would get into such a state that I would sit down to a bacon and egg and the table would appear to be moving away from me. I thought "Crikey, how long am I going to have to put up with this?" But the pay was good. It was a case

of getting really stuck in and saying "To hell with it, get it while it's there."
And this is the way it went, but the elderly chaps couldn't stand the pace.'
(Joe Dennis, quoted in Pagnamenta and Overy, 1984, p. 14)

That worker also put his finger on the other side of Fordism, the issue of
mass consumption: 'The pay was good.' When Ford introduced his assembly line he also increased the pay of his workers, or at least those able to
meet the rigorous rules of individual and family behaviour demanded by
the firm's euphemistically titled 'Sociology Department'. Ford's '$5 day'
was denounced by some of his fellow industrialists as being both danger-
ously socialist and doomed to failure as the increased wage bill cut into the
company's profits. But the move was far from socialist; it was simply a recognition, far-sighted for the times, that the wage increases would be more
than compensated for by the massive increases in labour productivity that
his new production techniques allowed. These new production techniques
in turn allowed production to cater for a mass market. Much to the chagrin
of his critics, Ford's profits soared.

Until Ford came along production in what Hobsbawm (1968) calls the
'archaic era of industrialization' was essentially geared towards the middle
class and the relatively few rich. The demand of the masses was for food,
shelter and clothing. However, it was these masses that offered the largest
potential market.

What the mass production factories offered was the possibility of dramatically increasing the productivity of the workers employed within them,
cutting the prices of the articles produced and allowing wage increases
which did not, in themselves, threaten profitability. The extension of credit
also helped to bring more goods within the spending power of the mass of
the population. This widening of the market was delayed by the two World
Wars and the government's policy of wage and social security cuts in the
1930s' slump (Hobsbawm, 1968). Even then, some growth in real wages
occurred, partly due to the establishment of Fordist consumer goods industries. However, it was only when the Second World War ended that anything truly resembling a 'mass production – mass consumption' economy
could be established. Since 1950 labour income has accounted for 70 per
cent of the UK's GNP compared with 56 per cent in the years before the
First World War (Lee, 1986). Individual wages were also bolstered by the
'social wages' of the Keynesian welfare state (most importantly in the form
of health, education and retirement provision) and by state management of
capital and labour conflicts over the scale of, and balance between, these
two sources of income. It is these socio-institutional structures which the
regulationists call the mode of regulation, a concept already introduced in
Chapter 2.

This Keynesian-style mode of regulation is thus the consumption counterpart of the Taylorist/Fordist labour process. The two together, to retain
the regulationists' terminology, combined to form the *Fordist regime of
accumulation*.

Summary of section 4.2.1

• Fordism is defined as a system of mass production and mass consumption.

• Fordist mass production is characterized by a labour process based around the fragmentation of tasks and the assembly line.

• Fordist mass production is regulated by a mass market bolstered by Keynesian welfare measures.

4.2.2 Explaining the rise and decline of Fordism: some theoretical issues

There are very important differences in the ways in which the two schools theorize the development of the Fordist regime, differences that are rooted in the two opposing positions that they take on the notion of historical and structural change.

'Natural laws' versus 'accidents of history'

The institutionalists, as represented by Piore and Sabel, explicitly reject what they characterize as the acceptance by the Marxist (or what they call 'neo-Marxist') regulationists of a 'natural law' or 'narrow path' of technological and industrial development and emphasize instead the role of 'social struggles' and the 'accidents of history'. For Piore and Sabel it is necessary to '... conceptualize a world in which technology can develop in various ways: a world that might have turned out differently from the way it did, and thus a world with a history of abandoned but viable alternatives to what exists' (1984, p. 38).

Technological choices, in this 'world of all possible worlds' were, of course, made, but what were more important at these 'branching points' or 'technological divides' were the 'particularities' of a nation's political and economic 'circumstance'. Thus, for example, the United States went further down the path of mass production in the early nineteenth century because:

> ... labour, especially skilled labour, was in short supply; there were no guilds to restrain the reorganization of production; and an affluent yeomanry – whose ancestral diversity of tastes had been erased by transplantation to the New World – was willing and able to purchase the crude standard products that early special-purpose machines tools turned out. Raw materials such as wood were abundant enough to make the inefficiency of the machines economically inconsequential. Because employers needed labour-saving machinery and because customers bought the machine-made goods, the American turn in the direction of mass production was natural. (Piore and Sabel, 1984, pp. 40–41)

For Piore and Sabel, however, there was no economic 'destiny' or 'iron law' at work in this departure. The path that was followed at this crossroads – to borrow the term used in Chapter 1 – was in the direction of mass production. An alternative, it is argued, would have been to follow the route based around craft skills. Contingent political and financial power were the deciding factors. But the choice could have been different – just as, in the institutionalist schema, there are also alternative paths on offer, as we will see below, at the 'second industrial divide' which the 'crisis of mass production' is said to have produced.

The Marxist approach of the regulationists contrasts sharply with that of Piore and Sabel and their followers. The regulationists are interested precisely in discovering what Piore and Sabel call 'natural paths' and 'general laws'. Their Marxist framework is, as Aglietta admits, revealed in the very use of the term 'regulation' which '... denotes the need for an analysis encompassing the economic system as a whole. *The analysis should produce general laws that are socially determinate*, precisely specifying the historical conditions of their validity' (1979, p. 15, emphasis added). The aim of the theory is '. . . the study of the social laws governing the production and distribution of the means of existence of human beings organized in social groups' and '. . . of the transformation of social relations as *it creates new forms that are both economic and non-economic, that are organized in structures and themselves produce a determinant structure*, the mode of production' (ibid, p. 16, emphasis added).

In certain respects the regulation school can be viewed as a variant of the theories that conceptualize the capitalist economic system as evolving through a series of qualitatively different stages of development (Green and Sutcliffe, 1987). The theory of long waves, discussed in Chapters 1 and 2, is clearly one such approach. Others have been based on stages in the development of competition (proceeding through competition to monopoly capital and, in some versions, to a third stage, state monopoly capital), the changing dominance of capitalist enterprise (with, for example, small localized firms being superseded by national monopolies and these in turn by the growth of multinationals), and stages of dominance or 'hegemony' of individual nations in the internationalization of capitalism. You will remember from Chapter 1 that this notion of the changing relative status of nations within the global economy is one strand in the regulationist school's argument and one we will refer to again in section 4.4. But it is the other 'stages theory' that this school deploys – the notion of the progressive unfolding of the way in which labour is organized and controlled in the production process, the labour process – which is important in the context of this discussion.

In the regulationists' view Taylorism/Fordism represents a qualitatively distinct stage in the historical development of the labour force within capitalism. The previous stages out of which it evolved are identified by Marx as:

1 'simple co-operation': where, by bringing large numbers of hitherto independent workers together to carry out similar tasks, capitalists benefit from the savings that accrue from the increase in the scale of production and the savings from the sharing of tools and buildings;

a stage succeeded by,

2 **'manufacture'**: based on the division of labour within handicraft production. With workers assembled together, the collection of separate tasks that each of these workers performed is broken down into a series of detailed operations and workers allocated to each of these. Thus workers come to specialize on only one part of the production process with implications for the levels of skill required (and the related value of labour power) – the technical division of labour that we referred to earlier;

developing into,

3 'modern history' or 'machinofacture' – where control of the labour process shifts decisively in favour of the capitalists. Marx argues that the hierarchy of skills which persisted in the stage of manufacture is demolished by the introduction of mechanized machinery which wrests control of the nature and pace of their work from workers, who are now reduced to little more than unskilled minders of the machinery to which they are allocated.

Marx did not live to see the transformation of 'modern industry'. He died in 1883, the same year that Frederick Taylor graduated in mechanical engineering. Change it did, and for the regulationists the way in which Taylor, and later Ford, steered the labour process was not, to paraphrase the title of a chapter in Piore's and Sabel's book, one of 'blind decision' but ultimately determined by the demands of capital accumulation. The direction was towards even greater subordination of workers to capitalist control.

In the regulationists' schema, as we have seen, it is this control which allows the appropriation of 'surplus value' and choices of production technology are guided accordingly. In this view hierarchies of craft skills and compressed technical divisions of labour which Piore and Sabel see as being viable alternatives in both the past and future are in fact impediments to the extraction of value and, hence, to the overarching process of capital accumulation. We will return to this point, but first it is necessary to digress for a moment to have a closer look at 'skill' and how it fits into arguments about the changing labour process.

Labour process change and the notion of skill

It should be clear from the discussion so far that running through the debates over the changing labour process is the question of skill composition and development. A landmark book in these debates was Harry Braverman's *Labour and Monopoly Capital: The Degradation of Work in the Twentieth Century* published in 1974. Building on Marx's analysis of the changing labour process, a basic thesis of Braverman's book, as the subtitle suggests, is the long-run tendency inherent in capitalism for the deskilling and fragmentation of work. You only have to think back to Extract 1 on the introduction of the assembly line at Ford's motor plant to appreciate the power of this argument.

This thesis has been challenged in more recent work, however. While it is not possible to do proper justice to the subtleties of some of these arguments in the space available here, there are key strands of the critique that you should consider. The first is based on a growing body of evidence that the impact of some new production technology is to change the nature of the skills required and/or extend them rather than simply downgrade them – 're-skilling' and 'en-skilling' as opposed to 'de-skilling'. A second argument against the simple de-skilling thesis concerns the role of labour in the labour process. In this view labour is not simply passive in management-directed changes in the labour process. Workers have some say in the way in which production technology is introduced and the pace and direction of labour process changes, either through formal negotiation between trade union and management representatives or informal modification of working practices.

Another argument which recognizes the participation of both management and workers in the labour process highlights the variety of strategies that the former pursue. Some may be de-skilling, others may not. Thus Friedman (1977) contrasts a labour process distinguished by *responsible autonomy* (where, as the term suggests, workers – usually the most skilled or 'core' workers – are allowed some control over their working arrangements) with one of *direct control* (where less skilled workers are left little scope for influencing the routine work to which they are all allocated). Others point to the fact that management cannot simply coerce workers into complying with rigidly predetermined work patterns but rather seek to secure the co-operation of the workforce – what Burawoy (1979) rather nicely refers to as 'the manufacturing of consent'. As we will argue in section 4.3, this aspect of labour process development is an important feature of some of the recent trends in regional differentiation in the United Kingdom where companies, particularly overseas ones, are actively 'manufacturing consent' in the localities in which their new ventures are located. As *Hudson* (1988) points out, these firms are increasingly weighting the 'social skills' of their workforces (essentially their receptiveness and malleability towards corporate goals) above more technical skills. This last point is particularly important for it underlines the fact that *production is a social process*. It follows, therefore, that the place of 'skill' within production is similarly socially constructed.

Just think for a moment about what the term **skill** actually means. If you consult a dictionary you will most likely come away with a definition on the lines of 'knowledge allied to dexterity'. But this still leaves open such critical questions as how these faculties are to be measured and by whom. Some of the most perceptive insights on these questions have come from feminist critiques of the social and economic role of women.

In this context the attempts by feminist writers to relate the *gender division of labour* to the broader social division of labour are most relevant. In making this link these writers emphasize the way in which women have generally been accorded the role of child-rearing and unpaid domestic work and go on to argue that this role helps structure women's participation in production (see, for example, Rowbotham, 1973, and Beechey,

1983). The gender division of labour has been interwoven, within production, with the technical division of labour – the fragmentation of tasks and the related skill composition of the labour process being 'gendered' into 'men's work' and 'women's work'. In the footwear industry, for example, the two basic labour processes are the cutting of the leather (or 'clicking', as it is known in the industry) and the sewing of the shoe uppers (or 'closing'). These two processes have had a rigid gender demarcation, with men doing the 'clicking' and women the 'closing'. Ask yourself why this has been the case. Is there some genetic difference in the physical and mental make-up of the sexes that somehow makes women naturally more suited to sewing than men? Or is this gender division of labour rather the reflection in the workplace of broader processes of gender differentiation operating in society as a whole?

Management, via 'work study engineering', clearly has a leading role to play in the determination of the labour requirements of particular production processes and management is a male-dominated occupation. Some writers have also demonstrated the role of male-dominated trade unions in establishing and maintaining a gendered division of labour (such as Cynthia Cockburn's (1983) study of the printing industry). The demarcation between 'men's work' and 'women's work' is thus a socially conditioned one. And so too is the accreditation of skill to gender-differentiated tasks. Thus 'clicking' in footwear is not just 'men's work'; it is also classed as skilled, work while women's 'closing' is given only 'semi-skilled' status. This skill designation in the technical division of labour is not determined in some neutral fashion by the technological characteristics of the production process. Much broader processes to do with the role of patriarchy and the formation of ideology in society as a whole are at work.

In this context it is worth considering for a moment why so much attention in the Fordism debate is given to the car industry. We have already seen that it is not especially important in employment terms. There are other industries that are equally important employers and that have production based around assembly lines (electrical domestic appliances, for example) which could just as well typify Fordist manufacture. But in many of these industries, unlike in car production, it is women who work on the assembly lines. Is there some connection between the relatively scant attention paid to these industries in the Fordist debate and the gender composition of their workforces? Similarly, could it be something to do with the 'maleness' and macho image of the car factory that explains why it crops up time and time again in the literature?

Finally, given that skills are constantly being reshaped both technically and socially, the institutional organization of training and 'creditation' has obvious importance. Given the dramatic decline in formal opportunities for skill training in the UK in recent years (with, for example, the number of engineering apprenticeships in the early 1980s being below a quarter of that three decades earlier) and the steep rise in youth unemployment, public sector training initiatives have taken on an increasingly important role in reshaping labour markets. Thus, for example, it is argued that the Youth Training Scheme has acted to create a new intermediate structure of sub-apprentice skills in the engineering industry inserted between the atrophying craft skills and the secondary, unskilled workforce (see Peck and Haughton, 1987). But it is more than simply technical skills which are being reshaped. Thus the increasing emphasis in these training initiatives on developing 'social skills' and 'work attitudes' could be interpreted as a public sector reflection of the private sector 'manufacturing of consent' that we referred to above.

'Skill', then, is clearly a concept which needs to be labelled 'handle with extreme care'. Certainly, to return to our discussion of the debate over Fordism, the regulationists and institutionalists handle skill very differently in their accounts of the evolution of the labour process – a result of their very different theoretical approaches.

Determinacy and indeterminacy in the theories

The institutionalists' position is much less 'deterministic' than that of the regulationists. As was noted above, craft skills in Piore and Sabel's view could have formed the basis for an alternative production system to Fordism at the 'first industrial divide' and, as we shall see in section 4.3, could still be at the core of the phase that they see as Fordism's successor. For support, they could turn to the arguments of a growing number of writers on the labour process that there is '. . . no determinative link between the logic of capitalist accumulation and the development of the labour process' (Littler, 1982). They could also cite some of the writers who have questioned the Braverman 'de-skilling' thesis.

Their critics, however, might argue that this and other aspects of the institutionalist argument assume too much indeterminacy and hence are theoretically unsatisfying. We have already seen that the institutionalists see de-skilling as a necessary tendency in the development of the labour process. The argument that there was no clear economic case for the eventual success of mass production is not very convincing. The economics of Ford's Model T set out in Extract 1 would certainly question it. Thus, for example, Williams, Cutler, Williams and Haslam (1987) examine the technical organization of Ford's car factory and the relationship of levels of investment to the cost savings from price reductions and labour saving and definitely conclude that: 'Ford's combination of process innovations had an overwhelming advantage over the craft methods of production . . . used hitherto'; and '. . . there never was a choice because there was not a viable craft alternative to the mass production of complex consumer durables' (p. 420).

The institutionalists' indeterminate view of the advent of mass production and Fordism is mirrored by their openness as to why they consider this 'regime' to be in crisis. Two alternative theories are suggested by Piore and Sabel. The first focuses on a series of 'external shocks' to the system (including labour unrest, global food shortages and the oil crises of 1973 and

1979). These shocks, it is argued, were responsible for setting off the inflationary spiral which prompted recessionary policy responses and a break-up of mass markets as a result of the consequent depression of demand and investment.

The second theory of crisis that Piore and Sabel offer concerns what they see as internal structural problems of mass production: these essentially boil down to difficulties over a mismatch between productive capacity and the level and composition of national and international demand. This reveals itself in mass market saturation and fragmentation as the ownership of the characteristic Fordist consumer goods becomes widespread and the rigid and standardized production set-up proves incapable of adapting flexibly to increasingly differentiated and customized patterns of consumer demand.

Piore and Sabel's neutrality over these two theories would not be shared by the regulationists. External shocks are precisely that – external to the system. What is important in their theorizing is the internal logic of the system out of which the crisis unfolds. Indeed they would take issue with the institutionalists over the very notion of 'externality'. Labour and social unrest, for example, would not be seen as external and contingent but firmly rooted in the workings of the system itself, embedded within, and understandable in terms of, the social relations of production. Externality has to be judged in relation to the conceptual framework: what is included and what is not.

It is worth pausing for a moment to consider what we have been saying about the differences between the two theories over determinacy in the light of what you learned about other theories in earlier chapters. While the regulationist argument is more deterministic than that of the institutionalists, it is less deterministic than, for example, some long-wave interpretations of economic change. The regulationists do see the necessity for a qualitatively different regime of accumulation to resolve the crisis of Fordism but they do also accept that the eventual form that it takes is not fixed and will be shaped by, for example, the outcomes of struggles between labour and capital. Compare that position with the views of some of the long-wave theorists who see economic change being subject to the regular, inexorable workings of the long-wave cycle from which there is no escape.

Where the two schools' theories of the crisis of mass production do seem to touch is in the notion of structural problems internal to the system and the acceptance of breakdown on both sides of the production-consumption scale. However, even here there are substantial differences of emphasis. The regulationists, for example, place more stress on factors related to the production/labour process, isolating the two main disruptive tendencies already referred to in Chapter 2 – labour unrest and the technical problems of co-ordinating production (the 'balance delay' factor to which we will return in the discussion in section 4.3). The institutionalists, in contrast, tend to concentrate more on problems associated with matching output and capacity to demand, emphasizing the problems of market saturation and fragmentation already referred to.

Summary of section 4.2.2

• While both schools agree that the Fordist regime is in crisis, this agreement is based on very different theoretical positions concerning the notion of historical and structural change.

• The institutionalist school, as represented by Piore and Sabel, is much less deterministic in its theorizing than are the regulationists, emphasizing much more the non-determined nature or 'contingency' of the changes they study. In sharp contrast with the regulationists, who have a firm notion of a structure in which changes are a necessary consequence of its workings, they do not seek to discover general systemic laws.

• The regulationists' relatively more deterministic view of the evolution of the labour process sees the latter developing in a series of stages. Inspired by Marx, they see the process of capital accumulation as the driving force of this evolutionary change.

• The notion of 'de-skilling' is central to the regulationists' position on labour process change. This notion has been criticized, however, for ignoring the extent to which new production technology can create new skills as well as remove old ones and for underestimating the active role that labour can play in resisting the 'de-skilling' of the labour process. Managerial strategies towards skill are complex and changes are introduced in a social context in which management and workers interact. A radical critique of the whole notion of 'skill' has come from feminist writers who underline the point that skill is socially constructed and that this recognition is the key to understanding why both the social and technical divisions of labour are 'gendered'. Training has a key role to play in the social recomposition of 'skill'.

4.2.3   Defining Fordism

Defining Fordism: the emphasis on manufacturing and the question of structure

One of the most striking features of the Fordism debate is the leading role given to the manufacturing sector by both the institutionalists and regulationists. This is not to suggest that service sectors have had no influence on the development of what the two schools would recognize as Fordism. The transformation of retailing from small shops to large multiple shops and department stores was both an accompaniment to and a promoter of the development of mass production. Nor is it to suggest that services are somehow not produced and have no labour process. Office work provides a classic example of the implementation of Taylorist/Fordist techniques in the service sector (Guiliano, 1985). Similarly the labour processes of a wide range of service industries are likely to be affected by recent technological developments in the form of 'electronic monitoring' through, for example, the surveillance of work performance offered by computerized 'point-of-sale' cash registers in shops and data entry operations in offices.

The fact remains, however, that, as was argued in Chapter 2, it is the failure of the labour process to develop in key service sectors on Taylorist/Fordist lines that generally receives most attention in the regulationist argument. In particular, it is the difficulty of introducing Fordist labour processes into the production of goods forming part of the 'social wage' (such as health and education) that is seen as contributing to a 'regulation crisis' by hindering the raising of productivity and a consequent lowering of cost (as, for example, Diane Perrons (1986) argues).

The leading role in shaping the Fordist regime is unambiguously given to the manufacturing sector. Yet, as was noted in the discussion of deindustrialization in Chapter 2, manufacturing employment in the UK has been in a relatively long-term decline. Manufacturing currently accounts for just under a quarter of total employment and a similar amount of GDP. This begs the question, therefore, of whether the importance of manufacturing to the UK economy is more than a simple function of its relative size. Is it more to do, perhaps, with its economic role and structural position?

Activity 4.1

Table 4.1 might help you to make up your mind. It shows the output growth rates by broad sectors in selected periods since the mid nineteenth century. Compare the different sectoral growth rates in the different periods. How does manufacturing fare in this comparison? Answer the following questions and then check your answers with those on page 182.

(a) In which periods was the growth of total gross domestic product (GDP) relatively high?

(b) In these periods which sector had the highest growth rate?

(c) Comparing the periods of fastest growth of total GDP between 1951 and 1973 with the much slower growth rates of the years since then, what stands out?

Empirically, then, the growth of manufacturing does appear to have been closely associated with the growth – and decline – of the UK economy as a whole. This association, of course, does not in itself imply any necessary causal connection between the two growth rates. A theoretical explanation is necessary for that and at the heart of this explanation lies the notion of structure.

While manufacturing in terms of its overall size within the economy may be subordinate to other sectors, it may still be dominant structurally. Think for a moment of the motor that drives the machine or the heart and brain

Table 4.1 Weighted[1] sectoral output growth rates (per cent per annum), United Kingdom, 1856–1983

	1856–73	1873–1913	1913–24	1924–37	1937–51	1951–64	1964–73	1973–79	1979–83
Agriculture, forestry, fishing	0.03	−0.01	−0.05	0.06	0.08	0.12	0.11	0.01	0.03
Mining, quarrying	0.19	0.12	−0.05	−0.02	−0.05	−0.02	−0.07	0.55	0.23
Manufacturing	0.61	0.51	0.14	1.04	0.81	1.14	1.11	−0.21	−0.70
Construction	0.11	0.04	0.11	0.22	−0.08	0.23	0.11	−0.11	−0.12
Gas, water, electricity	0.02	0.06	0.05	0.16	0.08	0.13	0.15	0.00	0.00
Transport, communications	0.21	0.24	0.10	0.15	0.19	0.18	0.28	0.09	0.01
Commerce	0.59	0.52	−0.50	0.44	−0.05	0.74	0.75	0.46	0.43
Public and professional services	0.12	0.22	0.08	0.16	0.39	0.21	0.27	0.40	0.17
Ownership of dwellings	0.12	0.10	0.02	0.09	0.03	0.07	0.09	0.11	0.05
GDP	2.00	1.80	−0.10	2.30	1.40	2.80	2.80	1.30	0.10

[1] The growth rate of each sector is weighted by its share in GDP

Source: Lee, 1986, Table 1.4

that regulate the body. What is important in these 'systems' is the functional relationships between their constituent 'sub-systems'. What drives the car? Which organs in the body are crucial for maintaining life? Thus, in relation to the question of whether the deindustrialization of Britain matters, an answer based on some notion of structure might be 'yes'. Manufacturing, in such a view, might be seen as playing a key role as the 'motor' of the economy – producing the goods on which services depend, forcing technological development and, through exports, making a critical contribution to the balance of trade. This is a question which will be taken up again in Chapter 6.

Defining Fordism: grouping industries on the basis of their labour and production processes

Not only do the theories of Fordist crisis concentrate on manufacturing, they also prioritize sectors within it – those based on mass-production techniques. And just how important are these? To answer this we will first need to consider the various ways in which manufacturing production is organized. Figure 4.2 is an attempt at classification. It shows the link between production scale, the degree of repetitiveness of production and the basic form of production process. It also indicates the way in which the four basic processes – jobbing, batch, mass and process – overlap to some degree.

Activity 4.2

Look closely at the different production processes shown in Figure 4.2. Where would you locate the manufacture of the following products: detergents, televisions and aeroplanes? The industry examples in the figure should guide you.

Check your answers against those on page 182.

Now consider the different technical divisions of labour associated with the production processes and industries listed in Figure 4.2. Think about the degree of automation of the process, the extent to which the process has been broken down into separate operations and the related training and skills required of the operatives.

Chemical plants, for example, have a much less extended technical division of labour than, say, the engineering and assembly processes where the production/labour process is generally broken down into a much larger number of specialized operations. Some processes have particularly high levels of craft skills (such as those in small-batch engineering of precision equipment) and others have more automated production where workers 'supervise' often virtually self-regulating machinery (such as in the continuous flow processes in the chemicals industry). This variation and complexity sometimes applies within industries and even within factories. Thus,

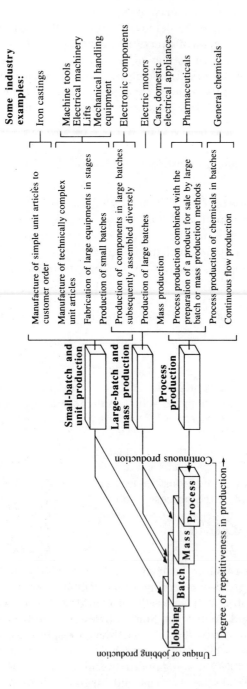

Figure 4.2   Manufacturing production processes
Source: Adapted from Wild, 1972, pp. 12–13

for example, in the car industry there are extensively automated production processes (such as body-stamping), highly labour-intensive assembly operations (in, for example, trim and final assembly), processes still partly dependent on craft skills (in transmission manufacture) and production based on non-engineering processes (the sewing of car seat covers and upholstery – processes in which 'skill' designation has been a highly contentious issue).

So where do Fordist processes fit in all this? If you look at Table 4.2 you will see different industries' share of manufacturing unemployment and net output in 1968, around the time that most regulationists would see as the high point of Fordist production in the UK. Vehicles, generally presented as the archetypal Fordist industry, is clearly important on both counts, but – as you will also see – mechanical engineering is even more so.

Table 4.2 Percentage share of manufacturing employment and net output, selected industries, 1968

Industry	Employment (000)	% share all manufacturing	Net output (£ million)	% share all manufacturing
Chemicals	407.6	5.2	1334.2	8.7
Mechanical engineering	977.2	12.5	1963.0	12.8
Instrument engineering	171.2	2.2	299.3	2.0
Electrical engineering	753.7	9.6	1375.3	9.0
Vehicles	788.4	10.1	1578.7	10.3
(of which, motor vehicles)	457.0	5.8	945.6	6.2
Textiles	666.2	8.5	1058.3	7.0
Clothing and footwear	445.1	5.7	484.2	3.2

Industries are Orders of the 1968 SIC (except 'motor vehicles' which is MLM 381 of the 1968 SIC)

Source: *Census of Production: Industry Analyses*, 1968, London, HMSO

Another glance at Figure 4.2 will tell you that mechanical engineering is dominated by batch production processes. Indeed, it has been estimated that around 50 per cent of all UK metal-working and engineering production is in job lots of less than 100 units and 80 per cent of less than 500 (Kaplinsky, 1984). Another estimate puts the number of workers directly involved in assembly-line work in Britain (in 1982) at 700 000, only 12 per cent of employment in manufacturing (and some 3 per cent of total employment). A more recent survey (in 1986) found 31 per cent of the plants surveyed used assembly lines but only one half of these lines were mechanically paced (cited in Williams *et al.*, 1987).

Given the continuing importance, then, of small-scale, non-assembly-line production, the obvious question is why do the regulationists and institutionalists place so much emphasis on large-scale mass production? Their argument in defence of this emphasis would be one based on the notion of structure that we touched upon earlier. They would argue that most small-batch producers are in the capital goods sector (i.e. producing the actual machinery and equipment needed to produce the whole range of manufactured goods) and that what are important in the Fordist mode of regulation are (mass-produced) consumer goods. Just as manufacturing drives the economy as a whole so, in this view, it is consumer goods that take the leading role in manufacturing growth in the Fordist phase, creating the demand for capital and intermediate goods.

Table 4.3 gives a breakdown of output growth rates by different manufacturing sectors in different periods since 1924. Look at the different sectoral performances over this period. Important consumer goods industries are in the van of growth over the 1950s and early 1960s with electrical engineering (which includes the important electrical consumer durable industries) and vehicles showing the fastest growth rates. The picture changes, however, thereafter. While electrical engineering continues to lead growth in the 1964–73 period, vehicle production drops dramatically, its place taken by the capital-goods-dominated mechanical engineering sector. Both the regulationists and the institutionalists might argue here that this represents the first signs of the impending crisis of Fordist consumer goods production. But, if this is the case, what is the explanation for the patterns of growth since 1973, that major turning-point in the international and national economy? Electrical engineering continues to grow, albeit at a dramatically reduced rate, while decline is led by sectors dominated by capital and intermediate goods and small-batch production – other 'metal industries', mechanical engineering and iron and steel. That classical Fordist industry, vehicles, has actually declined at a slower rate than these predominantly non-Fordist sectors.

Activity 4.3

Figure 4.3 and Table 4.4 show absolute growth over the period since the mid to late 1960s for the three main divisions of production: consumer goods (industries, such as food and drink, manufacturing products for consumption), intermediate goods (industries, such as textiles and chemicals, whose output is used in the manufacture of other products) and capital goods (industries producing the machinery and equipment needed to produce the output of all three divisions).

(a)   Which division grew fastest over the period shown? (See Figure 4.3.)

(b)   Within the three divisions, how did individual sectors fare and, in particular, those associated with the Fordist regime? (See Table 4.4.)

Intermediate goods production (including energy) grew fastest, finishing the period with output over 30 per cent above the 1968 level. A comparison of

Table 4.3 Weighted sectoral output growth rates in manufacturing (per cent per annum), United Kingdom, 1924–83

	1924–37	1937–51	1951–64	1964–73	1973–79	1979–83
Food, drink, tobacco	0.40	0.20	0.27	0.29	0.08	-0.03
Chemicals	0.19	0.34	0.46	0.52	0.27	-0.10
Iron and steel	0.20	0.13	0.18	-0.01	-0.21	-0.34
Electrical engineering	0.28	0.38	0.50	0.56	0.07	0.07
Mechanical engineering and shipbuilding	0.21	0.53	0.37	0.54	-0.23	-0.45
Vehicles	0.48	0.34	0.48	0.08	-0.10	-0.31
Other metal industries	0.31	0.22	0.16	0.08	-0.31	-0.60
Textiles	0.21	0.03	0.01	0.19	-0.12	-0.20
Clothing	0.20	-0.10	0.10	0.07	0.01	-0.14
Paper, printing, publishing	0.21	0.21	0.32	0.22	-0.03	-0.29
Bricks, pottery, glass, cement	0.18	0.11	0.15	0.15		
Timber, furniture	0.18	0.00	0.07	0.12	-0.03	-0.21
Leather and other manufactures	0.15	0.11	0.13	0.19		
Total manufacturing	3.20	2.50	3.20	3.00	-0.60	-2.60

There is some lack of sectoral continuity of definition between the pre-1973 data and the later reclassified data

Source: Lee, 1986, Table 11.2

Table 4.4 Output change by division of the economy, 1968–79

Consumer goods	Output change (%) 1968–1979
Broadcasting equipment	+169
Pharmaceuticals	+135
Soft drinks	+102
Dresses, lingerie etc.	+ 69
Overalls/men's shirts	+ 67
Watches & clocks	+ 64
Toilet preparations	+ 57
Other drinks	+ 55
Weatherproof outerwear	+ 54
Furniture	+ 50
Surgical instruments	+ 46
Pottery	+ 43
Women's/girl's outerwear	+ 38
Fruit & vegetable products	+ 37
Domestic electrical appliances	+ 37
Soap & detergents	+ 34
Brewing & malting	+ 32
Other printing	+ 26
Milk & milk products	+ 23
Paper manufacture	+ 20
Cocoa, chocolate etc.	+ 17
Printing/publishing	+ 16
Bacon curing etc.	+ 15
Other electrical goods	+ 15
Toys etc.	+ 14
Hosiery	+ 13
Food industries n.e.s.	+ 12
Tobacco	+ 11
All manufacturing	**+ 11**

Intermediate goods	Output change (%) 1968–1979
Plastics n.e.s.	+ 93
Vegetable oils	+ 85
Paint	+ 47
General chemicals	+ 44
Synthetic resins	+ 42
Glass	+ 37
Aluminium	+ 34
Mineral oil refining	+ 28
Lubricating oils	+ 28
Dyes & pigments	+ 21
Man-made fibres	+ 16
Rubber	+ 11
All manufacturing	**+ 11**

Capital goods	Output change (%) 1968–1979
Electronic computers	+676
Photographic/copying equipment	+178
Radio & electronic components	+118
Industrial engines	+106
Scientific/industrial instruments	+ 43
Mechanical handling equipment	+ 38
Pumps, valves & compressors	+ 26
Radio, radar & defence products	+ 19
Construction equipment	+ 14
All manufacturing	**+ 11**

+ 10 Miscellaneous manufacture	+ 10 Grain milling	+ 10 Ordnance & small arms
+ 8 Other textiles	+ 10 Stationery	+ 4 Engineers' small tools
+ 8 Dresses n.e.s.	+ 8 Fertilizers	+ 2 Insulated wires & cables
+ 7 Made-up textiles	+ 2 Cotton spinning	− 1 Other machinery
+ 1 Bedding etc.	+ 2 Abrasives etc. n.e.s.	− 3 Locomotives/carriages etc.
− 2 Biscuits	0 Jute	− 4 Telecommunications
− 3 Miscellaneous stationer's goods	0 Timber	− 7 Industrial plant
− 5 Sugar	0 Paper packaging	− 9 Office machinery
− 6 Motor vehicles	− 1 Metal n.e.s.	− 15 Agricultural machinery
− 6 Carpets	− 1 Textile finishing	− 22 Aerospace equipment
− 7 Jewellery	− 4 Miscellaneous wood & cork	− 23 Shipbuilding/marine engineering
− 9 Footwear	− 6 Cement	− 27 Machine tools
− 11 Mens/boys outerwear	− 10 Paper and board	− 31 Electrical machinery
− 14 Leather goods	− 12 Wire	− 60 Textile machinery
− 15 Bread and flour confectionery	− 12 Leather & fellmongery	
− 17 Cutlery etc.	− 14 Hand tools & implements	
− 21 Brushes & brooms	− 15 Animal & poultry foods	
− 28 Motor cycles/cycles	− 16 Iron and steel	
− 28 Linoleum etc.	− 16 Steel tubes	
− 33 Fur	− 16 MLH 322	
− 42 Hats, caps, millinery	− 19 Narrow fabrics	
	− 22 Rope, twine & net	
	− 25 Iron castings	
	− 28 Wooden containers/baskets	
	− 30 Bricks	
	− 32 Bolts, nuts, screws	
	− 33 Shops & office fitting	
	− 35 Coke ovens/manufactured fuels	
	− 35 Other base metals	
	− 35 Weaving cotton etc.	
	− 40 Woollen & worsted	

n.e.s. = not elsewhere specified

Source: Index of Industrial Production

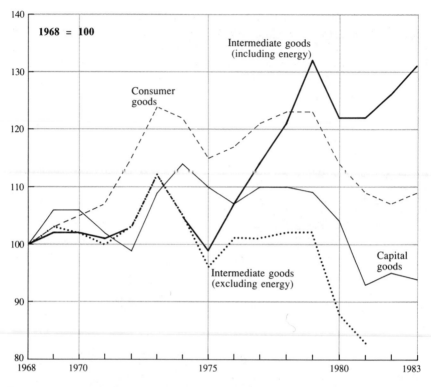

Figure 4.3   Output change 1968–83: broad divisions of the economy

the pattern of output growth in intermediate goods production including energy with the pattern excluding it shows the importance for the economy as a whole of North Sea oil production in the years since the mid-1970s, for it is the exploitation of this oil which lies behind that sharp rise in the second half of the period.

Within manufactured goods (i.e. excluding energy production) Figure 4.3 shows that the consumer goods division grew the most, peaking in 1973 and ending the period with output 9 per cent above the 1968 figure. In contrast, output in both capital goods and manufactured intermediate goods ended the period below the 1968 base figure.

Table 4.4 shows that, over the period shown (covering the two manufacturing output peaks in 1968 and 1979), the consumer goods division has both the largest number of industries growing at or above the all manufacturing average (28, compared with 12 in intermediate goods and 9 in capital goods production) and the highest proportion (28 out of 49 or 57 per cent, compared with 12 out of 43 or 28 per cent and 9 out of 24 or 38 per cent for intermediate goods and capital goods manufacture respectively).

However, none of the consumer goods sectors can match the massive output growth of the (then predominantly capital goods) computer sector (recording an increase of 676 per cent). And to complicate matters further, there are also some very marked differences within consumer goods production. Compare the output growth of those two classical mass production consumer goods industries – vehicles and broadcast-receiving equipment. Output of the former fell by 6 per cent (the 'crisis of Fordism'?) while that of the latter increased by 169 per cent ('crisis delayed'?).

To say the least, then, we are left with a rather confusing empirical picture. Some Fordist sectors are growing while others are declining – but more slowly than non-Fordist sectors – when the system or regime that they structure – Fordism – is supposed to be in crisis.

The economic relationships between industries are complex and it could be, for example, that a decline in an industry like vehicles could precipitate a much greater decline in a supplying industry like steel. But these interrelationships need to be specified. The regulationists do at least talk about different 'Departments' (capital goods, on the one hand, and consumer goods differentiated between those for workers and those for 'luxury' consumption, on the other) although these are rather unwieldy for the matter in hand. The institutionalists, on the other hand, are unashamedly cavalier in their categorization of industries. Thus, Sabel (1982), for example, sees Fordism simply as '. . . a shorthand term for the organizational and technological principles characteristic of the modern large-scale factory' (p. 33). This is a rather imprecise conceptualization.

Summary of sections 4.2.2 and 4.2.3

• Manufacturing is given a leading role in the shaping of the Fordist regime. This emphasis is dependent on some notion of manufacturing's structural role in the economy.

• It is arguable that the notion of a Fordist regime is constructed on a somewhat idealized definition of the production and labour processes in manufacturing industry. Production and labour processes are varied and complex and such an all-encompassing term as Fordism certainly has to strain to capture the actual variety and complexity of these processes.

4.3   Crisis resolution: neo-Fordism and flexible specialization?

4.3.1   Neo-Fordism and flexible specialization

Piore and Sabel's theoretical indeterminacy towards the causes of the 'crisis of mass production' is again matched in their analysis of the way in which this crisis can be resolved. Again two alternatives are offered at this crucial turning-point – this 'second industrial divide'. The first is the patching-up and re-ordering of the existing regime into what they call 'multinational Keynesianism'. This they see as operating very much on the lines advocated by the Brandt Commission's (1980) report of the global 'north-south' debate, with more demand being pumped into the system through policies raising purchasing power in 'less developed countries' of the Third World. The other alternative, and the one clearly favoured by Piore and Sabel, is the development of a new production system based around what they call **flexible specialization**. This system is possible because of the increased production adaptability offered by new manufacturing technology although once again the indeterminacy of their theoretical position reveals itself in the qualified nature of their championing of this post-Fordist alternative:

> There is no hidden dynamic of historical evolution. No law of motion of capitalist development makes the spread of flexible specialization the inevitable outcome of the crisis of the past decade. (Piore and Sabel, 1984, p. 281)

Compare that with the regulationists' position:

> Capitalism can escape from its contemporary organic crisis only by generating a new cohesion, a neo-Fordism. (Aglietta, 1979, p. 385)

It is interesting, however, that, despite the basic theoretical differences that these two quotations expose, once again the regulationists' (necessary) neo-Fordist regime bears close similarities with the institutionalists' (possible) flexible specialization future. Both are centred around new production technology. Thus, according to Perrons (1981), neo-Fordism:

> ... reconstitutes the totality of the production process through the use of electronic information systems and computer programming. This enables a fully integrated and self-correcting machine system to be introduced ... not unlike Fordism these techniques can also be applied to small batch production. (Perrons, 1981, p. 92)

4.3.2   Flexible production technologies and the changing labour process

As *Martin* (1988) points out, flexible production technology is part of a new wave of technological innovation based around the microprocessor. If the mechanization of the assembly line can in a sense be seen as the technological key to 'Fordist' production then it is the microchip that lies at the core of 'neo-Fordist' and 'flexibly specialized' production. Extract 2 is taken from *The Robot Age*, a book written by Peter Marsh in 1982. It gives a simplified but nevertheless instructive account of how this innovation has helped to shape the evolution of manufacturing processes from the Fordist one described in Extract 1.

Activity 4.4

Read through Extract 2 and jot down, or underline, what you think are the main implications of the new manufacturing systems for both the labour process and the scale and flexibility of production. Focus especially on the way in which both job numbers change and the relationship of workers to the process equipment is altered as the computerization of the system is increased. Try also to pick out what the extract has to say about the regulationists' concept of 'balance delay'.

Extract 2

The effect of computer-controlled production

Work is already well advanced on designing computer-controlled production cells. Here, a workshop would have several machine tools, each with its own range of tools in a bandolier from which it can automatically pick an implement for a specified job: in this way a machine can work for (say) half-an-hour with a cutting mechanism, then switch over to drill a hole in another piece of metal. The instructions that tell such a machine how to operate – for instance which tool to pluck from the bandolier and then how to use it – are normally lodged in a microcomputer that forms part of the equipment's control mechanism. In most factories that use these so-called numerically-controlled machine tools [...] a human is responsible for giving the machine its instructions. He [sic] also has to stand by to adjust the hardware while it operates. But in the new concept of the production cell, the operator's job is done by another computer, a highly-ranked supervisory machine whose role is similar to the foreman in a factory run by humans.

Such a 'supervisor' computer could control anything up to ten or twenty individual machines. It sends instructions to them in much the same way as a human overseer first formulates a strategy for getting jobs done and then tells other people to actually do the work. In engineer's jargon, such production cells of machines controlled by other machines are called direct-numerically controlled systems. Japan has been a leader in using such equipment [...]

With these systems, there is less work for people. A separate operator for each computerised machine tool is no longer required. Now a conventional, that is stand-alone, computerised or NC tool can do something like five times as much work in the same time as an old-fashioned, manually-controlled machine in which a person has to guide the mechanism through every stage of its fashioning actions. So with perhaps one operator for three machines in the new, direct-numerically-controlled system, the output for each operator is increased by a factor of something like fifteen, compared with the old way of making things. The production cells still, however, need someone to feed instructions to the central 'master' computer. They require workers to scurry from one machine to another to load raw bits of metal and take off finished products.

But efficiency can be increased even further with a second type of production system that has appeared in the past few years. In this equipment, a central computer not only controls each separate machine tool under its charge; it also arranges for the blocks of metal being machined to travel from one tool to another by some transport mechanism. The latter can vary according to taste. It can be a

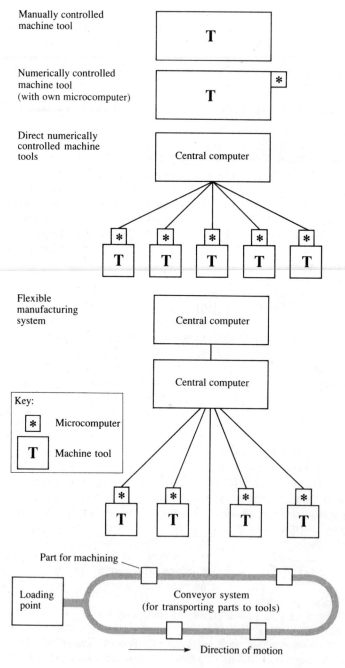

Figure 4.4 Evolution of computerized manufacturing systems

conveyor belt that carries parts around the system; it can be a sequence of robots that grab the components and place them in the relevant machine tool at the appropriate moment; or, most imaginatively, the transport equipment could comprise a series of unmanned trolleys that trundle around the factory floor and bear a load of raw parts from one point to another. The transport concept immediately cuts out the need for workers who put the components in place on the various machines.

The key factor of these systems is their flexibility. Not only does the supervisory computer tell the machines under it to execute a wide range of functions; it also directs the transport mechanism to carry parts round the system in whatever manner the computer decides is most efficient. Thus in a system comprising machines A to D, the central computer could ensure that a part due for a series of complex machining operations visits first A, then C, before going back to B and on to D. At each point on the tour around the system, the part would be machined in a different way until it emerges as a finished product. The next component that enters the system could then travel in an entirely different sequence. You can now appreciate the difference between this method of making things, and the inflexible automation of the transfer line, where there is no chance of varying the set sequence in which parts travel through the system: it is A to B to C to D, or nothing at all. The new equipment had to have a name; and engineers have coined for it the title 'flexible manufacturing system' – uninspiring but factual enough. Figure [4.4] shows a typical design, together with an indication of how the hardware has evolved from earlier machining systems.

Source: Marsh, 1982, pp. 100–4

The labour-saving aspect of the new systems stands out, as does the way in which control is progressively shifted from the machine operator to the computer-controlled machinery (or, more accurately, to the in-built operating software). The potential for increasing output is also clear with even the individual direct numerically controlled production cells increasing the output of the reduced number of operatives fifteen-fold. The full-blown flexible manufacturing systems have even less need for labour and output per worker is increased accordingly. But what really distinguishes the latest manufacturing systems is that adjective 'flexible' which denotes in particular the way in which production can be readily shifted from large-scale mass production of standardized items to small batches of customized products. In the Fordist set-up this was either technically infeasible or prohibitively expensive. With flexible manufacturing systems firms can shift production scale without any significant impact on overall operating costs – enjoying in the process what have come to be called *economies of scope*. These economies thus augment the *economies of scale* (the reduction in cost per unit of output) that the manufacture of standardized products in long production runs offer.

Extract 2 also compares the operating flexibility of new manufacturing systems with the inflexibility of production lines on the Fordist model. This is where the question of balance delay is touched upon. Marsh underlines the degree to which production sequences using flexible manufacturing systems can be varied (in his example, '. . . first A, then C, before going back to B and on to D'). It is the inflexible production sequence of 'A to B to C to D, or nothing at all' of the Fordist production line that is affected by the problem of balance delay. The work-cycles between all those points have to be synchronized to operate in sequence. Those between C and D depend on the successful completion of those between B and C and those between B and C can only be performed when those between A and B have been finished. Given the need for this sequential synchronization of tasks, it is not difficult to see how a break or delay in one work-cycle will interrupt the whole system. Flexible manufacturing methods help to avert this problem of 'balance delay'.

Flexible manufacturing systems, of course, are part of just one aspect of the overall production process – manufacturing. Design and co-ordination remain and it is automation of, to use Kaplinsky's (1984) terminology, these two other 'spheres of production' and ultimately the computerized integration of all three spheres that are the goal of the latest technological developments. This is where the fully automated factory that has haunted the debate over changing manufacturing technology will finally come into its own. Figure 4.5, taken from Marsh (1982), gives an idea of what such a factory might look like. It is a factory of this type that truly, to use the regulationists' phrase quoted earlier, '. . . reconstitutes the totality of the production process'.

The flexible technologies are important not only for the opportunity that they offer for widening the variety of production on Fordist mass production lines; they also enable small-batch production itself to be automated both technically and in terms of the economics of production as the costs of microprocessor-based equipment falls. Thus, Piore and Sabel see the potential for a proliferation of small companies using the new technology to compete in market niches both sectorally and geographically. In the latter case, one scenario that Piore and Sabel endorse is the reappearance of the networks of small firms that constituted the old nineteenth-century industrial districts which lost out at the first industrial divide. New technology in this context is also seen by the institutionalists as offering re-skilling and en-skilling possibilities as former craft skills are extended to incorporate the computer systems knowledge that the new technology demands. Again, in this scenario, the craft skills that were downgraded at the first industrial divide might return with a vengeance at the second.

There is more to flexible specialization, however, than the production technology. The term is generally used to refer to a whole productive system or systems. Thus, Scott and Storper, for example, define 'flexible production systems' as '. . . forms of production characterized by a well-developed ability to shift promptly from one process and/or product configuration to another and to adjust . . . output rapidly up or down without any strongly deleterious effects on levels of efficiency' (quoted in *Hudson*, 1988). This definition clearly refers to the economies of scope that we mentioned above but it also takes on board questions of the way in which single firms

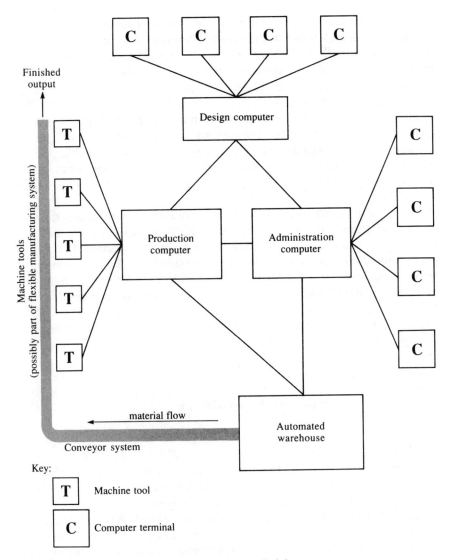

Figure 4.5 Possible layout of computer-controlled factory
Source: Marsh, 1982, p. 109

and factories relate to one another in, for example '. . . ensembles of flexible production sectors' including '. . . selected high technology industries . . . revitalized craft speciality industries, and . . . producer financial services' (Scott and Storper, 1988, quoted in *Hudson*, 1988). An important aspect of such agglomerations of flexibly specialized activities is the Japanese system of sub-contracting – the *just-in-time* or *kanban system* – whereby firms operate with a minimum level of stock inventory, drawing in supplies as and when they are needed (hence 'just in time') from a network of suppliers located in close proximity to them in order to minimize possible interruption to production. In this way, then, the spatial organization of production is as much part of flexible specialization as the aspatial production technologies.

The increased flexibility in utilization of labour is also frequently referred to as a key element in the overall flexible specialization system (see, for example, *Martin* (1988)). This refers to the way in which firms seek to achieve 'numerical flexibility' (through, for example, the use of temporary workers to meet cyclical fluctuations in output) and/or 'functional flexibility' (through the transferability of skills within production and across the technical division of labour). This aspect of flexible specialization will be taken up in Chapter 5.

There is also the other side of the flexible production coin, namely the way in which consumption is structured. Just as Fordism was defined in terms of both its production and consumption features, flexible specialization is also seen by its proponents as having a two-sided structure. As far as consumption is concerned, most emphasis is placed on the growing differentiation in consumer demand and switch away from the standardized products of Fordist mass production – alongside the dismantling of Keynesian welfare provision. Such shifts in consumption patterns, it is argued, demand flexibility in production.

4.3.3   Neo-Fordism: the evidence

Flexible production technology

So what is the evidence for this shift to a neo-Fordist, flexibly specialized future? It is fragmentary but what there is does caution against an uncritical acceptance of some of the claims of its proponents.

The first difficulty is periodization. Some writers date neo-Fordism in the UK from the early to mid 1970s (see, for example, Perrons, 1981, and *Martin*, 1988). But there are clear difficulties with this if one actually looks at trends in the introduction of new technology of the neo-Fordist type (i.e. robotics, computer-controlled machine tools, flexible machining systems and fully automated plant). It is generally agreed by commentators on industrial technology that the key turning-point for the introduction of flexible automation on a world scale was 1979/80. Prior to this date such key technologies as programmable logic controls and computer numerical controls were still relatively undeveloped and, importantly, the examples that were available were prohibitively expensive. The flexible production that did exist prior to the turn of the decade was concentrated in particular countries, most notably Japan. Thus, for example, Marsh (1982) points out that in 1977 there were eighty direct numerically controlled machining systems in Japan compared with just three in Britain.

Moreover, this relative undevelopment of flexible production techniques has been particularly true for the manufacturing operations that are given pride of place in the 'Fordist/post-Fordist' schema – assembly. Assembly operations have proved particularly difficult to automate 'flexibly'. One-off standardized products have been difficult enough, never mind variations within product ranges. This is reflected in the fact that in the 1970s there was only one assembly robot commercially available (made by Olivetti). But even if assembly operations are excluded, the extent of automation generally has tended to be exaggerated in popular accounts and especially with regard to the much vaunted 'computer-integrated manufacturing' (the almost totally automated factory), the pinnacle of flexible automation. In 1985 a group of consultant engineers set out to report on the 'state of the art' of this technology in the UK. This proved impossible as the group could not find a single genuine example of the technology actually in operation on which it could report!

This is not to argue that there are not important changes going on in manufacturing technology on the lines of the flexible specialization model, just that they are doing so much later, much more slowly and much less pervasively than is sometimes suggested.

Changing consumption patterns

What about the consumption side of the flexible specialization coin?

The institutionalists' concept of market saturation and fragmentation can be questioned. It is arguable, for example, that markets are in fact saturated in the way that Piore and Sabel suggest. As Williams *et al.* (1987) point out, there is little hard evidence to support their claim. Even in older consumer durables with relatively high levels of market penetration (like washing-machines and televisions) there are still opportunities for sales growth. In addition to the normal replacement demand there is, for example, a growing market for second televisions and second cars. And recall how companies, by changing product technology, can create 'new' markets and new products. This recreation of mass markets is central to the system. The replacement of black-and-white television sets by colour ones is an obvious example but there are others. Think of all the new products that have emerged in the last few years building on existing technologies and introducing entirely new ones: teletext televisions, video-cassette recorders, personal stereos, compact disc players, microwave ovens and so on. All of these are being produced and sold on a mass basis.

What about market fragmentation? The argument suggests that new demands for less standardized, more personalized products are being created which mass production is unable to handle. While there are certainly signs of moves in this direction there does not appear to be any truly convincing evidence that this threatens mass production, with producers unable to cope. Take cars. There is clearly a trend towards greater product differentiation. The days of Ford's single-coloured Model T are long gone.

But, as Williams *et al.* (1987) point out, all the volume car firms are able to handle more customized demand (such as cabriolets and sports coupés) on the back of the four or so basic model lines that they all now operate. If anything, the big firms are now moving towards a smaller number of basic models (and more standardized, volume-produced and interchangeable components). Competition within these differentiated market segments is intense and, as Williams *et al.* (1987, p. 427) point out, '. . . there will be trade winners and losers', but in their views this '. . . process does not threaten the system of large-scale production, any more than the fact of bankruptcy threatens capitalism'.

A final point, directed more towards the institutionalists who see more of a role for small firms in their neo-Fordist scenario than the regulationists do in theirs, concerns the question of scale and international competition. Stone's (1984) discussion of the competitive strategies of Japanese companies makes particularly interesting reading in this context. He looked at the production of what is termed 'mechatronics'. These are engineering products covering the range of those principally electronic (such as personal computers, calculators and so on) and those chiefly mechanical (like cameras). They comprise the bulk of the modern consumer durable market. What comes across most strikingly in the study is the crucial importance of production scale for the Japanese companies involved: 'Capacity is built up rapidly because achieving the rapid growth path is conditional on reaching high production volumes. High volumes drive prices down, through the economies of scale in assembly and in component manufacture' (Stone, 1984, p. 39). The high investments in production required are not a deterrent because '. . . the volume production and marketing process is geared to depreciating or liquidating these investments quickly, through high production volumes, which are sold quickly' (ibid., p. 45).

The question of scale is a crucial one in current debates over industrial policy. Thus it is often argued that UK corporations should concentrate on 'niche' segments within larger volume markets. Indeed the argument is often extended to the nation as a whole (raising some knotty questions, incidentally, about whether it is possible to talk about a national economy as a single entity in this age of multinational capital and interdependent economies). The notion of flexible specialization is often put forward to support this strategy. Yet, as Stone (1984) points out, it carries the risk of complete exclusion from the market. And recent UK industrial history provides plenty of evidence for this – from motor-bikes to televisions and radios. The US has its examples, too, and it is interesting to speculate about the coincidence of the emergence of the notion of the 'crisis of mass production' in the US with a period of dramatic and sustained loss of domestic markets to overseas, notably Japanese, producers. As Stone's study shows, the Japanese companies winning market share are volume producers. Is it not possible that this changing competitive position, this new form of international uneven development, is being mistaken by some as a crisis of the mass production system as a whole?

Scale still appears to be dominant in a whole range of markets, requiring major investments in research and development and production. The current trend towards international mergers and joint ventures is one reflection of this. New flexible technologies are being introduced but, at present, these are dominated by the large companies in an attempt to match flexibility with mass production. If Williams *et al.* are correct, these firms '. . . will not use [these flexible technologies] to create a workforce of independent craftsmen', whatever Piore and Sabel might think to the contrary, for 'new generations of computer-controlled equipment may deliver a more varied output but they do not restore an economic system based on redeployable productive resources and low fixed costs. That is a world which we have lost' (1987, p. 433).

Summary of section 4.3.3

• Despite the basic differences in underlying conceptualization, there are similarities in the two schools' views of the 'regimes' that they see evolving out of Fordism (the institutionalists' flexible specialization and the neo-Fordism of the regulationists), especially in terms of the production technologies that they see at the core of the new regime.

• The new flexible technology comprises a constellation of products and processes based on 'computer-integrated manufacture' or the 'automated factory', robotics and computerized, numerically controlled machine tools. This new manufacturing technology, it is argued, allows production economies previously confined to large-scale production to be realized at a wide range of scales: small batches can now be produced as cheaply as massive volume runs.

• Flexible specialization is defined as a productive system and as such is taken to include not only the organization and nature of production technology within individual firms and factories but also the way in which firms and factories relate to one another in, for example, customer-supplier networks. An increased flexibility in the use of labour is also argued to be a key feature of this system.

• Flexible production is mirrored by, and in turn encourages, increasingly customized patterns of consumption as the Fordist standardized markets become saturated and fragmented.

• While there is some evidence of flexible specialization, the evidence so far suggests that there is still a long way to go before any judgement can be made. The new flexible technology is being introduced much more slowly than some accounts would suggest and the evidence on market saturation and fragmentation would still caution against an uncritical acceptance of some of the claims of the two schools. The same qualification applies to the institutionalists' argument relating to the resurgence of the small firm. Large-scale production still dominates key consumer markets.

4.4   The geography of Fordism, neo-Fordism and flexible specialization

4.4.1   The geography of Fordism and neo-Fordism: the debate

An important feature of the whole Fordist/post-Fordist debate has been its concern with geography. Thus, while Fordism and neo-Fordism, as we have seen, have been put forward by their proponents as categorizations of national and even international economic systems or regimes, questions concerning the internal geography of these systems have also been central to their analysis.

In the regulationist school some of the most interesting work has been concerned with exploring the geography of 'the crisis of Fordism' at the international level. Thus, for example, Lipietz (1987) traces the insertion of newly industrializing countries into the international division of labour back to the crisis of Fordism in the advanced capitalist countries in the 'centre'. He dates this crisis to the early 1970s.

Having exhausted the possibilities of raising productivity through expanding the scale of production on Fordist lines, firms in the 'centre' were forced to seek out new locations offering the potential for raising labour productivity and maintaining competitiveness through their pool of cheap and malleable labour. This search was facilitated, he argues, by the splitting up of the labour process on Taylorist/Fordist lines. (Lipietz makes a relatively crude three-fold distinction between conceptual and organizational functions, skilled labour and unskilled labour.) Peripheral regions within the developed countries at the centre were the first to receive relocated unskilled tasks and then countries on the 'immediate outer periphery' such as Portugal and Spain. Gradually, however, Third World countries were incorporated either through what Lipietz calls 'Primitive Taylorization' or 'Peripheral Fordism' – distinguished, as the names suggest, on the extent to which the unskilled, labour-intensive tasks were mechanized but also in terms of the relative development of the local market for consumer goods.

What is particularly interesting about Lipietz' formulation is the way in which it attempts to combine the regulationist theory of crisis with that of the new international division of labour which was discussed in Chapter 1. The peripheral countries, in his argument, were being inserted into a new international division of labour because of the crisis of the production/ consumption regime in the centre. Their previous role in the old division of labour had been as a supplier of primary goods to the centre or as a (relatively limited) market for the centre's manufactured goods. The crisis of Fordism at the centre brought these areas into a new international division of labour in which they became producers of manufactured goods.

Think back to the discussion of 'spatial divisions of labour' in Chapter 2 and the way in which these are conceptualized as evolving through the superimposition of a new division of labour onto a previous one to produce a new combination. The same approach is also clearly applicable to what Lipietz is describing at international level. In Lipietz' schema the decentralization of production is clearly associated with an attempt by firms in the centre to prolong their Fordist production regime. Notice the way in which space is being used by the companies involved to maintain their competitiveness.

Other writers in the regulationist framework have extended the analysis to incorporate the geographical implications of neo-Fordism. It is here that the debate becomes confusing. For decentralization is also presented as a basic feature of the geography of neo-Fordism and the debate tends to blur at the edges, with moves in some accounts being attributed to Fordism extending its geography in an attempt to survive (as in the Lipietz argument outlined above) and in others to a qualitatively different regime of production, neo-Fordism. Thus, for example, in her discussion of the industrialization of Ireland, Perrons (1986) argues that peripheral economies were attractive to Fordist producers in the centre not simply because of their lower overall wage costs but also because:

> ... the introduction of the more automated or neo-Fordist labour processes, based on electronic information systems with automatic feedback mechanisms to counter the problem of the balance delay time and worker resistance meant that locations in peripheral areas were technically possible ... Thus it was possible to establish small units of production in geographical isolation from other plants belonging to the same company. (p. 251)

But, of course, it was also possible for companies to decentralize production using the old Fordist techniques. Indeed this seems to have been the case in Ireland:

> ... from the late 1960s and 1970s US, European and Japanese capitals came to Ireland and established larger plants *using Taylorist and Fordist labour processes* giving rise to the superimposition of a more modern industrial system. (ibid., p. 254; emphasis added)

So what is special about the geography of neo-Fordism? Oberhauser (1987) attempts to show this in her study of the post-war restructuring of the French car industry. She distinguishes two distinct periods of geographical reorganization of production and relates these periods to the shift from Fordist to neo-Fordist production within the industry. In the period up to the mid-1970s, she argues, the French car producers decentralized Fordist, semi-skilled assembly work from the Paris region to the rural provinces in an attempt to exploit the cheaper and more malleable labour in these areas. The crisis of Fordism, beginning in the early 1970s, inaugurated a new geography of production associated with the shift by the car producers to neo-Fordist production techniques. Reorganization occurred both intranationally and internationally. Within France production was automated using robots and flexible manufacturing technology of the kind described in section 4.3 and the labour process organized around shorter production lines and group working. Employment contracted. Alongside this in situ change in production technology, the industry moved towards a 'just-in-time' system for its component supplies. Remember what we said earlier about the flexibility that this system offers manufacturers and the need for the suppliers and the customers to be located close to each other to exploit this flexibility to the full. The geographical implications are fairly obvious. As Oberhauser notes, the shift to a 'just-in-time' system meant that '. . . supplier firms and automobile manufacturers became financially interdependent and geographically more concentrated' (1987, p. 454). At the same time as production was concentrating intranationally, however, Oberhauser argues that there was also an international decentralization: '. . . the transformation in production from Fordism to neo-Fordism extended the spatial division of labour from the national level to the international level' (p. 454). This dispersal involved, for example, the location of production in North America and Spain.

This distinction between intranational spatial concentration, on the one hand, and international decentralization on the other, is important for it gives an insight into what appears to be a basic theme in current writing on the geography of 'Fordism in crisis' – namely the tension between centralizing and decentralizing pressures in the reorganization of production.

This dichotomy comes out particularly clearly in the work of Alan Scott and Michael Storper on the geography of flexible specialization in the US. These authors claim to detect a tendency for high-tech industry to adopt a spatial pattern characterized by both 'agglomeration networks of flexible, customized production' and a decentralized pattern of 'routinized production' (Scott and Storper, 1987). While the latter could be part of a Fordist geography, it is the former (on its own or in combination with the latter) which would appear to be what distinguishes the geography of neo-Fordism.

Much of the writings of people in the institutionalist camp would seem to chime in with these arguments. Thus, for example, Piore and Sabel's scenario of regional 'conglomerations of craft-based federated enterprises' (on the lines of those currently operating in areas like Prato and Emilio Romagna in what has come to be called the 'Third Italy') clearly fits in with Scott and Storper's agglomerations of customized producers. And Schoenberger in her (1987) study of the US car industry stresses the countervailing tendencies for spatial dispersal and reconcentration.

What appears to set the institutionalists most clearly apart from others writing in the field, however, is their emphasis, yet again, on the indeterminacy of the processes at work, on their conviction that the spatial patterns are not determined by the technological characteristics of production and labour processes. In Schoenberger's words: 'The new technologies and organizational methods may alter the locational possibilities and constraints faced by the firm, but they in no sense dictate the outcome' (p. 211).

This argument does provide a useful counterweight to the tendency in some of the writing in this area to present the fragmentation of production and the introduction of the new flexible production technologies as having a necessary geography. While clearly, for example, the 'just-in-time' system has a spatial pattern built into its very structure, the fact that flexible automation facilitates the dispersal of small production units does not mean that this disperal will take place. An equally plausible argument can be made for investments in such technology having quite the opposite effect. In this argument, investment in automated production reduces the need for (living) labour. The cost attractions of cheap, unskilled and/or 'green' labour are reduced accordingly and other cost considerations such as proximity to suppliers and customers increase in relative importance. Indeed quite convincing arguments on these lines have been deployed to point to the vulnerability of the production decentralized to the Third World in the 1960s and 1970s (Lipietz, 'Primitive Taylorism' and 'Peripheral Fordism') to being repatriated to the First World (Rada, 1981; Kaplinsky, 1984).

The need in all this discussion of the changing geography of production is to avoid creating what Andrew Sayer (1985) neatly describes as 'spatial stereotypes' which '. . . freeze, and then present as universal, relationships which are contingent and historically specific'.

4.4.2 Fordism and neo-Fordism and the UK's changing economic geography

The main contours of Britain's changing economic geography in the postwar period were sketched out in Chapter 2. You will recall that what stood out in these changes was the 'break' in the mid to late 1970s from a pattern of interregional convergence in economic 'well-being' to one of increasing divergence. The period of convergence, you will also recall, was associated with the decentralization of production from the core of the South East and West Midlands to the peripheral regions.

This decentralization of production, in the context of relative national economic growth succeeded by increasing relative decline, could be viewed in a regulationist perspective as Fordism seeking to survive in a growing period of crisis. Thus, it could be argued, the earlier moves to overcome the labour shortages associated with the 'overheating' of the core regions were gradually replaced by more desperate moves to find cheaper and more malleable labour to preserve competitiveness on the Fordist model. The decline of industry in the inner cities (with its older, less productive production) would also fit into this view.

The so-called shift to neo-Fordism from the mid to late 1970s is more complicated, however, and does not appear to have been associated with a changing geography that neatly fits into some of the scenarios (Sayer might say stereotypes) that have been put forward. Certainly the period has not been marked by the decentralization that some proponents of neo-Fordism might expect. On the contrary, at a national level, there has been a relative spatial concentration with a loss of some of the production decentralized in the earlier period (and job loss associated with that which survived) and a decline in both the number of interregional moves of branch plants (and the number of jobs associated with them) and the distance of these moves (Townsend, 1987).

On the other hand, what does seem to have occurred which might fit in with some aspects of a post-Fordist scenario is the growth in direct investment abroad (that is, investment in actual production facilities) as part of the increasing openness of the UK economy discussed in Chapter 1. So intra-national retrenchment has been accompanied by a degree of international decentralization.

There has also been a spatial concentration of production in the new waves of investment with, for example, recently arrived Japanese companies in consumer electronics (where the UK is on the receiving end of overseas direct investment) clustering around each other in South Wales. Indeed, as *Martin* (1988) argues, the new waves of investment have generally been highly spatially selective, avoiding most blatantly the older industrial regions and especially those areas within them most tied to former waves.

Hudson (1988) looks at the changing economic fortunes of the older industrial regions. He is highly sceptical of the notion of conceptualizing social and economic change in terms of national regimes of accumulation like Fordism and even more so of attempts to apply such concepts in regional analysis. Whilst acknowledging the decentralization of Fordist production to the older industrial regions in the 1950s and 1960s, he is adamant that the scale of labour market changes associated with this introduction of 'new' industries and 'new' Fordist labour processes was quite limited and, in many cases, temporary as these branch-plants shed labour or closed completely in the 1970s. Interestingly, he also discusses the consumption side of the Fordist regime, arguing that the transformation to mass-consumption life-styles in the older industrial regions was limited and uneven and '. . . at best a pale shadow of what Fordism was meant to be about'.

But if Fordism is difficult for Hudson to come to terms with in the context of Britain's older industrial regions, neo-Fordism is nigh on impossible, notwithstanding the fact that he is able to find evidence of a whole range of recent changes in production and employment in the older industrial regions that many would seize upon as classic features of flexible specialization. These changes include a shift towards increased subcontracting, part-time and casualized working, single-union agreements and negotiation of the kind of 'flexible' working conditions that will be discussed in the next chapter. For *Hudson* (1988), however, these changes: '. . . do not constitute a transition to a new "post-Fordist flexibility" but rather a selective re-working which reproduces, in modified form, pre-Fordist and Fordist methods of production' and '. . . a reflection of a shift in the balance of power between capital and labour'.

On the last point Hudson's arguments begin to fit in with research that focuses on the role of the re-making of management-labour relations (especially by foreign-owned companies) in older industrial regions. As *Morgan and Sayer* (1985) found in their study of the South Wales electrical engineering industry, the new Japanese companies are increasingly seeking to mould labour practices around the goals of the firm as a whole and not just the production and labour process – actively 'manufacturing consent' and attempting to change working attitudes and behaviour.

Extract 3 gives an example of this in a company recently located in an older industrial region in Scotland. Notice the firm's highly selective recruitment policy (the term 'uncontaminated' in this context speaks volumes) and its package of working conditions similar to those discussed by *Hudson* (1988). Whether this is an example of flexible specialization remains an open and contentious question, as must the one that heads this chapter.

For all the necessary openness about the extent to which a major shift in the regime of accumulation has occurred, what is clear is that the context and conditions in which people work have been undergoing considerable change. This is the subject of the next chapter.

Extract 3

New town looks to the young and skilled

Ms Liz Murgitroyd spends her working days fixing chips to printed circuit boards in Mitsubishi's video recorder manufacturing plant at Livingston, West Lothian. She does not belong to a union; she is a Material Girl.

A chart above her head shows her weekly performance rating; another at the end of her assembly line portrays that of her quality circle. Among the Material Girls' competitors are the Young Ones, the Maniacs, the Thunderbirds and the Misfits.

The pop culture names have been chosen by workers whose average age is 18.2 years. Two-thirds of them are female. A giant poster of the Girls' spiritual leader, the pop star Madonna, hangs in the single-status canteen nearby.

A string of US and Japanese companies have settled in Livingston in the 1980s, bringing with them different working traditions. Strong emphasis has been placed on flexibility and performance; unions have been given a frosty reception.

West Lothian has been one of Britain's worst unemployment blackspots since a contraction in manufacturing and mining there, but the number of permanent jobs in Livingston – 15,719 last year – is expected to continue growing at the rate of 940 a year.

Yet for most semi-skilled workers consigned to the pool of unemployed, the growth of Livingston provides little comfort. New companies have shown particular interest in two distinct groups: skilled workers already employed by other companies, and school-leavers.

According to Mr David Balfour, commercial director of Livingston Development Corporation, the latter are seen as 'uncontaminated'. The experienced assembly line worker may have been exposed to such contaminants as traditional working practices and British shop stewards.

Mr Ernest Barnard, operations director of Ferranti Infographics, a small Livingston software company, says: 'This area has been notoriously highly unionised over the years and employers tend to think that if you have been in a union environment, it will have worked its way into you.'

Two Japanese companies, Mitsubishi and NEC Semiconductors, have adopted a policy of recruiting only teenagers as assembly workers. Both say they want workers without preconceived ideas about working practices, who are adaptable to training.

At Mitsubishi, 280 operators work a 39-hour week assembling video recorders. The more overt of Japanese traditions, such as managers wearing uniforms and compulsory physical exercises in the morning, have been dropped quietly. However, the emphasis on performance remains.

Ms Murgitroyd has worked at Mitsubishi for three years and is a grade 2 operator. Operators aged over 18 years earn between £116.50 and £130 a week: the annual pay award made to each individual varies across an 8 per cent range according to his or her rating.

The company has introduced what Mr Jim McCulloch, its personnel officer, refers to as a 'bastardised' system of quality circles, splitting its operators into teams which strive to attain performance targets for attendance, housekeeping and 'zero defects'.

Mitsubishi has firmly resisted approaches from the EETPU electricians' union, arguing that its elected staff consultative committee – which meets monthly to discuss workplace issues and prepares an annual wage claim – eliminates the need for union recognition.

NEC also employs about 280 operators, whose average age is 18.5, and places a heavy stress on harmonising working conditions. Mr Bill Gold, personnel manager, links its emphasis on mutual loyalty between company and employee to its rebuffing the EETPU.

He argues that the company needs a young workforce, open to frequent retraining, because of the rapidly changing nature of the semiconductor business. 'We cannot offer them a long-term job. But we are guaranteeing them long-term employment,' he says.

Such a targeted selection process is not found at all Livingston's foreign-owned non-union plants. Unisys, the US company, employs several former employees of Leyland Vehicles at nearby Bathgate – a plant known for its turbulent industrial relations history before its closure in 1986.

One is Mr Drew McLaren, aged 47, a supervisor on a document encoding machine assembly line. He says: 'I was very surprised when I came here at how good the management was, considering that it had a captive workforce and could demand everything from us without giving very much back.'

The company, which employs 250 hourly-paid workers from a wide age range, describes its relationship with employees and reasons for rejecting unions slightly differently. Mr Duncan Millar, personnel manager, says: 'Our philosophy is that we can do better than any third party for our staff.'

Among the perks Unisys offers all its staff is free life and private health insurance, and five weeks' holiday. A similar story is told at Apollo Computer, a small US company, where personnel manager Mr Graham Steven was formerly an ASTMS white-collar union shop steward.

Apollo places particular emphasis on single status for all staff, to eliminate what Mr Steven calls 'petty jealousies'. He says: 'A lot of people have a view of central

Scotland as an extension of Red Clydeside. But we have found no resistance to any of our ideas.'

The combination of single-status working conditions, performance-related pay and non-unionism has proved potent even to British companies. Livingston Precision, a small contract engineering company, has abandoned recognition of the Amalgamated Engineering Union.

Workers there are paid a monthly salary based on performance. Mr Ben Reilly, managing director, cites his apprenticeship in the 1960s at an electronics company with 'five grades of canteen and four grades of toilet' as the motive for not following traditional industrial relations practices.

Ms Murgitroyd gives a clue to one reason why employees have accepted new ways of working. Asked about the pressures of meeting performance targets, she says: 'Sometimes it gets me down, but it's OK. I reckon I'm lucky to have a job.'

Livingston Development Corporation is trying to persuade companies to train local unemployed people for skilled vacancies rather than poaching from each other. It is backing a West Lothian joint project set up for this purpose.

In Livingston, the Young Ones have reason to be grateful for their youth. At the moment, older job seekers without specific qualifications and skills can face a hard task finding work.

Source: John Gapper, *Financial Times*, 18 January 1988

Summary of section 4.4

• An important feature of the whole Fordist/neo-Fordist debate has been its concern with geography at both international and intranational levels.

• An important strand of work has been concerned with the decentralization of production from the First to the Third World in the 1960s and early 1970s. This shift, it is argued, represented an attempt by Fordist producers to maintain their profitability. In this argument the regulationist theory of crisis is integrated with the notion of a new international division of labour.

• Decentralization of production has also been put forward as a key feature of the geography of neo-Fordism, though it is not always clear how this geography differs, if at all, from that also seen as being associated with Fordism.

• A basic feature of the geography of neo-Fordism is the tension between decentralization and concentration of production. New production systems like 'just-in-time' and agglomerations of flexibly specialized firms point towards spatial concentration. But there is a danger of assuming that new flexible production systems, or older inflexible ones for that matter, have a necessary geography. Care has to be taken to avoid creating spatial stereotypes.

• The decentralization of production in the UK in the 1950s and 1960s could be interpreted as a spatial response to the crisis of Fordism. The spatial pattern that could be associated with neo-Fordism is less clear. It would appear, however, that the spatial concentration of production has thus far tended to outweigh spatial dispersal.

● Major new waves of investment have been spatially selective, avoiding in particular the older industrial regions. The extent to which these regions were ever part of a Fordist regime is still an open debate. So too is the question of whether some of the new patterns of working in these regions actually constitute a change towards flexible specialization. What does appear to have been important, however, has been the emphasis, especially by Japanese companies recently established in the UK, on the re-moulding of management-labour relations.

Answers to Activities

Activity 4.1

(a)   1924–37 and especially 1951–64 and 1964–73.

(b)   Manufacturing with average annual growth rates of 1.04, 1.14 and 1.11 per cent respectively.

(c)   The way in which manufacturing shifts from being the fastest growing sector to the most rapidly declining one (with average annual growth rates of −0.21 and −0.70 per cent in 1973–79 and 1979–83 respectively).

Activity 4.2

Detergents are examples of a chemicals product manufactured in batches using process production techniques.

Televisions, archetypal consumer durables of the period since the Second World War, are assembled on a mass production basis.

Aeroplanes, more complex and larger-scale products, are manufactured by small-batch and unit production methods.

Further reading

The two key texts in the whole Fordist/post-Fordist debate are ones which have been referred to in the course of this chapter, Michel Aglietta's *A Theory of Capitalist Regulation* (London, New Left Books; 1979) and *The Second Industrial Divide* by Michael Piore and Charles Sabel (New York, Basic Books; 1984). But, be warned, Aglietta's book is quite a difficult read.

If you find it hard going, then Alain Lipietz' *Mirages and Miracles: The Crises of Global Capitalism* (London, Verso; 1985) (also recommended as further reading for Chapter 1) offers a more accessible account of the regulationist position, albeit with more emphasis on explaining the changing economic interrelationships between the First and Third Worlds.

Harry Braverman's *Labour and Monopoly Capital: The Degradation of Work in the Twentieth Century* (New York, Monthly Review Press; 1974) remains a seminal text on the changing labour process, stimulating a whole school of writing on the subject. Some of the critiques of Braverman's work appear in Stephen Wood's edited collection, *The Degradation of Work? Skill, De-skilling and the Labour Process* (London, Hutchinson; 1982).

Two other edited collections give very readable accounts of various aspects of the labour process debate including questions of skill, the gender division of labour, women and domestic work and accounts of experiences of different labour processes. These are Kenneth Thompson's *Work, Employment and Unemployment* (Milton Keynes, The Open University Press; 1984), a set book for the Open University course, *Work and Society*, and its companion Reader, Craig Littler's *The Experience of Work* (Aldershot, Gower in association with The Open University; 1985).

Most of the latest writing on the geography of neo-Fordism and flexible specialization is from a North American perspective. A comprehensive overview of the UK situation has still to be written. However, Ron Martin's article, 'Industrial capitalism in transition: the contemporary reorganization of the British space economy', in the associated Reader (Massey, D. and Allen, J. (eds) (1988)) gives a thumbnail sketch of the broad features of this new geography and raises a number of related economic and political issues.

Two contrasting views on shifts towards 'flexibility' and the re-making of management-labour relations from different parts of the British Isles also appear in the associated Reader. Hudson's 'Labour market changes and new forms of work in "old" industrial regions' focuses on the North East, and Morgan and Sayer's article discusses South Wales. The latter appears in their *Microcircuits of Capital: Sunrise Industry and Uneven Development* (Cambridge, Polity Press; 1988) which provides an up-to-date and challenging account of the changing geography of electronics production, both internationally and within the UK.

5   Fragmented firms, disorganized labour?

John Allen

Contents

5.1   **Introduction**   185

5.2   **The dispersal of industry**   186
5.2.1   The decline of regional economies   187
5.2.2   Disorganized spatial structures?   188
5.2.3   The demise of the large firm?   192
5.2.4   Fragmentation strategies   195
Summary of section 5.2   200

5.3   **The restructuring of the labour market**   200
5.3.1   The flexible workforce?   201
5.3.2   Assessing the evidence   204
5.3.3   The rediscovery of flexibility?   211
Summary of section 5.3   213

5.4   **Trade unions at the crossroads**   213
5.4.1   The changing face of trade unionism   214
5.4.2   Fragmented unionism   222
5.4.3   Disorganized labour?   224
Summary of section 5.4   227

Further reading   227

5.1 Introduction

Flexibility, as noted in the last chapter, has become a rather broad term under which different theorists have subsumed a range of different developments. Although it is not yet clear what kind of 'flexible' economy is emerging, flexibility has been given as a clear example of how labour processes and product markets are changing in the present period. In this chapter we explore other ways in which the economy is said to be in the process of being restructured along flexible lines.

The focus will be upon changes that have or are likely to have a major impact upon the organization of people's working lives. Fewer people today, for example, work in giant industrial workplaces. Many of the larger factories have disappeared and along with them the certainty, for the male worker at least, that a job meant lifetime employment. New patterns of work have emerged. Full-time employment has fallen while part-time work, temporary employment and homeworking have increased. At the workplace, long-standing demarcations between jobs are being called into question as the issue of multi-skilling is placed on the agenda by employers. In the face of many of these changes, the trade unions have declined in both membership and bargaining strength. They have begun to question their role and their base in today's changing economy. A sense of labour in transformation is apparent. Collectively, do these changes represent a fundamental shift in the way that working life is structured in contemporary Britain? This is the broad question which guides the selection of topics discussed in this chapter.

I stress broad, for we cannot deal with all of the topics that have a bearing on this question in one chapter. The changing pattern of work and industrial organization is in itself an enormous subject and so too are some of the claims that are made about the extent and pace of such changes. I intend therefore to consider three issues which, in different ways, have been taken as indications of a move towards more flexible and spatially dispersed structures of work and industrial organization.

Each of the three issues has been addressed in earlier chapters. In the next section we look at the decline and fragmentation of many of the large industrial firms in the old 'heartlands' of the British economy and the emergence of a more dispersed industrial structure. The focus here will be upon the extent and significance of the shift in production away from existing large plants into smaller plants and small firms. The following section examines some of the changes occurring in the social composition of the labour force and the breakdown of established labour market patterns. The reorganization of workforces within firms to achieve greater 'flexibility' will be one of the major threads of this section. Finally, in section 5.4 we take up the related issue of the changing structure of trade unionism and the significance of a more dispersed and fragmented labour market for the structures of collective work organization.

As before, the central question that will be asked of each set of changes is whether it represents a structural change in the organization of the economy, or a limited and perhaps temporary response to the full-scale economic recession of the late 1970s and early 1980s, one which is therefore potentially reversible. As the changes we are examining are still working themselves out, any answers to this central question will be tentative and subject to further debate. Despite the incipient nature of many of these changes, some theorists have spoken of the emergence of a new, 'disorganized' phase of capitalism (Offe, 1985; Lash and Urry, 1987). This is a broad historical thesis and one which figures throughout this chapter, particularly in sections 5.2 and 5.4. Other theoretical accounts that we shall examine are more restricted in their scope, aimed at explaining discrete changes in the short to medium term. In each case, as in previous chapters, we shall be looking at how these theories construct their explanations, rather than simply outlining their different views.

5.2   The dispersal of industry

The following points about a more dispersed geography of industry since the 1960s have been referred to in earlier chapters: the collapse of manufacturing in the cities and major conurbations; the decentralization of manufacturing jobs away from the major industrial centres to the rural periphery; the reorganization of industries as firms fragment their operations and locate different parts of the production process in a variety of places; and the growth of service industries in provincial towns and cities. At a general level these changes reflect differences in the locational requirements of the currently expanding industries from those in decline and also, to some extent, they reflect the declining international competitiveness of much of Britain's manufacturing industry. Another factor associated with industrial dispersal, not previously noted, is the marked decentralization of the population from the old, established, urban industrial centres and conurbations. Most of these trends should strike a familiar chord. What is of interest to us now is the relationship between this more dispersed pattern and the organizational structures of firms and their workforces.

According to Lash and Urry (1987), a significant aspect of this process of dispersal is the demise of distinct regional economies which were formerly dependent on a small number of long-standing industries and the emergence of more diverse regional structures with fewer differences between regions in terms of their industrial mix. Associated with this process of regional diversification is the break-up of large firms or large plants which have tended to dominate the industrial landscape of the major industrial cities. Both trends are supported by available evidence, some of which you will be aware of from Chapters 2 and 4. Disagreement has arisen, however, over the significance and the nature of the changes involved, particularly in relation to the fragmentation of large firms and the parallel growth of small plants. To set these issues in context, we shall first address the subject of regional diversification and the spatial dispersal of industry.

5.2.1 The decline of regional economies

The distinctive pattern of regional development in the United Kingdom, laid down over previous decades, has been well documented. From the latter half of the nineteenth century to the inter-war depression, most regions, though not the South East, were characterized by sectoral specialization, often dominated by a small number of industries. Some of the major differences were outlined in Chapter 2 with different regions at the core of successive waves of industrial development. Before the inter-war depression, among the best-known examples were coal and steel in Wales, Scotland and the North East, textiles in the North West, shipbuilding in the North, and clothing and footwear in the East Midlands. By the 1950s many of these regional specializations, although less pronounced, were still evident and included the concentration of vehicles and engineering in the West Midlands. Industrial towns like Sheffield and Coventry, built on steel and engineering respectively, had a strong presence in their regions; and companies like Swan Hunters in Tyneside, Scott Lithgow and John Brown on Clydeside, and Rolls Royce in Derby were inextricably bound up with the symbolism of place and distinctive work cultures. The difference between regions was largely an *inter-sectoral* division of labour, which represented itself on the map as a split between the traditional heavy industries in the 'north' and the modern consumer industries in the midlands and the South East (Marshall, 1987).

By the mid-1960s this pattern of industrial concentration within different regions had markedly weakened and with it the distinctiveness of regional profiles. The processes involved are those set out earlier in connection with the spatial dispersal and the decline of industry. Each process has in some way contributed towards the flattening of regional profiles. Job loss in manufacturing has been greatest in the regions and conurbations that were dependent on a manufacturing base. The growth of the service industries, as noted in Chapter 3, has exhibited a more even distribution in comparison with manufacturing, largely attributable to the expansion of public services in the 1960s and early 1970s. And, as noted in Chapter 2, the decentralization and disintegration of industry have contributed towards a more complex *intra-sectoral* division of labour between regions, with different stages of the production processes within the same industry located in different areas.

Putting all this together does not lead to the conclusion that all regions are becoming alike; there may be a greater *convergence* of regional industrial structures, that is, an increased similarity in the types of industry to be found across the regions, but within regions there are signs of increased *divergence* (Fothergill and Gudgin, 1982). The geography of industry, it would appear, has become more fine-grained, with, for example, the Medway towns declining amidst the relative prosperity of the South East, the south Cheshire area prospering in the declining North West, the co-existence of growth and decay in the towns of the Central Valley in Scotland and so on.

Before considering the significance of this new geography of industry, it is worth noting that the divergence of industrial structure within regions does not imply that the 'region' has lost all meaning as a social category. Cooke (1985), for example, has argued forcefully that a region such as South Wales, despite the erosion of its heavy industrial base, retains a symbolic significance, that is, as an entity which people identify with and to which they attach a certain cultural and political significance. Class characteristics and identities within the region may have been forged by a set of industries which are now in decline, but their influence persists and informs present-day cultural and political forms. In this sense, they remain regional characteristics. Part of Cooke's argument is to show the different periodizations of change, the different pace at which cultural, political and economic changes can occur. Our concern in this section, however, is primarily with economic change and, since the 1970s, the dispersal of industry and the decline of distinct regional economies have become features of a new pattern of uneven economic development. The question to be asked is: does this pattern represent a fundamental, long-term shift in the spatial structure of the UK economy or the latest phase of uneven development which will, in the short to medium term, give rise to a renewed pattern as the locational requirements of industries change?

5.2.2   Disorganized spatial structures?

Arguing the former are Lash and Urry in their book, *The End of Organized Capitalism* (1987). Their thesis considers a number of the advanced capitalist economies and takes account of more than changes in the economy. Its value here is the importance that Lash and Urry attach to the shift from regional distinctiveness to local diversity as one indication of an emerging 'disorganized' phase of advanced capitalist economies. A truncated version of their argument runs something like this.

'Organized' capitalism refers to a set of structures put in place at the end of the nineteenth century both from 'above' and from 'below'. Organization at the top was primarily achieved through the collective actions of banking and industrial capital and from below by the actions of organized labour, the trade unions and the political parties which represented the interests of labour. In the UK the process of organization began at the bottom rather than at the top. The role of the state as an active agent of organization occurred later, typically in the inter-war period. By the 1960s and

1970s the organizational structures – economic, social and spatial – put in place by these agents had entered into some kind of crisis which signalled the end of organized capitalism and the emergence of a new, disorganized phase. The list of organizational structures in crisis is not considered in detail here, but includes, among others, the regulation of national markets by nationally based corporations, the establishment of national bargaining structures by the collective organizations of labour and the growth of corporatist forms of organization to achieve national objectives. Associated with these organizational forms is, according to Lash and Urry, a particular *spatial fix*, a set of interconnected spatial structures which are in the process of dissolution. It is this aspect of their thesis that is relevant here.

The features of this spatial fix are those mentioned earlier: the development of distinct regional economies shaped by a small number of industries and organized around large plants in the major urban centres. And the reasons offered to explain the dissolution of this spatial fix, a process currently under way, are also familiar to you from Chapters 2 and 3, namely the spatial deconcentration and dispersal of industry, and the use made of local diversity by industry to fragment their operations and situate them in a variety of locations. The key point to note about this process of dissolution is that, in Lash and Urry's view, it is an *orchestrated* process. Whereas the pattern of regional specialization laid down during the phase of organized capitalism was, in their view, largely an unplanned pattern produced by the actions of a large number of separate companies, under disorganized capitalism the development of a more complex spatial division of labour is a planned development internal to multinational corporations (1987, p. 90). Thus the process of disorganization, of spatial dispersion, is rather paradoxically taken to be one that *is* organized from 'above'. (See *Cooke*, 1987; *Martin*, 1988.)

I have stressed the spatial aspect of their thesis in order to show how changes in the geography of industry are viewed as part of a broader shift in the organizational structure of the UK economy, and of capitalism in general. A major strand of this argument accords with the view of uneven development expressed by Doreen Massey in Chapter 2, in that she, too, emphasized the relations of control that structure the different functions, the different economic activities, that places perform in the wider national, and international, economy. The point is put rather differently by Lash and Urry, who refer largely to the ability of global corporations to structure the organization of space 'from above', but the substance of the view is similar. The two views of uneven development differ, however, in their respective accounts of historical periodization, over the number of different phases of uneven development and over their relative time-span. Let us briefly compare the two views.

As can be seen from Table 5.1, Lash and Urry refer to three historical periods or stages of western capitalism – liberal, organized and disorganized each of which has an associated spatial pattern of development. In this sense their account of social change is a considerable improvement over broad theories of change which neglect the uneven geography of social change and treat societies as a unified whole.

The spatial organization of the liberal phase varied greatly but in general it was characterized by highly localized developments which subsequently

Table 5.1
Temporal and spatial changes in liberal, organized and disorganized capitalism

Phase of capitalist development	Predominant temporal/spatial organizational/ structures	Spatial changes within each territory	Predominant means of transmitting knowledge and executing surveillance
Liberal	Large-scale collapsing empires that had been built up around dynastic rulers or world religions; emergence of weak nation-states.	Growth of tiny pockets of industry. Importance of substantial commercial cities as well as the expansion of new urban centres in rural areas.	Handwriting and word of mouth.
Organized	Nation-states within the ten or so major western economies increasingly dominate large parts of the rest of the world through colonization.	Development of distinct regional economies organized around growing urban centres. Major inequalities between new industrial and non-industrial regions and nations.	Printing developed through 'print-capitalism'.
Disorganized	Development of world economy, an international division of labour, and the widespread growth of capitalism in most countries.	Decline of distinct regional/national economies and of *industrial* cities. Growth of industry in smaller cities and rural areas, and the development of service industry. Separation of finance and industry.	Electronically transmitted information dramatically reduces the time-space distances between people and increases the powers of surveillance.

Source: Lash and Urry, 1987

gave way to the development of more distinct regional economies at the end of the nineteenth century as capitalism entered its organized phase. The precise timing of this development varies from country to country, but broadly speaking organized capitalism began 'in most western countries in the final decades of the nineteenth century as a consequence of the downward phase of the Kondratiev long wave which began in the mid 1870s' (ibid., p. 3). By the 1960s and 1970s, as noted above, the structures of organized capitalism and its associated 'spatial fix' are seen to be in a process of dissolution, giving way to a new phase of disorganization. Thus the period from the late nineteenth century to the 1960s is represented as one distinctive pattern of uneven development which, in turn, has given way to a more dispersed pattern of geographical change. Whether this new phase of development is also linked to the rhythms of Kondratiev's long waves is not clear in Lash and Urry's thesis and neither is the explanatory weight that they attach to such cycles. Nonetheless, the breakdown of the uneven geography of capitalist development into three distinct phases does give a clear indication of what are taken to be the overarching changes in the spatial structure of Britain since the late nineteenth century. And it is the general level at which their account is conducted that distinguishes it from the temporally discrete account of successive forms of uneven development outlined by Doreen Massey in Chapter 2.

There, in section 2.5, the duration of successive phases of uneven development in the UK appeared to be of a short-term nature and linked to more specific changes within the division of labour in society. Thus the decentralization of industry from the central regions to the periphery that occurred in the 1960s and 1970s, a process which is part and parcel of the emergence of Lash and Urry's disorganized phase of capitalism, had by the late 1970s and early 1980s given way to a process of reconcentration of production and the closure of peripheral sites (*Cooke*, 1987). As Chapter 4 noted, among the new growth sectors of the economy, in both the manufacturing and the service industries there are tendencies towards the recentralization of production within British industry. In this sense it may be premature to speak of the spatial deconcentration of industry as a distinctive feature of a new phase of British capitalism. This particular pattern of uneven development within the UK may be associated with a short-term rather than a long-term change in the structure of British industry.

The differences between Lash and Urry's view of uneven development and Massey's view, in terms of the time-span of successive phases of spatial change, reflect the scope and abstraction of the questions asked in the two accounts. By identifying broad historical phases in capitalist development, Lash and Urry draw attention to equally general questions about the nature of spatial changes within the different phases. Disorganization therefore implies spatial deconcentration, a spatial scattering that is translated as the decline of industrial cities and of the 'region'. In contrast, the account of spatial changes in Chapter 2 is mainly concerned with successive developments in the post-war period and draws attention to the need to question the changing locational requirements of different industries over that period. (See also *Massey*, 1988.) The two accounts of uneven development are not incompatible; they overlap in a number of respects, descriptively and conceptually. The latter account, however, which aims to explain discrete changes in the spatial structure of industry in the short term, cannot be easily subsumed under the general historical framework of the former interpretation. Why? Because Lash and Urry's argument rests upon the validity of their *interpretative* framework – the periodization of capitalism into distinct phases with associated spatial patterns. And as *Cooke* (1987) has argued, such a broad framework underestimates the ability of industry to reorganize spatially in the short to medium term. A phenomenon worth examining, then, is the changing organizational structure of industry in the post-war period.

5.2.3   The demise of the large firm?

Lash and Urry's argument that the spatial fix of organized capitalism is in the process of dissolution connects with the trend towards the fragmentation of large firms within the manufacturing sector and the growth of small plants and the rise in the number of small firms. What we appear to be seeing is a fall in the average size of plants, in terms of the numbers employed in separate workplaces, and an increase in the number of small firms. From the 1950s up to the 1970s the average numbers employed in plant and firms in the manufacturing sector grew significantly. In 1959 a quarter of all employees in the manufacturing sector worked in plants employing 10 000 or more. By 1978 this figure had increased to just over a third of all workers. A similar growth in the proportion of employees is also apparent in workplaces employing 1000 or more over roughly the same period (Fogarty, 1986). Since the late 1970s, however, a number of factors have contributed towards an overall reduction in the average numbers employed in plants and firms.

The obvious factor is the run-down of manufacturing capacity which, as noted in the previous chapter, has led to job losses in the mass production industries and large manufacturing firms in general. As Table 5.2 indicates, the number of firms employing more than 999 workers dropped considerably in the early 1980s. Two other interesting trends have emerged.

Activity 5.1

(a)   Although the number of firms (enterprises) employing more than 999 employees has declined since the early 1970s, what is the nature of the trend in column 2, the number of plants (establishments) that firms operate?

(b)   Now examine column 3, the average number of workers employed per plant (establishment). What kind of trend is emerging here? How does it relate to the above trend?

Table 5.2 Establishment analysis of manufacturing enterprises with more than 999 employees, United Kingdom, 1973–82

Year	Number of enterprises	Establishments per enterprise	Average employment per establishment
1973	828	12.4	459
1974	847	12.3	457
1975	808	12.7	443
1976	795	12.9	411
1977	781	13.5	415
1978	769	13.1	419
1979	751	13.2	413
1980	704	14.5	367
1981[1]	627	14.9	343
1982[1]	582	15.0	338
Percentage change, 1973–82	−29.7	+21.0	−26.4

[1] Revised definition, 1981–2

Source: *Business Monitor* PA 1002, in Shutt and Whittington, 1987

The most striking feature is that employment within plants of the remaining large firms has shrunk and yet, *at the same time*, those firms have also increased the average number of plants that they operate (Shutt and Whittington, 1987). The decline in average plant size, then, is not solely attributable to lay-offs caused by a deepening recession; it can also be traced to the fragmentation of large firms.

The reduction in the size of plants by the large manufacturing firms should not, however, be translated as a reduction in the economic concentration of manufacturing industry. Multi-plant ownership and large industrial corporations are two sides of the same coin. From Figure 5.1 you can see just how far the degree of economic concentration has risen in manufacturing industry since the turn of the century.

Between 1950 and 1970 the top one hundred manufacturing firms increased their share of total net output from just over 20 per cent to just over 40 per cent. Since that date, according to the available figures, the degree of economic concentration has stabilized around 40 per cent. This figure is almost certainly an underestimate as such figures do not take account of the fact (noted in Chapter 3) that major corporations now tend to operate in a number of markets. So today, if you are working in a small plant, it is likely to be owned by one of a small group of companies. In 1986, for instance, over one and a quarter million workers – some 5 per cent of the total workforce – had jobs with the forty largest manufacturing firms in the UK (*Labour Research*, 1987).

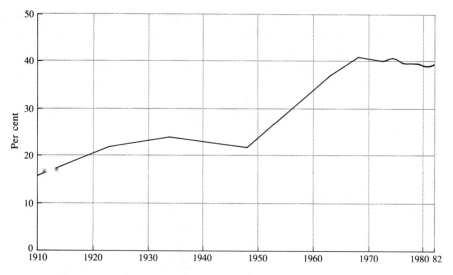

Figure 5.1 Share of the hundred largest enterprises in manufacturing net output, United Kingdom, 1909–82

Source: Prais, 1976; Business Monitor *PA 1002*

The contemporary corporation therefore bears little resemblance to the dominant image of the giant firm organized around a few large plants within one industry. It is perhaps best to think of the modern large firm as an entity which controls its operations through a variety of strategies – through the ownership of plants, franchising, licensing agreements, subcontracting arrangements and so forth – in a range of markets and which employs people in a variety of workplaces and locations. The fragmentation of the operations of the large firm, then, should not be read as a fragmentation of control. We shall return to this point after considering other factors that have led to a reduction in the size of workplaces.

One factor which has contributed to the reduction in the average size of workplaces is the growth of employment within small firms. Within manufacturing the share of total employment in small firms fell during the 1950s and 1960s, rose slowly in the 1970s and increased significantly in the early 1980s. Moreover, in comparison with the mid-1970s, the death rate of small firms fell in the early 1980s (Rainnie, 1985). Some of this growth is likely to be accounted for by the rise of small firms in high-technology industries, although the current indications are that these are few in number with limited potential for job growth (see Gould and Keeble, 1984). A far greater number of small firms, as we shall see, are likely to have grown in response to changes in the organization of large firms.

The largest number of small firms, however, are not in manufacturing but in the service sector. The size of workplace in many of the service industries has generally been smaller than in manufacturing. Think of the number of small business offices and the multitude of small retail firms. This raises an interesting point. With the decline of manufacturing generally, and large firms in particular, the rise in the *share* of total employment within small firms has to be seen in the context of the *structural shift* in the UK economy from manufacturing to services. Put another way, as the proportion of manufacturing employment in the economy declines, so the share of service sector employment grows, and with it the proportion of employment in small firms. This is not to deny that there has been a growth of small firms in the economy; it is merely to situate this growth in a broader structural context.

Within the service sector, too, there has been a growth in the number of service firms since the mid-1970s. Much of this growth, as indicated in Chapter 3, is attributable to the externalization of services by the larger manufacturing and service firms. Many of these activities such as cleaning, catering, security and a range of business services have been contracted out to small service firms. A similar process of externalization has occurred between large and small manufacturing firms, as we shall shortly see. Finally, it is also important to bear in mind that many public sector services, in particular central government services, are organized around large establishments. This is changing, albeit slowly; nonetheless the point is significant when it is recalled that much of the debate concerning organizational size and the fragmentation of workforces has revolved around *private* and not public industries.

5.2.4 Fragmentation strategies

So far, a number of trends have been isolated which point towards a reversal of the shift towards organizational centralization in the 1950s and 1960s. Are these trends an indication of a new disorganized phase of capitalism, heralding the demise of the large firm, or a limited organizational response to economic recession? As with many of the questions in this book, our answers will be open-ended. One way of approaching this question is to assess whether the processes of fragmentation are *formal* rather than *actual* (Rainnie, 1985). By this, I do not mean that the trends identified are false or over-emphasized; the signs of fragmentation are clear enough. They are not at issue. The issue is the *kinds* of economic relationships that exist between large firms and small firms, and between large enterprises and their small plants, in a period of economic restructuring. To talk, on one hand, of the decline of large firms and, on the other hand, of the growth of small firms and small plants, may divert attention away from the links between firms. In particular, it may serve to obscure the forms of market and non-market interactions between firms and the economic circumstances in which those forms are *altered* and *remade*.

One example which neatly illustrates the nature of some of the relationships involved is the role of small firms and small plants in the current period of restructuring. To date, one of the clearest accounts of the kinds of relationship operating between large and small units of production has been given by Shutt and Whittington (1987). Following Tarling (1981), they identify two general types of small firm – *independent* and *dependent*. Independent small firms are loosely divided into two kinds. One kind competes in the market with large firms, often by intensifying the work process, that is, by working both labour and machinery harder. In some cases, they can profitably fill gaps in the market created by the withdrawal of large firms in a period of recession. The other kind of independent small firm does not compete with large firms, but operates in small, specialized or local 'niche' markets, often by adopting the advantages of new technologies. Dependent small firms complement the operations of large firms, for example, through subcontracting arrangements to meet fluctuations in market activity or to service the peripheral needs of large firms. In that sense, they are dependent upon the requirements of large firms and the success of those firms.

Shutt and Whittington go on to argue that the growth and fortunes of each of these types of small firms are, in different ways, locked into a set of relationships which are largely determined by the actions of larger firms. The thrust of the argument is that the growth of small firms is partly explained by the fragmentation strategies of large firms. In the wake of recession, the use of small firms by large firms enables the latter to displace the fluctuations of the market onto the former. The use of small firms and the shift of production into smaller plants also, it is argued, enable large firms to gain a more effective control over the labour processes within their plants and in other small firms. The shift of production away from existing large plants into smaller decentralized units, for example, is seen to reduce the power of organized workforces and enhance the ability of the company to introduce flexible working practices.

Three different types of fragmentation strategy are identified, which are summarized in Table 5.3. The use of the strategies varies from industry to industry and individual firms may use them in combination, separately or in tandem with strategies of labour market flexibility (see section 5.3.1). Each strategy involves a different form of relationship between large and small units. Decentralization of production involves the break-up of large plants into a number of smaller plants, with formal ownership responsibilities retained by the large firm. Devolvement strategies involve the transfer of ownership responsibilities to smaller firms, whilst the larger firms retain a guaranteed revenue through licensing or franchise agreements. In this way the larger companies avoid the responsibilities of labour organization and are protected from the fluctuations of the market. Finally, disintegration strategies are also characterized by the shifting of ownership responsibilities onto smaller firms, but in this case the large firms retain control through their market power. This may take the form of contractual agreements between large and small firms whereby the latter are dependent upon the 'make or buy' decisions of the large firms. Small firms, in this instance, can be locked into a relationship with larger firms which enables the latter to control 'at a distance' the operations of the small firms without having to shoulder the responsibilities of ownership (Sayer, 1985). So, even if you are working in a small firm, as opposed to a small plant that is, the economic prospects of the firm may still be locked into the dynamics of the larger firms. Examples of two of the three types of fragmentation strategy are given in Extract 4.

Table 5.3   Fragmentation strategies

Large firm strategy	To manage	Outcome	Large firm/small unit link
1 Decentralization	Demand risk. Labour process control. Innovation risk.	Small plants	Ownership
2 Devolvement	Demand risk. Labour process control.	Small firms	License, franchise
3 Disintegration	Demand risk. Labour process control. Innovation risk.	Small firms	Market-power. Ability to re-purchase.

Source: Shutt and Whittington, 1987

Extract 4

Fragmentation strategies in the North West

Kelloggs

Kelloggs provides an instance of decentralization of production which originated from management's need during the late 1970s and early 1980s both to reassert control over the labour process within the firm and to cater for product innovation ... Kelloggs, which operates in twenty countries throughout the world, had first established its breakfast cereal plant at Trafford Park, Manchester, in 1938. Trafford Park became the second largest cereal factory in the world, producing over 10.25 million packets of cornflake and rice crispies per week and employing 2,085 people in 1980. Forty years of continuous production at one site in an expanding product market produced a strong trade union organization. At the same time, growing consumer demand for healthier food products combined with criticisms of its monopolistic position in the United Staes, was forcing the company into a vigorous new product development programme originating from its Fort Custer research centre.

   In the late 1970s, Kelloggs UK had already begun the process of decentralizing production away from Manchester. Printing operations were first separated out and hived off to new plant at Irlam. Then, as new products were introduced, new plant was opened up in Skelmersdale to produce waffles and in Wrexham for Super

Noodles, bran products and muesli. Following the prolonged ten-week strike at the Trafford Park plant in 1979, management decentralized production further by developing new 'buffer' warehousing units (in Farnworth, for example) away from the main manufacturing facility ... During the early 1980s, production and employment continued to expand at Wrexham, while Trafford Park contracted as new production technologies were introduced ...

Chloride

Chloride provides an example of both decentralization and dis-integration in the North West. Swinton, near Manchester, was Chloride's original site, dating from 1891. By the mid-seventies about four thousand people were employed at the site, making automotive, motive power, standby and defence batteries. There were about two thousand shopfloor workers, almost all male, organized by the TGWU. A Combine and a Joint Negotiating Committee linked Swinton with the automotive batteries plant at Dagenham but not with Chloride's other smaller plants. However, Michael Edwardes, Chairman since 1971, was implementing a divisive divisionalization programme through the Group, which had already split Swinton into four separate profit centres (*Financial Times*, 22 July 1975). Moreover, in 1975, work had begun on a new plant at Over Hulton, a few miles from Swinton ...

The new Over Hulton site opened in 1979, and four hundred workers were shifted from Swinton to make the motive and multipower batteries. The two sites remained part of the same TGWU branch, and initially negotiated together. However, in 1981, Chloride ended these joint negotiating procedures too.

The recession brought 1,100 shopfloor redundancies in the years 1980 and 1981 at Swinton. The 140 compulsory redundancies of August 1980 had been made with no notice. Decentralization and dis-integration accelerated.

Originally, there had been two lead smelting furnaces at Swinton and one at Dagenham. In 1972, Chloride had bought a company with smelters at Abbeywood, London, and at Wakefield. These smelters had received heavy investment, Swinton's very little, while Dagenham's was closed down. As demand turned down, Swinton's first furnace was closed in 1979. The second Swinton smelter was closed in 1981, but the threat of strike action helped to win the thirty workers involved redeployment elsewhere on the site.

Swinton also had a joinery shop, making wooden battery cases. Its manager was offered the work on a sub-contracting basis, and in 1980 a separate company called KLS Joinery Services Ltd. was set up on the nearby Wardle Industrial Estate. Chloride gave guarantees for the new company's overdraft and leases to the amount of £375,000. Only forty workers were taken on by KLS, about forty other joiners being made redundant. The workers who were taken on had to take a pay cut of about 10% and had their wages frozen for the first year of operations.

1980 also saw the similar break-up of the printing department, whose manager set up a new firm on another nearby industrial estate, taking only about thirty of the forty women who had formerly been employed at Swinton. In the same year, the Kings Lynn separator plant was sold off, with supplies henceforth being bought-in from France, Spain and Germany ... by 1985, there were only nine hundred people employed at Swinton, of which 485 were shopfloor TGWU members.

Source: Shutt and Whittington, 1987

Such strategies are also likely to have spatial implications, of which the most significant is probably the break-up of the spatial concentrations of employment in the old industrial centres and the growth of small firms and small plants in different locations. In Shutt and Whittington's view the deliberate dispersal of investment and contracts is likely to occur where the main reason for fragmentation is the reassertion of control over the labour process. Dispersal, in this instance, as we shall consider in section 5.4, may be part of a wider strategy by large firms to undermine union organization across plants and devolve responsibility for pay and working conditions to 'local' management. Although there will be exceptions, the geography of dispersal is seen by Shutt and Whittington to favour the more sparsely populated regions and thus reinforce the shift in employment from the cities and conurbations to the smaller towns and peripheral rural areas. But there is no inevitability about this pattern of dispersal. If fragmentation continues, it may well take a spatially reconcentrated form, with clusters of firms supplying one another in central locations. Disintegration strategies, for example, may involve little spatial dispersal; the firms involved may be a stone's throw away from each other.

No spatial form, then, can be 'read off' from the strategies of fragmentation. But what of the strategies themselves: do they represent a long-term and irreversible feature of industrial organization? Much depends upon whether the strategies are short-term responses to the economic downturn of the late 1970s and 1980s, in which case it is possible that large firms will respond to an economic upturn by recentralizing employment. For example, they may reabsorb the activities of small dependent firms within larger plants or re-enter the markets currently served by small independent firms. But, if the arguments of Piore and Sabel spelt out in Chapter 4 are valid, then the fragmentation of larger firms may be the result of fundamental shifts in the organization of production and the reorganization of control networks, in which case the trend towards smaller workplaces and smaller firms may well continue. Either direction is possible.

Whatever the outcome, and it may well vary from industry to industry, two points are important to bear in mind. First, whether the future geography of the firm is one of spatial concentration or dispersal, it is likely to be substantially different from the geography laid down by the older, larger manufacturing firms in previous decades. In that sense, the spatial fix established by large firms within the old industrial centres which shaped distinctive regional economies is in the process of dissolution. Left to market forces, if economic recovery involves the recentralization of employment within some industries, it will not necessarily take place in the 'old' manufacturing cities and regions, with their established patterns of labour organization and work practices. Second, if the trend towards the fragmentation of the firm continues, this does not necessarily imply that there will be a similar economic deconcentration of industry. The ownership and control of industry remains relatively concentrated, as indicated by Figure 5.1. The form of the relationship between firms may change: for example, large firms may no

longer own their small counterpart, but they may well control them through
devolvement strategies. In this instance the process of fragmentation is
formal rather than actual insofar as a clear relationship of dominance and
subordination is involved, despite the actual separation of ownership (Rainnie, 1985).

Summary of section 5.2

• Changes in the post-war structure of the economy, in particular from the
1960s onwards, have eroded the distinctiveness of regional economies and
placed greater importance on the differences of industrial structure within
regions.

• According to Lash and Urry, the development of distinct regional
economies organized around a handful of industries in major urban locations is a characteristic spatial structure of 'organized capitalism'. Under
'disorganized capitalism', this particular 'spatial fix' has begun to dissolve
and a more dispersed geography of employment, favouring the rural
periphery and smaller cities, is emerging. The long-term character of this
new pattern of uneven development is unresolved.

• Since the 1970s there has been an overall reduction in the average size of
workplaces as employment in large plants has fallen and the number of
workers in small firms has increased. Large manufacturing firms have increased the number of plants they operate, whilst reducing the numbers
employed in each plant. The growth of employment within the service sector
has also contributed to the rise in the number of small firms in the economy.

• No disagreement has arisen over the nature of these changes, but there
are different views about the significance of such trends: whether they
represent long-term changes of a disorganizing kind or short-term organizational responses to recession.

5.3   The restructuring of the labour market

Alongside the debate over the changing size and organization of the workplace, a related debate has arisen over the changing composition and structure of the workforce, and the organization of work. And the two are
connected. The break-up of the large firms, the reduction in the average size
of workforces and the establishment of production in new locations are
linked in certain ways to changes in the proportion of male and female
employment, the growth of part-time and temporary work and the introduction of new ways of working. In short, the restructuring of the workplace is
bound up with the restructuring of the workforce and the nature of work.
Today, you are not only more likely to be working in the service sector, in a
small firm, perhaps, or in the public sector, but there is also a greater

likelihood that you will be employed on a part-time or temporary basis. In 1987, for example, one in five workers were employed on a part-time basis, and the number of temporary workers had been put at over one and a half million, some seven per cent of the total workforce (Hakim, 1987).

Statistics of this kind, however, can only take us so far. The fragmentation of the **labour market** requires interpretation, and this is our concern here. In this section some of the arguments for and against the view that firms are restructuring their internal labour markets into a *core* and a *periphery* workforce to achieve greater flexibility and efficiency from their employees will be explored. Section 5.3.1 sets out the theoretical views of Atkinson (1984, 1985) and others who argue that the core/periphery model is a new, structural feature of the labour market, one born of recession but likely to persist because of changes in technology and the structure of markets. The evidence for this view is assessed in section 5.3.2. The contrary view, that much of the core/periphery argument refers to established features of the post-war labour market and that recent trends are little more than adjustments to familiar patterns of labour segmentation, is discussed in 5.3.3.

5.3.1 The flexible workforce?

On the basis of case-study research, Atkinson has argued that firms are dividing their workforces into 'core' and 'peripheral' groups in order to achieve different kinds of flexibility. A model of the new flexible firm is set out in Figure 5.2. Core workers comprise the full-time, permanent employees of a company who enjoy job security and high earnings in return for performing a wide range of tasks that cut across 'old' skill demarcation lines. They are *functionally flexible*. As the nature of a firm's operation changes, as their markets for different products alter, so core workers acquire and use a variety of skills to perform different tasks. Typical members of this core are managerial and professional staff and the multi-skilled worker. The central characteristic of this group is that their skills are not readily available in the wider labour market. The firm therefore will attempt to retain this group of workers and separate them from the external labour market.

Around the core is a series of outer layers, each representing a different group of peripheral workers. The first peripheral group are also full-time workers, but they enjoy less job security and career prospects than the core group. They are hired from the external labour market to fill specific jobs, usually of a semi-skilled nature. Lack of career opportunities and the routine nature of the tasks performed encourages a high degree of labour turnover. They are *numerically flexible*. The second peripheral group includes part-time workers and a variety of temporary workers ranging from agency staff, people on short-term contracts, government training schemes to home-workers. They perform the same type of tasks as the first peripheral group, but they are employed on a contract basis designed to supplement numerical flexibility. They are hired and laid off in accordance with the fluctuating levels of a firm's production. The availability of this source of labour enables

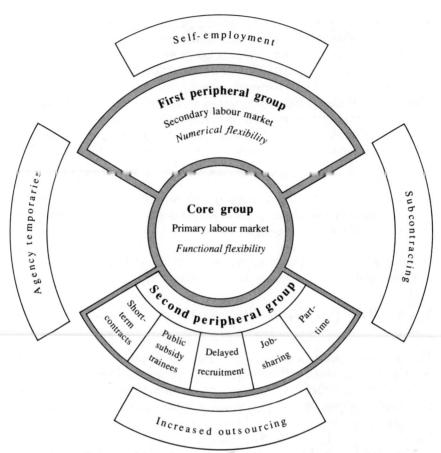

Figure 5.2   The flexible firm   *Source: Atkinson, 1984*

firms to increase or decrease the number of workers employed in response to market trends. As the scale of a firm's operation changes so, in turn, the size of this peripheral group increases or decreases. Finally, there is a group of external workers not employed directly by the firm who perform either very specialized or very routine tasks such as cleaning or security. Numerical flexibility is achieved by employing workers through the use of subcontracting arrangements, outsourcing, self-employment and so on.

The model is an 'ideal-type', one which fits few companies, although a number are seen to approximate to its general features. To date, this precise pattern of segmentation is acknowledged by Atkinson to be limited to a handful of mainly foreign-owned firms, concentrated in particular industries. The significance of the 'flexible firm' for Atkinson, however, is not limited to these few examples, for two reasons. Firstly, because he believes that firms are beginning to restructure their internal labour markets in this direction. The term *internal labour markets* refers to the structure of jobs and promotion ladders within a firm which are insulated from the market mechanisms that govern the supply of and demand for labour outside a firm.

And, secondly, because he considers that the changes in the national labour market noted earlier also point to developments in this direction.

Evidence in support of the former contention is restricted mainly to case-study materials and surveys of changing work patterns within firms. One of Atkinson's frequently quoted studies, *Changing Working Patterns and Practices* (NEDC, 1985), involved a survey of seventy-two firms employing 660 000 people in the food and drink industry, engineering, retailing and financial services and claims that sixty-four of the seventy-two firms had increased the numerical flexibility of their workforce since 1980. The strategies varied from firm to firm, but the general claim was that firms were making greater use of peripheral workers to meet fluctuations in demand. Just over two-thirds of the firms had increased their employment of temporary workers, the majority in the previous five years. Nearly three-quarters had increased their use of subcontractors and almost one-fifth had made greater use of self-employed workers in the previous five years. Similar evidence of firms attempting to achieve greater flexibility in work organization was also found in a study of thirty-one firms by Atkinson and Meager (1986).

Evidence on the extent to which firms are attempting to gain greater functional flexibility from a core of permanent, secure workers is also acknowledged by Atkinson to be rather thin and, at present, limited to a number of large, capital-intensive firms in the manufacturing sector. The actual number of firms which have segmented their workforces along the lines of the core/periphery model is also few in number. Some of the better-known examples are set out in Extract 5.

Extract 5

Core/periphery examples

- Control Data employs about 230 supplementals on 3-month and 10-month contracts to 'act as a buffer, protecting its 900 permanent employees'. The 'supplementals' have less good sick pay, holiday pay and pension provision.

- Manual workers at Findus, Long Benton, are divided into two groups. The first have a special clause added to their contracts saying that their employment could be terminated at any time, at one hour's notice without union approval. The second group do not have this insecurity clause.

- In Shell Carrington, all civil work (that is bricklaying, painting, etc), and some other work, such as lagging, is now contracted out; there are no civil craft workers on site and the company has ceased to recognise UCATT who used to organise there. When back-up is required, it now goes straight out to contractors without consultation with the unions. Many ex-Shell employees are now returning to work on a self-employed or 'Fixed-term Contract' basis. So, it is not the job being made redundant, but the worker/union member.

Source: Centre for Alternative Industrial and Technological Systems, 1986

If, however, a broader notion of flexibility is adopted, one that includes various combinations of changes in shift patterns and working hours, the promotion of team working, the reduction of demarcation lines, retraining to acquire additional skills, inter-union flexibility and so on, then the extent of 'flexibilization' is greater. Even where such changes have been taking place, however, they may be partial or incomplete (Income Data Services, 1986). Interestingly, the main movements in this direction have often been contingent upon the development of new sites and the recruitment of a new workforce. The movement of industry, that is, the dispersal of plants to new locations, is thus wrapped up with attempts by firms to secure greater flexibility from their workforces and their technology. Geography here is thus an integral aspect of the restructuring of the workforce and the introduction of new work practices. The establishment of new plants in new locations, however, is no guarantee that such changes have taken place (ibid., 1986).

How, then, should the arguments for the 'flexible firm' be assessed? Two forms of assessment are open to us. The first is methodological. How convincing are the types of evidence used to support the flexible firm thesis? The second concerns the substantive claims made for flexibility. Is the interpretation of the evidence convincing? We will tackle the issue of evidence, before taking a closer look at alternative interpretations of the recent changes in the structure of the labour market in section 5.3.3.

5.3.2   Assessing the evidence

Atkinson draws upon two kinds of evidence to back up his argument: case-study materials and the wider, national changes in the external labour market. The first kind of evidence, the use of case studies to support a general argument raises a perennial problem for researchers, namely how to make sense of broad, national changes through knowledge of a limited range of case studies. How representative were the case studies? Interestingly, Atkinson made no claims to representativeness. Neither of the two main studies referred to above were representative of either the four sectors chosen in the study of seventy-two firms or representative of the economy in the study of the thirty-one firms. In the larger study the selection of the firms was guided by the acknowledged need of the firms to reorganize internally to maintain a competitive advantage and in the smaller study the firms were chosen because they had actually introduced measures to promote greater flexibility. Does this lack of representativeness, the acknowledged bias in the selection of the firms, undermine the thesis? It certainly exposes the argument to criticisms of exaggeration and overstatement (Casey, 1987).

The evidence from the 1984 Workplace Industrial Relations Survey, for example, does not confirm the 'flexible firm' thesis (Millward and Stevens, 1986). Covering the period from 1980 to 1984 and involving over two thousand establishments with over twenty-five employees in the private and public sectors, the survey found little evidence of substantial change in employment practices. The results indicate a small increase in the use of part-time workers, mainly in educational institutions in the public sector, no change in the use of workers on short-term contracts, a significant decline in the use of freelancers, and a substantial decline in the use of homeworkers and outworkers. On the basis of this evidence, in relation to establishments with twenty-five or more workers, there appears to be little use by firms of groups in the peripheral workforce in the first half of the 1980s.

Activity 5.2

Does the evidence of the 1984 Workplace Industrial Relations Survey invalidate the claim that the *direction* of change within firms is towards flexible labour practices? Consider the following questions:

(a)   The WIR Survey involved a sample of over 2000 establishments in contrast to the small-scale surveys and case-study materials presented by Atkinson. Is an economic change important only if it is statistically widespread? There are more small firms in the economy, for example, than large firms. Is the numerical dominance of small firms matched by a more significant role in the economy than that of large firms?

(b)   The flexible firm model is acknowledged as an analytical tool designed to aid our understanding of what is happening to the structure of labour markets. Is it possible to judge the validity of the model in isolation from some of the wider structural changes occurring in the economy? Consider the application of new technologies and the implications of flexible specialization for the way that goods and services are produced, and the consequences of the fragmentation strategies adopted by firms. None of these changes is representative of all firms in the economy. Does this diminish their *structural* significance?

We will return to this issue in section 5.3.3. First, however, there is another kind of evidence to consider.

The second kind of evidence used by Atkinson to support his argument, the wider trends in the external labour market, raises a different set of questions about the validity and extent of the 'flexible firm' model. If manufacturing firms are increasing their use of peripheral groups to obtain greater flexibility, we would expect to see a recent upturn in the proportion of peripheral workers in the total workforce. The evidence is not clear-cut, but there are some indications of growth in the peripheral workforce. Much of this growth, however, has taken place within the service industries rather than in the manufacturing sector and is not easily traced to service firms adopting 'flexible' strategies. A closer look at the three groups of workers which comprise the majority of the peripheral workforce – part-time labour, temporary workers and the self-employed – is required before any firm conclusions are drawn.

Part-time labour

Over the post-war period **part-time employment** has been growing steadily in the UK. As full-time jobs have declined, part-time working, and especially women's part-time employment, has become a major characteristic of the post-war labour force. As Figure 5.3 indicates, the number of part-timers rose by 4.7 million between 1951 and 1987, to account for some 23 per cent of

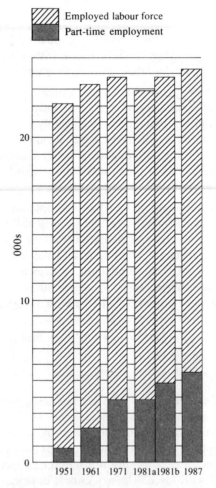

Figure 5.3   The growth of part-time work in Britain, 1951–87

Data for 1951, 1961 and 1971 refer to people aged 15 and over; data for 1981 refer to people aged 16 and over. The higher figure for 1981 and those for 1987 are derived from the Department of Employment estimates; all other figures are self-reported in the Censuses of those years. Part-timers are those usually working 30 hours or less per week excluding overtime and meal breaks.

Source: Data from Censuses of Population and Department of Population in Hakim, 1987, Table 7, p. 555

the total workforce. Increasingly, the dominant images of paid work as full-time and workers as male are at odds with the shifts in the labour force.

The most striking feature about part-time jobs, as noted in Chapter 3, is that the majority are concentrated in the service industries, in health and education, retailing, hotels and catering, and a wide variety of miscellaneous services. Unlike the public sector services, many of the private services are expanding and so too is the substitution between full-time and part-time employees (Robertson, Briggs and Goodchild, 1982). In contrast, part-time working in manufacturing fell in the 1970s, a loss of some 85 000 jobs and this trend has continued in the first half of the 1980s. In so far as the 'flexible firm' proponents look to manufacturing firms to support their argument, then, it is not borne out by the national trends.

We might reasonably suppose that these figures weaken Atkinson's argument. They certainly do not support it, but neither are they sufficient to undermine it. Despite the small, declining proportion of part-timers in manufacturing, some interesting trends have emerged. Beechey's (1987b) survey of part-time work in Coventry's manufacturing industry, for instance, identified a different set of reasons behind the use of part-time labour in the 1970s from that of the 1950s and 1960s. In the earlier period of sustained economic growth she attributes the use of part-timers primarily to labour shortages relative to wages or the inability of firms to attract full-time labour. In the 1970s, and the onset of economic recession, she found that part-timers were employed to maintain continuous production, 'to provide a flexible labour force over the working day or working week, and to fill in gaps and cope with overflow' (p. 157). The same empirical trend, therefore, the use of part-time labour, is attributable to a different set of causes in the two periods (see also *Hudson*, 1988).

The use of the term 'flexible', in this context, however, requires qualification. Beechey's use of the term does not possess the same connotations of 'disposability' that are implied by the requirements of numerical flexibility. The employment relation is not one of insecurity or instability, but it is one that involves flexibility of time. The same can be said for the use of part-time employment in the service industries, which is geared primarily to match working hours to periods of customer demand or operating requirements, thereby containing labour costs (Robinson and Wallace, 1984; Robinson, 1985). Overall, the use of part-time workers has enabled employers to cheapen labour costs by adjusting their labour requirements to the daily or weekly fluctuations in demand for products and services which can be foreseen but not evened out (Robinson, 1985, p. 28).

Furthermore, within the service sector this particular use of part-time labour appears to pre-date the onset of recession and reflects the type of jobs available within certain industries – low-skilled, low-paid, with limited career prospects – and their occupants: women. Not surprisingly, the growth and location of part-time work is a reflection of the growth of specific service industries and their geography; it is concentrated in the South East and South West, although the North West and Scotland also registered high growth rates (Townsend, 1986). It is odd, then, that Atkinson does not centrally consider in his work the largest employer of part-time workers – the service industries – or the reasons for their consistent use in the post-war period.

Self-employment

After part-time workers, the self-employed are the next largest group within the 'peripheral' workforce. The exact numbers of the self-employed are difficult to calculate, given the degree of overlap between the three peripheral groups. In the mid-1980s, for example, one-fifth of the self-employed were also part-timers, as were over half of all temporary workers (Hakim, 1987). That aside, it would appear that the number of self-employed has risen sharply since the late 1970s. Figure 5.4 shows that between the mid-1960s and the early 1970s, self-employment rose and then fell, rising again in the late 1970s and early 1980s to just under 10 per cent of the workforce, one in ten of the working population.

As with part-time labour, however, much of this growth is concentrated in the service sector. According to the 1984 Labour Force survey, three industries accounted for two-thirds of all self-employment – distribution, hotels and catering, and construction. Miscellaneous services accounted for a further 10 per cent, as did agriculture. The corresponding figure for manufacturing was around 8 per cent. The pattern mirrors the growth of services in the south outlined in Chapter 3, with just over half of the UK's self-employed concentrated in the three southern regions – the South East, the South West and East Anglia. The South East alone accounted for just over a third of all self-employment (Creigh *et al.*, 1986). These figures, then, add little support to the view that the growth of self-employment is connected with the adoption of 'flexible' strategies by manufacturing firms.

It is difficult to draw any clear conclusions, however, as the reasons behind the recent growth in self-employment are many and varied. They range from the substitution of self-employed workers for employees, the rise in the number of unemployed workers, to the introduction of government employment schemes which help the unemployed into self-employment and the growth of the privatization programme (*Labour Research*, 1986). The relative weight of these factors and the degree of permanence attached to the self-employment created is, at present, open to speculation.

Temporary labour

Compared with the data on part-time labour and self-employment there is an even greater difficulty in obtaining reliable figures on the growth and size of the **temporary labour** force in the post-war period. The distinction between 'temporary' and 'permanent' employment, for example, has no clear legal basis and is thus difficult to establish. Like the category of self-employment, the term 'temporary' is a rather fluid, imprecise term which

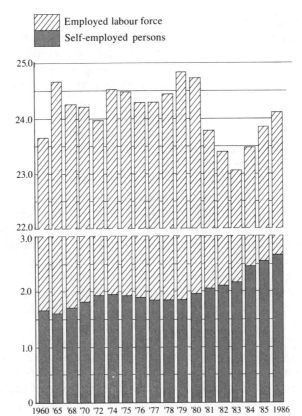

Figure 5.4 Self-employed persons as a proportion of the employed labour force, Great Britain, selected years 1960–86

Source: Employment Gazette, *February 1987, Historical Supplement No. 1, Table 1.1, p. 4*

has been interpreted in various ways. In recent surveys, estimates of the size of the temporary labour force varies from 6 per cent in the Policy Studies Institute study (Casey, 1987) to just under 8 per cent of the total workforce in the Institute of Manpower Studies study (Meager, 1986). Its rate of growth, however, is impossible to gauge as previous surveys were not conducted on a comparable basis. Nevertheless, some indications of the role of temporary labour in the economy can be drawn from the above surveys.

Both surveys show that temporary work is high among service sector employees, particularly within distribution, hotels and catering and miscellaneous services. There is evidence to suggest that the fastest growth of temporary work is in the public sector services, primarily education, health and public administration. Together, these two groups of industries account for nearly two-thirds of the temporary labour force. Many of the reasons given by employers for the employment of temporary labour were of a traditional nature – to cover for sickness, maternity leave and vacations, to cope with seasonal peaks, to cope with fluctuating workloads and so forth. There is, however, some evidence in the IMS survey to support the view that firms have increased their employment of temporary labour to avoid a commitment to employing permanent workers in the face of market uncertainty.

This is an interesting finding. Although this new use of temporary labour by firms was numerically less significant than traditional concerns, it does represent a potential trend towards a greater use of temporary labour. This view is lent support by the findings of a survey of seven hundred large employers (over 5000 employees) which indicated that just under a fifth *expected* to increase the proportion of temporary workers in their workforce over the five-year period 1985 to 1989 (CBI 1985a,b cited in Hakim, 1987). Expectations, however, are a rather different kind of evidence from current practices (the stress here is upon the difference, not upon the status of the two kinds of evidence).

The findings of the Policy Studies Institute are rather different in this respect. They found little evidence of the new reasons for the employment of temporary labour and suggest that the idea of the 'flexible firm' is over-stated, in as far as 'new' temporary working is restricted to only a small number of firms. The study concludes by reiterating the point that employers' use of temporary labour largely reflects traditional patterns rather than a new employment practice (Casey, 1987). The evidence on trends in temporary work is thus inconclusive and far from comprehensive.

What conclusions can be drawn from this brief review of the trends in the growth of the three largest groups of 'peripheral' workers? One point is evident. It is a dubious practice to cite changes in the structure of the *external* (national) labour market as confirmation of an argument about the increased segmentation of firms' *internal* labour markets. True, the structure of the labour force has been changing rapidly in recent years, but much of the growth of part-time labour, self-employment and temporary labour is attributable to the sectoral shift in the structure of the economy – from manufacturing to services. The growth of service sector employment and the decline of manufacturing have thus increased the proportion of 'peripheral' workers in the total workforce. Moreover, it is difficult to trace the majority of this increase to any new developments in employment practices, as is implied by proponents of the 'flexible firm' thesis. What we appear to be seeing is more of the same or rather a continuation of established trends. It could be argued, therefore, that those advocating the flexible firm thesis have 'stretched' the empirical evidence on labour market changes to support the thesis.

Is this a reasonable criticism? It may be reasonable, but I am not sure that it is an adequate criticism. If all that is being evaluated is the quantitative 'fit' of the model, then this overlooks the more abstract claims of the argument, that the emerging division between a core and peripheral workforce is connected with wider changes in the structure of the UK economy. Knowledge claims of this kind cannot be assessed directly on the basis of statistical trends, there is a qualitative dimension involved which requires that the interpretative framework and the connections drawn are also evaluated.

5.3.3   The rediscovery of flexibility?

There are two related ways in which the interpretative framework of the flexible firm thesis has been called into question. The first takes issue with the originality of the thesis and argues that many aspects of the flexibility argument refer to commonplace features of industrial relations practices in the post-war period (*Hudson*, 1988; MacInnes, 1987; Pollert, 1987). The second criticism is directed at the connection drawn between, on the one hand, flexible labour market practices and, on the other hand, the 'Japanization' of management styles and the potential of flexible specialization discussed in the previous chapter (Pollert, 1987).

The nature of the first objection to the flexible firm thesis is that employers have always sought flexibility of labour and flexibility of working practices from their workforces. There is nothing new about a core and a peripheral workforce, and nor is there anything particularly new about employers attempting to erode traditional job demarcations, reduce overtime working and alter shift patterns to obtain greater flexibility from their workforce. The latter, it is argued, is typical of productivity agreements in British industry in the 1960s and 1970s, with management encouraging workforces to bargain away inflexible working practices in return for wage increases (MacInnes, 1987).

As for the core/periphery model, this is seen as a reconstruction of existing dual labour market models, which split the workforce into primary and secondary type employment. In its initial formulation by Doeringer and Piore (1971) large, technologically advanced firms, with a considerable measure of control over their product, sought a relatively stable, skilled workforce. As the kind of skills required are relatively scarce in the labour market, employers sought to attract and retain such workers by providing good wages and secure working conditions. These workers enjoy primary type employment. In contrast, secondary jobs are to be found in firms operating in highly competitive markets and are characterized by low pay, instability of employment and poor working conditions. Workers in this section of the labour market are taken on and laid off in accordance with fluctuations in market demand. There have been many revisions to this dual labour market model: the identification of sub-markets within the primary sector, the overlap between the sub-markets, and the recognition that organized workers also influence the shape of these markets. The notion of a polarized workforce, however, is a persistent theme.

In this sense, the only real difference that is seen between the presence of a dual labour market in Britain in the 1960s and 1970s and now, is the economic climate in which calls for greater flexibility are being made, namely one of high unemployment and a weaker trade union movement. In this climate, the rediscovery of flexibility is considered to serve an ideological role for companies who are seeking a more flexible use of labour: it legitimizes casualization and unemployment in the name of 'progress' (Pollert, 1987).

Anticipating this kind of criticism, Atkinson and Gregory (1986) acknowledge the weakness of labour in the present climate to resist employers' proposals on greater work flexibility. Any response from labour, however, has to recognize the connection between wider changes in the organization of the economy and attempts by companies to introduce flexible working practices. It is, they argue, the *combination* of changes occurring – in the way that new technologies are changing production processes, and creating more effective decentralized management structures to co-ordinate an increasingly fragmented and dispersed labour force – that makes flexibility a new and structurally significant feature of economic organization. In this broader context, attempts by companies to implement flexible labour strategies should be seen as one of a battery of flexible strategies that are currently restructuring British industry. Examined from this angle, the long-term trends in 'peripheral' forms of employment discussed earlier have led to a major restructuring of the labour force in the 1980s. If this is so, then flexible work arrangements may be part of the shift from Fordism to neo-Fordism discussed in the previous chapter.

This leads on to the second reservation that has been expressed about the flexible firm thesis, which is that many of the connections drawn between flexible labour markets and other kinds of flexibility with respect to labour processes, product markets, management practices and the like are not yet in place. The scenario of flexible specialization outlined in the previous chapter, with its emphasis upon small-batch, customized production taking place in small, decentralized units, is a limited one. And so, too, is the adoption of Japanese management practices and forms of economic organization within British industry. Indeed, the attempt to attract Japanese and other foreign firms to Britain is not especially to do with widespread job creation; it is rather their role as innovators of management strategies and forms of work organization which is considered significant (*Hudson*, 1988). Talk of flexible firms in this context is thus seen as prescriptive rather than descriptive of actual trends (Pollert, 1987).

An evaluation of the impact and potential scope of these 'newer' elements is beyond the scope of this chapter. If, however, it is the case that the language of flexibility has been rediscovered by British companies, the potential is also there for its rediscovery by the labour movement. Flexibility of work can also mean that people should enjoy greater flexibility over their working lives – over working time, over the type of work done, and over job control. The direction of change within firms does not favour this view of flexibility, nor does the current economic climate and increasingly volatile markets. This view of flexibility, however, merely serves as a reminder that the breadth of the term, the number of changes that can be subsumed under the label of flexibility, also leaves it open to serve the interests of workers as well as employers (Beechey, 1987b).

Summary of section 5.3

• One of the claims advanced for the growth of 'flexibilization' within the British economy is that firms are beginning to reorganize their internal labour markets into core and peripheral workforces to achieve both functional and numerical flexibility.

• The evidence for this shift has been called into question for its lack of representativeness and the failure to recognize the long-standing use of peripheral labour in British industry. Against this, it is possible to consider the issue of *numerical dominance* separately from the question of *structural dominance*. Moreover, the degree of quantitative 'fit' between theory and evidence overlooks the qualitative dimension of theory assessment.

• In a qualitative vein, the flexible firm thesis has been criticized for its lack of originality, its rediscovery of dual labour markets in the UK and traditional productivity agreements. In defence of the flexible firms thesis, it is argued that it is one of a number of simultaneous changes taking place in the economy that are moving it in the direction of 'flexibilization'. It is a 'new' thesis in so far as it is part of a long-term shift in the organization of production and markets in the UK economy.

5.4 Trade unions at the crossroads

The debate over what is happening to trade unions in the UK is also wrapped around long-term views of what is happening to the UK economy. It has two versions. The first version bears a certain resemblance to the structure of the 'flexible firm debate'. It runs something like this.

There has been a rapid slide in trade union membership in the country since the late 1970s. What significance should we attach to this decline? Are the trade unions caught up in a trajectory of long-term decline, brought about by a shift in the balance of the economy from full-time employment in large, manufacturing plants to part-time workers in small, service firms? Or is the fall in trade union membership a short-term, cyclical phenomenon, a consequence of economic recession and an unfavourable political climate which has encouraged employers to withdraw trade union recognition? If the latter is the case, then there is nothing new about a fall in union membership; it has happened before, in the depths of the inter-war reces-sion, and the numbers rose in the subsequent economic upturn. If the former is true, then we are witnessing the inevitable demise of trade unionism in Britain.

Now, as far as I know, this is an illusory debate; no one holds either of these views in the form expressed here. True, no one denies the crucial significance of the rapid fall in manufacturing employment since the late 1970s and the impact of political legislation upon the organization and size of trade unions, but the real debate appears to be over how these short-term changes *in combination with* the longer-term changes in the structure of the economy and the labour force will affect the structure of trade unionism in the UK.

Approached in this way, the question of what is happening to trade unions in the UK appears more meaningful. Rather than speculate over their demise (it is still one of the largest union movements in the west; only Italy is comparable), it may be better to consider the changing direction of union-ism. What does the growth in employment in the service industries, the increase in white-collar workers and peripheral forms of employment, together with the decline in the size of workforces hold for the structure of unionism? Do the changes in the technology of production, of the kinds discussed in Chapter 4, which are altering the character of jobs and skills, and the increase in flexible working practices, add up to an irreversible shift in the direction of unionism? What direction is unionism likely to take if flexible specialization takes hold in various sectors of the economy. Like-wise, what would a post-Fordist unionism look like? On the political front, what are the long-term consequences for the trade union movement of the moves to privatize services or to decertify unions (for example, at GCHQ)?

The answers to many of these questions will only be apparent over time. Nonetheless, they are worth posing now as they convey something of the crossroads that confronts British trade unions. The various ways out of the crossroads will be addressed in section 5.4.3. Before doing so, we shall examine the nature of the transition period that, by all accounts, trade unions are going through. This is approached in two ways. First, section 5.4.1 charts the post-war changes in trade union membership and looks at some of the structural reasons advanced for its downturn since 1979. Then, in section 5.4.2, the focus shifts to the changes in the geography of trade unions and the impact that a more dispersed and fragmented industrial landscape has had upon structures of unionism.

5.4.1 The changing face of trade unionism

Figure 5.5 shows the rise and fall in trade union membership in Britain over the post-war period. Membership grew steadily through the 1950s and 1960s, followed by a period of strong growth in the 1970s. Between 1969 and 1979 membership grew by just under three million to reach an all-time peak

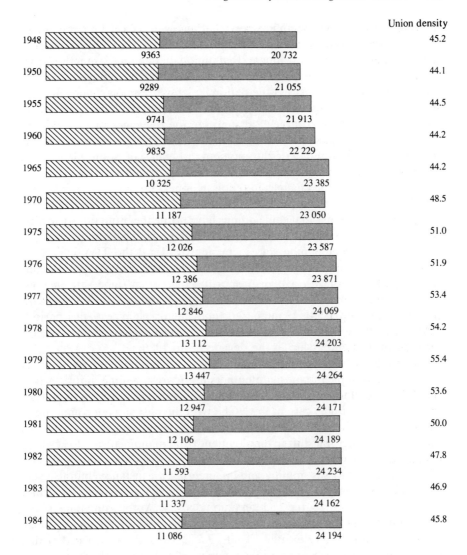

Union density

Year		Union density
1948	9363 / 20 732	45.2
1950	9289 / 21 055	44.1
1955	9741 / 21 913	44.5
1960	9835 / 22 229	44.2
1965	10 325 / 23 385	44.2
1970	11 187 / 23 050	48.5
1975	12 026 / 23 587	51.0
1976	12 386 / 23 871	51.9
1977	12 846 / 24 069	53.4
1978	13 112 / 24 203	54.2
1979	13 447 / 24 264	55.4
1980	12 947 / 24 171	53.6
1981	12 106 / 24 189	50.0
1982	11 593 / 24 234	47.8
1983	11 337 / 24 162	46.9
1984	11 086 / 24 194	45.8

Figure 5.5   Aggregate union membership and density in the UK, for selected years 1948–84

Source: Price and Bain, 1983; Annual Reports of the Certification Officer

of 55 per cent of the total workforce, that is, those in employment plus the unemployed. By the mid-1980s all the membership gains made in the 1970s had been lost and the density, that is, the proportion of the workforce in unions, had dropped to 45 per cent.

If, however, you exclude the unemployed from the workforce and consider only those in employment, you get a rather different picture – the fall in union density is less than half (Beaumont, 1987). This is not simply a statistical twist: how union density is measured has implications for any assessment of union strength in a period of recession. To include the unemployed in the workforce may give a distorted impression of union strength within industry: it would appear that union bargaining strength at the workplace has diminished considerably. To omit the unemployed from the calculation, however, distorts the national picture of union change and the impact that job losses have had upon the influence of the trade union movement in society at large. We shall see the relevance of this point in section 5.4.3 as it has some bearing upon how the direction of change within unionism is interpreted. For the moment, we can gain some idea of the impact of unemployment on union membership from Table 5.4.

The table shows the changes in union membership in the twenty largest unions in 1986 over the previous decade. Within the overall decline in membership, it is clear that some unions have borne the brunt of this decline whilst others have expanded. Despite amalgamations, the unions with a high proportion of their membership in manual trades – the TGWU, AEU, GWB, EEPTU and NUR – have suffered a disproportionate loss. In contrast, those unions with a high proportion of their membership in non-manual trades – BIFU, NALGO, NCU, COHSE and ASTMS – have, with the exception of the NUT, increased their membership over this period. TASS, the white-collar manufacturing union, also registered a significant increase in its membership in the decade up to 1986.

So what lies behind these changes? Clearly the rise in unemployment has had a marked impact upon the membership figures of some unions, while the growth of other unions, notably the NCU, reflects a process of merger between unions (in the case of the NCU, with the post and telecommunications workers in the CPSA). But there are more significant changes at work than this. The sectoral shift in employment from manufacturing to services discussed in Chapter 3 is one factor. The industries that have suffered considerable job losses, mining and engineering for instance, but also services such as transport, are also industries which traditionally have had highly unionized workforces, a high union density. At the same time, some of the fastest growing industries, those in the service sector, are among those with the lowest union densities. Table 5.5 sets out the contrast. On this evidence, it would appear that jobs are increasing in precisely those industries where trade unions have traditionally failed to organize the workforce.

It is hard to avoid the conclusion, then, that the sectoral shift from manufacturing to services has been a major factor in the overall reduction in the proportion of the workforce that is unionized in Britain. But this is not the whole picture. There are other considerations which cut across this conclusion. The first is that the growth sectors in manufacturing, such as the high-tech industries, also have a low proportion of union representation and this too works against the maintenance of union density in Britain (*Labour Research*, 1983). Secondly, even though the private sector services are poorly organized, union membership is on the increase in this sector, as is evident from Table 5.4. And, thirdly, any account of sectoral change also has to acknowledge the importance of union membership in the public

Table 5.4 The twenty biggest unions, 1986

Union (area of recruitment)	Number (% change since 1976)	Unions taken in since 1976
1 TGWU (transport and general)	1 377 944 (−29%)	agricultural workers, dyers & bleachers
2 AEU (engineers)	857 559 (−26%)	foundry & construction workers
3 GMB (general & municipal)	814 084 (−11%)	boilermakers & textile workers
4 NALGO (local government)	750 430 (+10%)	
5 NUPE (public employees)	657 633 (+1%)	
6 ASTMS (insurance, technical & managerial)	390 000 (+3%)	
7 USDAW (shopworkers)	381 984 (−7%)	
8 EETPU (electricians)	336 155 (−20%)	
9 UCATT (builders)	349 485 (−16%)	
10 TASS (manufacturing)	241 000 (+50%)	sheet metal workers, pattern makers, metal mechanics & tobacco workers
11 COHSE (health service)	212 312 (+6%)	
12 SOGAT (print)	199 594 (+3%)	NATSOPA
13 UCW (post office)	191 959 (−4%)	
14 NUT (teachers)	184 455 (−36%)	
15 BIFU (banking)	158 746 (+42%)	
16 NCU (post office engineers)	155 643 (+25%)	some transferred from CPSA
17 CPSA (civil servants)	150 514 (−35%)	some transferred to NCU
18 NGA (print)	125 587 (−17%)	SLADE
19 NUR (railway workers)	125 000 (−31%)	
20 NAS-UWT (teachers)	123 945 (+44%)	

TUC figures for December 1976 and 1986; ASTMS and TASS merged in 1987 to form MSF.
Source: *Labour Research*, Vol. 76, No. 9, 1987

service sector, the most highly unionized sector in the economy, higher, that is, than either manufacturing or private sector services. So the picture is not so much one of an increasingly non-unionized workforce, as one of a shift in the profile of unionism. The image of unionism as manufacturing-based is giving way to a service-based unionism, in both public and private services.

It is not all down to sectoral shifts, however; the issues discussed in sections 5.2 and 5.3, the changing size of the workplace and the changing composition of the workforce, also appear to have altered the profile of unionism. As the authors of the 1984 Workplace Industrial Relations Survey

Table 5.5   Employment changes and union density

Industry	Change in employment 1976–1986[1]	Union density 1984[2]
Banking, insurance & finance	+709 000	43%
Business services	+383 000[3]	21%
Hotel & catering	+211 000	21%
Wholesale distribution	+162 000	32%
Energy & water	−61 000	88%
Transport	−123 000	85%
Metals, mineral products	−290 000	68%
Vehicles & transport equipment	−322 000	81%
Metal goods & mechanical engineering	−493 000	55%

[1] *Department of Employment Gazette*, Historical Supplement, February 1987
[2] BWIR 1980–84 (Aldershot, Gower; 1986)
[3] Includes other services
Source: *Labour Research*, Vol. 76, No. 9, 1987

argue, 'the decline of union membership, union recognition and the closed shop in the private sector is clearly associated with the falling number of large workplaces employing predominantly male, manual, full-time employees' (Millward and Stevens, 1986, p. 298). Table 5.6 sets out the evidence behind this statement. Starting at the top, a fairly clear association is evident between size of establishment and union density. In small workplaces (25–49 employees) the average union density was 26 per cent, whereas in the largest workplace of 1000 or more the figure rose to 72 per cent. Moving down the table, you get a better idea of prevailing trends in union density. Workplaces that grew by 20 per cent or more between 1980 and 1984 had a low union density, while those that shrunk by 20 per cent or more had a much higher union density. There also appears to be a statistical relationship between the size of a firm and union membership levels. In firms of less than 100 employees union density averaged 20 per cent rising to just under 60 per cent in firms with 50000 or more workers. So, on this evidence, if you have a job with a small firm or work in a small workplace, it is less likely to be unionized.

Turning to the sections of Table 5.6 which look at workforce composition, it would appear that the shift away from manual work is associated with a decline in union membership. Only a quarter of the workforce is unionized in predominantly non-manual workplaces, compared with over a half of the workforce where the majority (over 70%) work in blue-collar jobs. Remember, however, that the table only refers to private manufacturing and private services; the public sector is not included. As much of white-collar unionism is concentrated in the public sector, we should be cautious about what the table tells us about the relation between occupational shifts and union membership. High unemployment among manual workers has certainly weakened the unions, particularly the job losses brought about by the closure of large manufacturing plants, but the growth of white-collar jobs does not suggest a pattern of decline. Rather, it signifies the changing face of unionism. Increasingly, the view that many people hold of the trade unions is at odds with the realities of work experience. The figure of the manual trade unionist in the large engineering works is no longer representative. Today's trade unionist is much more likely to be wearing a white collar and working in a service industry.

Activity 5.3

Apart from looking out for the kinds of information that may be relevant to data interpretation, there is a further reason for approaching this type of table with caution.

What we have been looking at in Table 5.6 are statistical associations between factors. Such associations, however, do not tell us whether one factor is the *cause* of the other. Bearing this point in mind, what does Table 5.6 have to say about the relationship between part-time work and union density? Look at the average union density for workplaces with over 40 per cent of part-time workers and compare this figure with the average union density in workplaces with less than 5 per cent employed on a part-time basis.

Table 5.6 indicates that a low level of union membership is associated with a high proportion of part-timers in a workplace and vice versa. But *why* should this association hold? Many women, as noted in section 5.3, are employed on a part-time basis. Is the statistical association a result of the part-time nature of work or of the gender composition of the part-time workforce? Or is the association attributable to both these factors? Or neither? The answer is likely to be significant for trade unions.

Until recently, trade unions have been rather slow to organize groups of workers on the periphery. There are, however, moves among some unions such as the TGWU, GMB and USDAW to go in this direction, to actively recruit part-timers in particular. There are also signs that some unions recognize, in Cockburn's words 'that a change in their attitude to women is needed if they are to survive into the 21st century' (1987, p. 7). Over the post-war period, female membership of trade unions has grown significantly and represents an increasing proportion of all union members – around

Table 5.6   Trade union density in the private sector in relation to the characteristics of workplaces, 1984

	Proportion of establishments with union density of: (row percentages)							Average density	Unweighted base	Weighted base
	0	1–24%	25–49%	50–89%	90–99%	100%	Not known			
All establishments	42	12	9	17	6	4	8	42	1189	1267
Size of establishment										
25–49 employees	52	9	7	14	5	5	7	26	223	663
50–99 employees	37	16	12	18	7	2	7	30	239	338
100–199 employees	27	16	11	22	7	5	9	39	206	156
200–499 employees	23	11	10	25	8	7	13	47	210	80
500–999 employees	13	3	9	25	18	2	22	60	165	20
1000 or more employees	5	4	5	39	24	4	16	72	146	10
Change in establishment size since 1980										
Decrease of 20% or more	29	9	15	22	10	5	7	60	329	226
Decrease of less than 20%	35	13	7	20	8	10	6	48	251	241
Stable	41	16	9	14	7	3	10	45	141	152
Increase of less than 20%	50	11	8	18	2	1	9	36	136	180
Increase of 20% or more	59	10	7	13	2	1	8	21	155	244
New establishment since 1980[1]	–	–	–	–	–	–	–	–	14	27
Not known	39	15	8	18	7	4	8	37	163	196

Size of enterprise										
25–99 employees	56	15	6	17	2	1	3	20	178	438
100–199	57	7	13	11	5	0	7	22	77	114
200–999 employees	42	11	11	17	7	3	7	35	181	170
1000–4999 employees	33	18	9	18	7	8	4	48	262	174
5000–49 999 employees	25	6	10	22	15	7	13	55	260	192
50 000 or more employees	24	8	7	19	6	4	29	58	131	94
Not known	29	7	16	16	4	13	10	57	100	84
Proportion of employees who were manual										
More than 70%	34	14	7	25	9	6	4	53	456	485
Between 31% and 70%	41	14	14	18	4	2	4	45	387	391
Between 0 and 30%	53	7	7	7	4	4	16	25	346	390
Proportion of employees who were part-time										
More than 40%	56	13	10	8	1	3	7	24	136	178
Between 6% and 40%	47	10	9	14	4	5	11	35	354	468
Between 0 and 5%	34	13	9	23	10	4	5	51	663	578

[1] Unweighted base is fewer than 20, therefore too low for percentages

Source: Millward and Stevens, 1986

one-third in the mid-1980s. As women rather than men are more likely to be employed on a part-time or temporary basis and as this appears to be the direction in which the labour market is moving, one can gauge the significance of Cockburn's statement.

If many of the changes in working patterns, for instance the growth of white-collar work, the expansion of peripheral forms of employment and the increase in the number of women in the workforce, are part of a long-term and irreversible trend, then it is difficult to avoid the conclusion that the trade union movement is at some kind of crossroads.

5.4.2   Fragmented unionism

Not only is the face of unionism changing, so too is its geography and this, in turn, is putting into place new structures of unionism (Massey and Miles, 1984). In the immediate post-war period, at the height of organized capitalism according to Lash and Urry, union membership was concentrated in the cities and the industrial regions whose pattern of growth was laid down in the late nineteenth and early twentieth centuries. Many unions were tied closely to particular regions, their geographies reflecting the location of the industries around which they were organized. The coalfields and the National Union of Mineworkers is an obvious example, but other regional specializations noted in section 5.2.1, such as textiles in the North West and clothing and footwear in the East Midlands, were also organized around single unions. Even among general unions, such as the Amalgamated Union of Engineering Workers, whose membership is drawn from a wide array of industries and occupations, membership was concentrated in certain industrial cities and regions. This spatial concentration of union membership, the unions 'heartlands' as they have become known, established the cities and the larger towns as the centres of trade unions, the site of union power (*Lane*, 1982). Looking back on this period, what is striking now is how, since the 1960s, these union heartlands have declined.

Today, the trade union membership has a more dispersed geography, the result of a catalogue of processes which you have considered in this and the preceding chapters. Following Massey and Miles (1984), we can group the processes broadly into one of three kinds – deindustrialization, the changing organizational structure of industry and the changing composition of the workforce. Deindustrialization, as you will recall from Chapter 2, has swept across the old regional bases of the industrial heartlands since the 1960s, taking with it large sections of the membership of both general and industry-based unions. The picture, however, is not simply one of membership loss; there have been gains over this period, but these have generally been in areas outside the old union bases. Figures 5.6 and 5.7 show the spatial levelling that has occurred among the membership of the National Union of Tailor and Garment Workers since the 1950s. According to Massey and Miles, this is not an exceptional pattern: the levelling of regional membership profiles is characteristic of a number of unions.

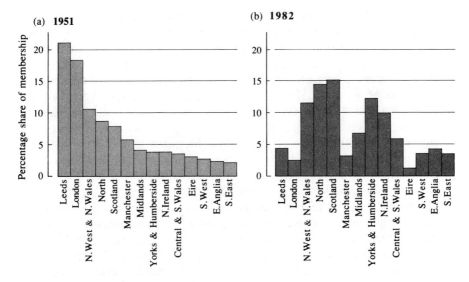

Figure 5.6 Membership of NUTGW for all areas

Areas are not the same size and may not conform to accepted definitions of name of region as union membership areas have been used. Membership areas with the same name among unions may not be of a similar geographic size, as the definition of the area varies among unions.

Source: Massey and Miles, 1984, Figure 1, p. 21

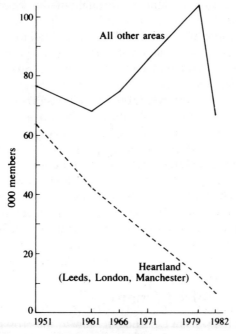

Figure 5.7 Membership trends for NUTGW, 1951–82, for heartland and other areas
Source: Massey and Miles, 1984, Figure 2, p. 21

Some of the major factors behind this pattern of spatial dispersal were discussed in section 5.2: the decentralization of employment, the fragmentation of the large workplaces and the relocation of plants from the cities to peripheral locations. These factors, according to *Lane* (1982), have produced a more fragmented union movement, and a less radical form of unionism. Many of the smaller towns and cities in which plants have been established lack a radical cultural tradition, they are isolated geographically from the old centres of union power, and the new workforces, although unionized in many cases, are more likely to be 'green' labour, that is, with no experience of union organization. Above all, the rise of multi-plant firms and their spatial dispersal has enabled firms to introduce more fragmented union structures such as single-union deals and plant-level bargaining (*Hudson*, 1988). The geographical reorganization of industry in this instance has been integral to the erosion of industry-wide and national structures of unionism that characterized industrial relations in the UK throughout the inter-war period and up to the mid-1960s. And it is this kind of feature, the breakdown of the *national* structures which organize labour, that Lash and Urry take to be one of the characteristics of an emergent disorganized capitalism (1987, p. 108).

The exception to this is, of course, the public sector unions which bargain on a national level. Their growth has patently contributed to the spatial evening out of trade unionism overall, although here the pattern represents a consolidation of membership rather than any particular weakening of labour organization. For example, throughout the 1950s up to the early 1980s, the National and Local Government Officers Association attracted more members outside of the London, West Midlands and North West conurbations than within them. A similar dispersal pattern of growth was also evident for the National Union of Public Employees in the 1970s (Massey and Miles, 1984). Besides, as was pointed out in Chapter 3, public sector service jobs are more evenly distributed across the country than either private sector service or manufacturing jobs, so a more spatially even unionism is likely to occur.

In this section we have been concentrating upon the changing geography of trade unionism in the UK over the post-war period and in particular upon the trend towards a more fragmented and spatially even pattern of unionism. There is some evidence here for the direction of unionism. In the final section we look at how this evidence and the trends set out in section 5.4.1 have been interpreted and what kinds of crossroads have been drawn up for British trade unionism.

5.4.3   Disorganized labour?

Lash and Urry (1987) have a particular view of the crossroads that British trade unions face. You will recall from section 5.2.2 that the process of organized capitalism within the UK began at the bottom, through the actions of organized labour in particular, at the end of the nineteenth century. Now, according to Lash and Urry, the key actors in the process of organization are also in a strong position to shape the new structures of disorganization that are being laid down. But in the UK this has not been so; the employers have been the central actors, shaping the new structures to meet their interests. Three reasons are advanced for the relative weakness of the British labour movement, the first of which gives us some idea of the crossroads that Lash and Urry have in mind.

One of the characteristics of disorganized capitalism is the labour market dualism referred to in section 5.3.3, the division between primary and secondary labour markets. This dualism, it is argued, has led to a dualism in the labour *movement*, a rift between workers in 'private-sector export orientated firms which bargain on a plant or company level, and (workers in) the public sector, on the one hand, and most declining sector firms, on the other, which bargain on a national level' (Lash and Urry, 1987, p. 274). Workers in the first category, in protected labour markets, are seen to identify with the firm rather than with the wider labour movement. The outcome of this identification is taken to be a shift towards company union-ism and increased tendencies towards sectionalism in the labour movement, in particular a split between unions operating in the export-orientated firms and public sector unions (ibid., p. 284). The growth of single-union and strike-free deals among Japanese and US firms in Britain is taken as evi-dence of the movement towards company unionism in the private sector, and an index of an increasingly disorganized labour force.

It is worth stressing that Lash and Urry do not see the growth of sectional-ism as a necessary consequence of labour market dualism. If workers in protected labour markets can realize and sustain a strong collective identity then, in their view, the growth of sectionalism in the labour movement can be avoided. Others, such as Atkinson and Gregory (1986), have similarly argued that core workers could use their bargaining strength to establish better working conditions among the less unionized periphery. This is an alternative direction: the spread of unionism among workers previously less organized, among part-time and temporary workers.

Of the two directions, Lash and Urry clearly think that unionism in the UK is moving in the former direction, towards company unionism. Part of the explanation for this movement lies with the two remaining reasons they advance for the UK's weakened labour movement. The first concerns the promotion of flexible working practices on employer's terms and the second, the introduction – again by employers – of new institutional forms of management-labour relations. In the latter case the stress is upon employers seizing the initiative to shape labour practices around the identity of the firm through such forms as quality circles, worker representation on company boards and profit-sharing.

Putting all this together, what this closely resembles is the shift from Fordism to neo-Fordism debated in the previous chapter. In many ways, therefore, the argument that contemporary capitalist economies are becoming increasingly disorganized is wrapped up with the view that mass production systems are giving way to flexible production systems within industry. And, if this is so, then the new work practices and the new forms of worker representation are seen to fit more easily into the structures of company unionism rather than the multi-unionism characteristic of the mass production industries. Under neo-Fordism, the old structures of unionism – industry-wide or national forms of collective bargaining – are said to be disappearing in favour of decentralized and differentiated negotiations on wages and working conditions (Bonefield, 1987).

One significant strand of the neo-Fordist scenario is the emphasis which it places upon manufacturing firms, in particular foreign-owned firms, and their core workforces as the locus of new structures of unionism. This raises an interesting question. It concerns the apparent hegemony of core manufacturing workers in the labour movement, reflecting perhaps the structural dominance of male, full-time, manual workers within British trade unionism. Why should this group of declining workers influence the direction of change? Are there any particular characteristics of the peripheral workforce which thwart attempts to shift unionism in this direction?

The reason most commonly cited is the high labour turnover among part-time and temporary workers – that they are not with one employer for any length of time. Places like McDonalds, the fast food chain, for instance, are said to have a turnover in London of around 200–250 per cent each year, which obviously poses considerable organizational difficulties. USDAW, with 40 per cent of its membership in part-time work, loses just under a third of its membership every year, some 100 000 members, owing to the high labour turnover in the industries it draws its membership from. Other factors mentioned include the kinds of work involved – often isolated service jobs in small workplaces; the unfamiliarity of established patterns of labour organization; and the marginal impact that unions have on the lifestyles of many young people entering the labour market for the first time. Finally, for many women the predominance of male values and priorities which permeate and structure the affairs of unions is itself seen to hold women back from involvement. Each of these factors represents an obstacle to unionism, although none can be said to put certain groups of workers beyond unionization. There is no necessary reason, for example, why unions should fare badly as the numbers of part-timers in the workforce rise. Besides, some unions, as noted earlier, have moved in this direction; a reflection perhaps of the kinds of jobs available to their membership and potential membership (*Hudson*, 1988).

Trade unionism in the UK may thus be shifting in more than one direction, a sign possibly of the labour movement dualism emphasized by Lash and Urry. In what sense, then, do these movements represent the disorganization of labour? Above all, it would appear that the breakdown of the national structures of unionism is of paramount importance. Whilst a falling membership and a changing spatial distribution of trade unionism have contributed towards this breakdown, the most important factor appears to be the actions of employers 'from above'. What is left out from this assessment, however, is the position of the public sector unions in the labour movement.

What is clear is, first, that the public sector has a highly unionized workforce organized around national bargaining structures and, second, that the latter are progressively being dismantled. There is an interesting parallel here between the decentralization of bargaining in the private sector and moves to fragment the public sector unions. In particular, the privatization of services, that is, the contracting out or selling off of the public service activities to the private sector, has begun to erode national bargaining structures and the coverage of collective agreements (Beaumont, 1987). Once again the action is 'from above', but in this instance carried out by the state. Whether this kind of state action is part of an irreversible, long-term shift towards the disorganization of labour depends upon the capacity of organized labour to resist movement in this direction. And that is partly why British trade unionism is at some kind of a crossroads.

Summary of section 5.4

• By the mid-1980s union membership in the UK was close to pre-1970 levels, the gains of the 1970s wiped out by deindustrialization. Employment growth in industries and among groups of workers with little history of union organization is shifting the profile of unionism – from manufacturing to services, from manual to non-manual workers, and from men to women.

• Geography has been an integral part of this shift, as the old heartlands of the labour movement have been eroded and a more spatially dispersed unionism has emerged. All this, in turn, has arguably led to a move away from industry-wide and national structures of unionism towards local or company-based structures.

• These empirical trends are open to interpretation. On the one hand, the labour movement may be witnessing the growth of sectionalism, with a split between a secure, unionized, core workforce organized at the level of the firm and a poorly organized periphery. Alternatively, the peripheral workforce may itself hold the key to the future direction of unionism, tilting the axis of organized labour away from the established structures of a labour movement built on manufacturing towards the interests of part-timers and women in the service industries.

Further reading

On the issue of work in general, Charlie Leadbetter and John Lloyd's book, *In Search of Work* (Harmondsworth, Penguin Books; 1987), is an accessible account of the changes in its organization and structure and, more specifically, the impact that such changes are likely to have upon our working lives.

A challenging appraisal of these changes from a feminist standpoint is provided in Veronica Beechey's *Unequal Work* (London, Verso; 1987).

If you wish to follow up particular aspects of changing work patterns then two journals, *Labour Research* and the government publication *Employment Gazette*, provide a continuous stream of informative articles and statistical trends. For instance, one recent article in the *Employment Gazette* is Catherine Hakim's examination of the composition of the flexible workforce, 'Trends in the flexible workforce' (Vol. 95, No. 11, November 1987).

Another dimension of work that you may wish to pursue is the question of informal work, that is, work done outside the formal economy governed by state legislation. Ray Pahl's *Divisions of Labour* (Oxford, Basil Blackwell; 1984) is a useful introduction to the representation of work in society and how its meaning has changed over time.

On the trade unions, a good source book to the anatomy of trade unionism in Britain is *Trade Unions in Britain* (London, Spokesman; 1985) by Ken Coates and Tony Topham. For a stimulating account of how trade unions have begun to respond to the growing number of women in the workforce, you should read Cynthia Cockburn's *Women, Trade Unions and Political Parties* (Fabian Research Series No. 349).

Finally, if you found Lash and Urry's arguments as outlined in this chapter interesting or provocative, it is worthwhile examining at first hand – in *The End of Organized Capitalism* (Cambridge, Polity Press; 1987) – the shift to disorganization in five western countries (the UK, USA, France, West Germany and Sweden). Phil Cooke's (1987) article, 'Spatial development processes: organized or disorganized?', is a useful appraisal of the geographical dimension of the disorganization thesis; it is reprinted in the associated Reader (Massey, D. and Allen, J. (eds) (1988)).

6 What is an economy anyway?

Doreen Massey

Contents

6.1	**Introduction**	230
6.2	**Does deindustrialization matter?**	
	1 The motor of the economy?	231
6.2.1	Propulsive industries	232
6.2.2	The nature of demand	235
6.2.3	Productivity	235
6.2.4	Innovation and technical change	236
6.2.5	Increasing returns to scale	237
6.2.6	Social implications	238
6.2.7	Geographical implications	239
6.2.8	The 'real' economy?	240
6.3	**Does deindustrialization matter?**	
	2 The question of exports	241
6.3.1	Definitions	241
6.3.2	The debate at national level	241
6.3.3	The debate at regional and local levels	244
6.4	**What is an economy anyway?**	247
6.4.1	Crowding out?	247
6.4.2	What is wealth?	250
6.4.3	The economic and the social	252
	Summary	257
	Further reading	258

6.1   Introduction

The previous chapters have raised a number of fundamental questions which they have not had space to explore; the purpose of this final chapter is to push some of those questions further. Its aim is partly to be the basis for a review, by looking at issues from new angles, and partly to be provocative of further thought. The questions will not be answered, for they are on-going debates rather than simple questions. Rather, the arguments from contending points of view will be presented. In this spirit of being speculative and of opening up questions, some of the Activities are also more open-ended, inviting you to join the debate.

If we are indeed at a point of structural change then it is a time for asking big questions, and the debates presented here revolve around three fundamental issues:

- the future shape of the UK economy . . . which raises issues about –

- the conceptualization of an economy . . . which leads into a theme which underlies the whole chapter –

- the social construction of concepts and categories.

The two sections which follow both revolve around the question 'does deindustrialization matter?'. They look at some of the arguments which have been made for the continuing necessity for a strong manufacturing economy, and at opposing arguments that services are now poised to take over the central role once held by manufacturing. There are two major issues here: the degree to which manufacturing is a necessary engine of growth, and the degree to which manufacturing is a necessary basis of UK exports. The arguments are 'social' as well as 'economic' and this leads into the final section which examines the use of this dichotomy in debates over the economy, and asks 'what is an economy anyway?'. For underlying all the positions outlined in the chapter are different ways of conceptualizing an economy. It is in this way that this chapter continues this and the related textbooks' concern with the evaluation of theories. Part of what this chapter is about is exposing their underlying assumptions. While sections 6.2 and 6.3 pick up mainly on Chapters 1, 2 and 3, section 6.4 draws primarily on Chapters 4 and 5. One thing runs through all the issues, however, and that is the importance of the geographical dimension. Sometimes this is because the answer to a question may vary depending on the scale of the analysis. Sometimes, and perhaps most importantly, it is because different policy-stances taken on the questions asked in this chapter imply very different futures for the cities and regions of the UK.

6.2 Does deindustrialization matter?

1 The motor of the economy?

One of the major changes in the UK economy which we have explored in this book has been the shift away from manufacturing and towards services, and the question which this obviously raises is: does it matter?

One's answer to this question will depend to some extent on an evaluation of the theories presented in Chapter 3 (the post-industrial and socio-technical approaches, and that of Mandel) and on which of those theories is found more convincing. But there is clearly an argument to be made that the shift in the balance of the economy from manufacturing to services is part of a 'natural' progression for advanced societies and that, although the process of transition may provoke difficulties, there is not a fundamental 'problem' nor is the process reversible. This argument can be made both at national level, about the economy as a whole, and about particular regions and localities.

Indeed since the 1970s there has been a shift in *regional* policy away from its previous exclusive concentration on manufacturing. Gradually, incentives have been made available to the service sector too. Implicitly – and sometimes explicitly – this has reflected an argument that the manufacturing sector can no longer be relied upon to revive the employment base (and the discussion *has* largely been in terms of jobs, rather than output or profits, for instance) of large areas of the country for many of which it had once been central.

The same shift of emphasis also happened on occasions at *local* level. A number of northern cities, built above all else on manufacturing, but which have seen their economic bases suffer a long decline, have begun to orient their employment policies for the future more towards services.

And yet, in spite of all this, there are many who argue that in fact services cannot simply take over from manufacturing its role as the core provider of national and regional income and of jobs. In that context, they would argue, the decline of manufacturing is indeed a serious threat to the UK economy and society.

Before going on, it is important to make a few points to clarify this claim.

First, such people are not necessarily arguing that the shift from manufacturing to services is problematical; what may be more at issue is the absolute decline of manufacturing. Thus Thirlwall (1982) writes:

> Indeed, it is well documented that in the natural course of the development process there are resource shifts first from agriculture to industry and then from industry to service-type activities, in accordance with differences in the income elasticity of demand for products as income rises, and with differences in the sectoral rate of growth of labour productivity. All industrial market countries, except Finland, have experienced a relative shrinkage in manufacturing since 1960. (p. 24)

Note here how Thirlwall's choice of a definition of deindustrialization is based on his identification of which phenomenon is causing the problem. Indeed, much of his paper is concerned with this, and it takes us back to the important issues of conceptualization raised in Chapter 2. Later in Thirlwall's paper there is a whole section entitled 'Does deindustrialization matter?', a question to which he gives an emphatic answer 'yes'. So, when it comes to matters of strategy and of policy, the definition of deindustrialization *is* important.

Secondly, it is not just at national level that manufacturing decline is seen as problematical, and that manufacturing industry is seen as a necessary core of a healthy economy. Thus Fothergill and Gudgin (1982) write: 'Despite the size and growth of service employment, the conclusion which emerges is that manufacturing has become the dominant influence on the pattern of urban and regional employment change in Britain' (p. 25).

Thirdly, quotations like the last one bring out an important point: that what is at issue here is manufacturing as a 'dominant influence'. This does not mean that it should necessarily be numerically dominant, for instance in terms of jobs. Indeed, we saw above that Thirlwall is not in the slightest exercised by a shift in balance from manufacturing to services. That could happen in a context in which all sectors were blooming with health. As was seen in Chapter 4 in the discussion of Fordism and flexible manufacturing, sectors (in the case of Chapter 4 defined in terms of their dominant labour processes) do not have to dominate in terms of size to be key to the dynamic of the whole. What is at issue here is whether or not services can take over that key role in the UK economy so long held by manufacturing.

Fourthly, there is therefore also an argument, at least implicitly, about the degree to which British deindustrialization is inevitable. It is certainly the case, as was shown in Chapter 1, that in international comparative terms employment in manufacturing has fared particularly badly in the UK. Part of the argument, therefore, concerns the question of whether this performance has been worsened by government policy decisions, for instance, and, if so, the degree to which its performance could be improved.

So why *is* manufacturing so often seen as a necessary **engine of growth** of an advanced economy? In fact, there is a whole set of often interlocking arguments.

6.2.1   Propulsive industries

First of all, it is argued that manufacturing industries are more likely to be propulsive, or dominant, industries. A **propulsive industry** is one which is highly integrated into the economy, local or national, in such a way that it can transmit growth to other sectors in that economy. One element of the argument here is that growth in manufacturing industries has multiplier effects on other sectors of the economy. In particular, growth in one manufacturing industry may transmit growth to other sectors through orders for its inputs, from both other manufacturing and service industries. This is the input-output or technological multiplier. Manufacturing industries, it is argued, in part simply because of the nature of their production processes, are more likely to be able to transmit growth in this way than are services.

Activity 6.1

Before you go on, what arguments are there against this position? Why might service industries also be propulsive – although perhaps in different ways – in a local or regional economy?

Hints:

- How is the composition of the service sector changing? (See Chapter 3, and *Wood*, 1986.)
- How might the presence of producer services be an encouragement to the growth of other industries in an area? (See *Daniels*, 1986, section 6.)

The power of the argument about propulsive industries varies with geographical scale. Clearly, although growth of a propulsive industry will have reverberative effects on other sectors, the degree to which that effect will help the local or national economy will depend on where those other sectors are located. At a national level it may lead only to increased imports. At a regional level the idea of a propulsive sector has been central to the theory and policy of 'growth poles'. In this policy, manufacturing investments were made in peripheral regions in the expectation that they would become foci for the growth of associated, and especially supplier, industries. All too often, it failed to work. From the steel-works of Southern Italy to the car-plants of Scotland, they failed to stimulate the development of components suppliers. Instead components were brought in from elsewhere.

What was at issue here was not whether or not the industries were propulsive – they were – but the geography of their effect. Certainly there seemed to be few cases where geographical constraints on suppliers were such that they *had* to locate in the immediate vicinity of the propulsive sector. Had they already been located there it might have been the local region which benefited from the multiplier effects, but certainly the need for geographical propinquity was not sufficient to stimulate the development of a *new* industry.

All these things are influenced by social and even political forms, and there have been numerous recent examples. One such is the Scottish electronics industries. The growth of this (very considerable) constellation of high-technology industry has been the product mainly of inward investment by large corporate, and often multinational, companies. This has had a number of effects, one of them – linking back to the discussion in Chapters 2 and 4 – is that as (decentralized) branch plants, they tend to have rather less

R & D and rather more physical production and assembly. According to the theory which says manufacturing industries are more likely to be 'propulsive', this could actually increase the possibility of multiplier effects, comparatively, from the Scottish plants. Yet in fact one of the problems most frequently pointed to in the Scots electronics industry is the lack of local components suppliers.

It is indeed often argued that branch plants may be less likely than others to stimulate growth in their local areas (Dicken, 1976). This may simply be because all ordering is done centrally from a headquarters which is in another region; or it may be that this branch is simply one in a chain of production in the ownership of the same company, and that it obtains its inputs from another plant of the same company, located in another region, maybe even another country (Massey, 1984; *Daniels*, 1986, section 6). So the social form of an industry – in this case the structure of its ownership – may influence the effectiveness and the geographical implications of a propulsive sector.

There have, of course, been attempts to control the geography of the multiplier effect. When the Nissan company agreed to establish a plant in Sunderland, part of the deal was that there should be 60 per cent 'local content'. What this meant was that 60 per cent of the local inputs, by value (and including labour), would come from local sources (although in this case 'local' meant the EC!). In spite of this very broad definition of 'local', however, the evidence as I write this does indicate that Nissan is indeed encouraging some of its suppliers to locate very close to its plant. The reason for this relates to the kinds of changes discussed in Chapter 4: the just-in-time system can increase the importance of proximity for suppliers and therefore increase the potential local multiplier effect even of branch plants of multinationals.

As was seen in Chapter 3, the service sector is becoming increasingly complex, and producer services in particular have been growing apace. Indeed the distinction between manufacturing and services is increasingly arbitrary. Services are an integral part of the whole production system. As *Wood* (1986) points out, the internal complexity of the service sector means that service industries themselves generate demand for other services, and therefore may promote growth among firms supplying such inputs. They also, of course, purchase from manufacturing industries. Thus Rajan (1985) argues:

> The evidence suggests that 20% of output of the service industry is used by the manufacturing sector in order for the latter to produce its own output. By implication, therefore, the manufacturing sector supports nearly 20% of the jobs in the service sector. On a similar criterion, the service sector supports about 7% of the jobs in manufacturing. (p. 54)

Moreover, it has been argued, some producer services may also be propulsive as *suppliers*. Whilst some companies provide their own producer services, many do not and the presence of such services may be an important stimulus to the growth of such companies. Their absence from a region will mean either that other industries there cannot benefit from their services or that they will incur greater costs in acquiring them from another region. The presence of producer services in a region may therefore both enable firms in that region to grow faster and attract new firms into the area (*Daniels*, 1986). Here, then, the relation is reversed and producer services are seen as propulsive because of their importance as suppliers of essential inputs.

The point in both cases is that service industry investment may in some cases even lead manufacturing to certain regions. Here we begin to stray into another argument, which we shall pick up again in the next section. For the moment let us pursue further the notion of 'engines of growth'.

Having propulsive sectors is fine for the transmission of growth to other sectors, but it is also necessary to generate and sustain the growth in the first place. Here, another bundle of arguments comes into play.

6.2.2 The nature of demand

It is argued that to have a growing economy it is necessary to have industries whose products have a high **income elasticity of demand**. You may have noticed this term in the quotation from Thirlwall earlier. To say a good has a high income elasticity of demand means that as incomes rise so demand for the good will also rise, so that growth will be further stimulated. In other words, such goods can provide an in-built dynamic of growth as an element in the system.

From Chapter 3 you will know that there is debate on this issue. Part of the argument for the post-industrial-economy thesis is indeed that as incomes rise it is demand for services, not goods, which increases. In other words, increasing income elasticity of demand is argued, precisely as part of the Fisher-Clark thesis, to be a particular characteristic of services.

Yet this is disputed, as was also pointed out in Chapter 3, by Gershuny and Miles (1983), who argue in reply that while this effect may be real, there is also the *price* elasticity of demand to be considered. This says that demand for goods is sensitive to price, though again this sensitivity varies by product. Thus, if services become more expensive in relation to manufactured goods, the price effect might outweigh the income effect. Gershuny and Miles (1983) argue that this has indeed happened for marketed final services (though not all services) in the UK.

This is a debate which is likely to continue.

6.2.3 Productivity

What this highlights is another widely discussed difference between manufacturing and services: the argument that *productivity has increased faster* in the former than the latter. For this reason, it is argued, manufacturing has a more dynamic impact on growth than do services. But this is output growth. The impact on employment may be contradictory. One of the criticisms made of the regional policy of the 1960s and '70s was that much of the regional grant money had been taken up by a few large firms whose subsequent investment programmes, although they may have made the plants themselves more competitive and therefore less vulnerable in the longer term, actually led to a *loss* of jobs. Such 'jobless growth' was characteristic, for instance, of the chemical industry of Teesside, which had received many millions of pounds of regional policy aid. It was partly in response to this contradiction of regional aid for manufacturing industry that policy attention began to turn to services. In contrast, it was seen in Chapter 2 that Aglietta (1979) argued that many consumer services are particularly hard to automate and therefore become drags on the overall growth of the economy.

Once again, however, this distinction between manufacturing and services is increasingly coming under challenge. Aglietta was only referring to consumer services, and *Wood* (1986), while agreeing with the position in general, points to parts of the service sector where there have indeed been significant increases in productivity. Barras (1984) also points out that productivity increases in services have varied over time. Most particularly, he shows that there has been a significant increase in productivity in private services since 1980 (p. 59). This has resulted in part from the effects of recession, which forced a labour 'shake-out' and the faster-than-usual scrapping of older and less productive capacity; but it also derives from a wave of capital investment in services in the late 1970s. Moreover this new capital investment embodies new, micro-electronic technology. It could, therefore, mark the beginnings of major productivity increases in certain services. He points to 'electronic funds transfer within financial services, point-of-sale debiting in distribution, viewdata and teaching programmes in education [the Open University is well ahead of the field here!], expert systems in health' and many other examples (p. 65).

This argument about productivity is related to two other arguments for the key role of manufacturing industry in any economy.

6.2.4   Innovation and technical change

The first of these is the argument that *innovations and technical changes* are more highly clustered in manufacturing than services. Thus the SPRU group's documentation of 'fundamental' innovations between 1945 and 1984 has been classified by sector, and this shows that the majority of innovations took place in manufacturing (Harris, 1987, p. 307). Moreover, while services were net importers of innovations made elsewhere, manufacturing sectors as a whole were exporters. This harks back to Chapter 4's discussion of the basis of Fordist process-innovation in manufacturing.

Such arguments, however, can again be questioned for talking of 'manufacturing' and 'services' as a whole. Some manufacturing sectors are more 'innovatory' than others, more likely than others to be the bearers of wider technological change to the economy; and *some* service sectors, such as banking, insurance and finance, and indeed R&D itself, probably are innovatory and the focus of technological development. Certainly, they are not all of the 'inevitably-labour-intensive-consumer-service' variety. Moreover, one of the reasons given for manufacturing's supposedly greater tendency to innovate is that while its capital investment is largely in machinery, a much higher proportion of the service sector's capital investment is in buildings. This is true; but again it could change in at least some service sectors if they really are on the verge of a micro-electronics revolution. Finally, pushing this issue even further, some would argue that the new technological developments of today are precisely blowing apart the classical distinction between manufacturing and services. Thus Thrift (1987) comments: 'the old division of the economy into a manufacturing and a services sector seems increasingly suspect. If the application of products is becoming more important than their production, then perhaps a division into information and non-information-producing categories is more useful' (p. 77).

6.2.5   Increasing returns to scale

The other argument about the significance of productivity increases in manufacturing concerns *increasing returns to scale*: that is, that productivity increases as output grows. It is sometimes argued that in manufacturing these returns are particularly high (Kaldor, 1966), occurring both through economies of scale in production and also, for instance, through agglomeration economies. If this is so, then a growing manufacturing sector can spark off a process of cumulative causation. As output grows, labour productivity increases so that regions with higher output levels will have higher productivity and therefore correspondingly higher wages, which in turn attract labour, with the result that output increases even faster. Moreover, growth in manufacturing will attract labour from lower productivity sectors within the economy, thereby increasing both output and labour productivity over the economy as a whole.

It certainly seems to be true that at the moment the service sector as a whole does not experience such increasing returns to scale. But once again it is not clear that this is true *in principle* for all services. Since much of this kind of increasing-productivity-with-growth comes from new investment in machinery, then if certain services do become more machinery-based the same kinds of increasing returns to scale could apply to them too.

The catch, of course, is that if indeed services do come to demonstrate equal ability to increase productivity, while this may be good for economic growth in that there will still be a good engine in the economy, the corollary is that services will not be able to provide sufficient jobs for us to have socially acceptable levels of unemployment. One reply to such 'technological pessimism' is that we have faced such crises before and yet

> ... have been confounded by each subsequent economic recovery. The reasons for pessimism are not hard to find, for it is much easier to perceive the labour-saving effects of technical innovations in established industries than it is to appreciate either the likely expansion of aggregate demand due to the price effects of technical progress, or to identify where new industries, based on new products or services, will arise to expand the demand for labour (Barras, 1984, p. 66)

Could it be the fifth Kondratiev?!

Many of these discussions, then, depend on making judgements about the medium-term future, and 'technological forecasting' is notoriously difficult. But behind all these rather detailed and technical arguments about the importance of manufacturing lie other, much broader and more general ones.

6.2.6   Social implications

First, there is a clear concern about the *social implications* of a decline in manufacturing employment, and a growth in service jobs. Here the concern is about the *relative* size of the two sectors, and above all about the *nature* of jobs. It may be that in a future economy the motor of growth could be provided by manufacturing, but that services would be the main provider of jobs. Both of these assumptions are, as we have seen, questionable, but suppose for a minute they are correct. What would that mean for the *quality* of jobs? Prowse (1987) writing in a *Financial Times* review of the period since 1979 reported:

> In the US, the debate about living standards and 'competitiveness' has also prompted economists to examine value-added and wages in different sectors. It seems that in different countries and in different historical periods manufacturing sectors have consistently been able to remunerate workers of a similar quality better than service industries. The moral seems to be that if the US wants to raise living standards and to provide more better-paid jobs, it will have to revive its manufacturing industry. Services provide a lot of jobs, but often not particularly attractive ones. Britain may have to learn the same lesson. (p. 37)

Indeed, as Chapter 5 showed, a significant proportion of the current overall changes in the labour market – in conditions of employment – is due to the relative growth of services. Certainly, the apparently greater difficulty of increasing productivity in a number of services might account for the lower wages, as the other side of the coin of the increasing numbers of jobs. What does seem to be true is that there is a serious polarization in types of employment within the service sector. Those who view a service economy with enthusiasm tend to point to financiers, computer analysts, lawyers and psychologists; the more sceptical point to hospital ancillary staff, the hotel and catering industry and the casualized work in the tourist industry.

Such a concern is often also one element in arguments from the labour movement. As we saw in Chapter 5, the proportion of part-time jobs is higher in services than in manufacturing; so too is the proportion of small firms. In both, high levels of unionization are harder to achieve. Services, thus far, have indeed been more difficult to organize so it is little wonder that some people in the labour movement view the collapse of manufacturing employment with such alarm. The combination of this collapse with the decline of mining and the growth of services, along with the changing geographical distribution of jobs, challenges the heartlands of the British trade-union movement (*Lane*, 1982; *Morgan and Sayer*, 1985). It even challenges a traditional notion of 'the working class' itself as largely composed of male, manual workers. We shall take up these issues again in *The Changing Social Structure* (Hamnett, McDowell and Sarre (eds), 1989). One reply, of course, is that unions, and the nature of unionism, are also currently being reorganized, and sometimes attacked, in manufacturing itself (*Morgan and Sayer*, 1985). Both Morgan and Sayer and Lane, moreover, show how location is being used in this context, for instance by employers opting for greenfield sites. Another reply is that some services, most notably those in the public sector, have very high rates of unionization, but it is precisely these sectors which are under attack from cuts and privatization.

6.2.7 Geographical implications

There is a similar concern that an economy based on services would also imply a highly unequal *geography*. Any comparison of the future geographies of manufacturing and services will, of course, depend on the balance of their constituent sectors. The geography of a manufacturing economy mainly based on new industries such as electronics would look very different from a more broadly based one. And the geography of a service-based economy would depend very much on the balance of different types of services (see Chapter 3 and *Allen*, 1988). *Martin* (1988) demonstrates the very clear inverse relation which currently exists between the decline of manufacturing and the growth of services. How much, then, will employment growth in services help the regions where manufacturing employment is being lost? Moreover, from *Daniels* (1986) it is possible to construct an argument that producer services may be part of a process of cumulative causation accelerating growth in the South East. Producer services are already concentrated in that region and their own increasing globalization is likely to reinforce that process; and this in turn is likely to encourage further growth in both these services and manufacturing. Services in this sense, as was argued earlier, may be a propulsive sector.

Activity 6.2

Is it not possible to use regional policy to encourage the decentralization of such services? Think back to Chapters 2 and 4 and the discussions of decentralization of manufacturing jobs to the regions which took place in the late 1960s and early '70s. Try to relate that discussion to services. There is helpful material in *Allen* (1988) and *Martin* (1988).

(a)   How easy might it be to attract services to peripheral regions? Might there be a difference between types of services?

(b)   Would the same kinds of problems attend the decentralization of service industries as happened with manufacturing? *Daniels* (1986), for instance, talks of the vulnerability of producer service growth in the regions to the 'branch-plant syndrome'.

(c)   Why might this 'syndrome' mean that even if decentralization were achieved it might not solve the problems of uneven development? (*Hudson* (1988) elaborates on some of the wider problems of branch-plant economies.)

(d)   What other kinds of solutions can you think of?

6.2.8   The 'real' economy?

The final general concern about the decline of manufacturing relates again to the notion of the 'real economy' and 'real jobs', though in a different way. Here the argument is that all service employment is in the end dependent on manufacturing. For consumer services (public or private) may provide jobs and income, and even demand, in the rest of the economy but, so the argument goes, ultimately they are dependent on people having incomes to spend on them. Consumer services in that sense live off the income multiplier from other, more basic, sectors ('the sectors which produce the wealth in the first place'). With producer services the argument is similar. They depend on the technological multiplier from manufacturing. Their very name means that they exist to service 'production'. The implication is that only manufacturing is 'production'. Without production, no producer services.

6.3   Does deindustrialization matter?

2 The question of exports

6.3.1   Definitions

Even if this were true – which we shall anyway question – few places in the
world, either countries or regions, have the whole range of economic activities. One aspect of the spatial division of labour, both international and
intranational, is that different areas will produce some but not all of the
world's commodities. So why cannot some areas specialize in services and
others in manufacturing?

At this point we encounter a theory, which brings much of the preceding
discussion together, and which has been one of the main planks in the argument for the importance of manufacturing. This is *export-base theory*.

The central point of export-base theory is that, in order to grow, an economy needs to bring in additional income by selling abroad (or, in the case
of a regional or local economy, by selling outside its area). An economy
needs to export. On this foundation a distinction is constructed between
basic industries and dependent (or non-basic) ones. Basic industries are
those which export, which sell their output outside the area. They thus
bring income into the area from outside. Dependent industries, by contrast, are those which sell their output in the local market. Since the size of
this market is, according to this theory, in the end determined by the income brought into the area by the basic industries, so the growth of the dependent sector is also determined by the fortunes of the basic industries.
This is thus an argument which has particular resonance in an economy as
open as that of the UK's, where it merges into the more general argument
that exporting is necessary to the UK because of its need to import so
much. But export-base theory more specifically is an approach which is
also used at regional and local levels. In itself, the theory does not argue
that only manufacturing can provide the exports necessary for survival and
growth, in other words that manufacturing is a necessary foundation of the
'basic' sector. In the debate about the UK and its regions, however, that
argument has been made most forcefully.

6.3.2   The debate at national level

At *national* level, as Chapter 1 showed, the United Kingdom for long survived in the international economy primarily by selling manufactured
goods. Moreover its overall position in the world economy means that the
UK is also very dependent on exports to pay for imports of things it does
not produce. As manufacturing imports have risen faster than exports, the

question arises as to what can take the place of manufacturing? As Chapter 1 pointed out, a more favourable balance on trade in primary products (fuel and food) has helped offset the problems, but the oil will not last forever. So can services take over? Instead of 'workshop of the world' could Britain become, for instance, 'banker-to-the-world'?

Many argue that services could not take over, and therefore that manufacturing must retain a central place in the British economy's trading relation with the rest of the world.

For these people, then, the first definition of deindustrialization outlined in Chapter 2 is particularly important. For Singh (1977) the problem is that manufacturing is not currently able, after satisfying demands of consumers at home, to sell enough of its output abroad to pay for import requirements at socially acceptable levels of output, employment and the exchange rate. In July 1985, a House of Lords Select Committee chaired by Lord Aldington argued that the decline of manufacturing exports posed a grave threat to living standards and to the nation's economic and political stability.

Those who argue for the necessity of a continuing manufacturing export base often make the following points.

1 It is difficult to increase earnings in the form of profits, interest and dividends, especially in the short term, because these are based on investments abroad (see Chapter 1) and consequently require an outflow of capital before the return flows back.

2 Consequently, any increased contribution to the balance of payments would have to come from 'private services'. These consist of tourism, sea transport and civil aviation, construction and financial services. Certainly in recent years the UK economy does seem to have performed better in these areas than in manufacturing. However, when one looks more closely it emerges that almost the whole of the surplus in this area, and much of the recent growth, comes from the City's financial services. Although earnings from, for instance, tourism can be considerable they are, argue the advocates of manufacturing, very vulnerable to shifts in exchange rates.

3 There is a problem of scale. Trade in manufacturing is massively greater than that in services. In the case of Britain it would require an increase of one third in our world share of trade in services to offset a decline in our world share of manufacturing of only one per cent (Sargent, 1979).

4 There would also be distributional implications, both social and geographical, of turning to services as the main basis for exports. This would be especially true if, as predicted, such exports were dominated by a few sectors, particularly financial services, and possibly tourism. Given what we have already seen of the social and geographical characteristics of these sectors, such a strategy could imply basing the economy's relation with the international world on highly polarized distributions, both in terms of income and social structure and in terms of spatial organization. In other words, there is a clear relation between the choice of strategy about the

UK's place in the international division of labour and social and geographical distributions within the country.

5   Finally, a strategy which prioritized the City would also close off policy options for the future. One small step by a future UK government in a radical direction and the world's financiers could overnight withdraw their custom and bring the economy to its knees.

The choice of a 'manufacturing strategy' is not unproblematical either. The electronics industry, one of the 'growth' industries, is itself in deficit and anyway has a highly unequal geographical distribution (see Chapter 2), and manufacturing generally is performing poorly. Here the arguments of people like Singh (1977) and Thirlwall (1982) link up with the debate in section 6.2. For British manufacturing turns out in fact not to be well-placed in terms of one of the supposed characteristics of manufacturing that make it a potential engine of growth: it does not rate well in terms of income elasticity of demand. In other words, the output is not of high-enough quality, not sufficiently 'up-market'. This is not due to the structure of home demand, for imports *are* in fact of this type. Nor is it a question of the sectors in which the UK specializes, for the imbalance can be found in each sector. The problem, it is argued, is the generally lower quality, design and general performance of the products of British manufacturing, in turn a result of lack of investment and poor management and management-worker relations. With attention to these, the performance of British manufacturing could be improved.

There are, however, those who would argue that services *can* take over manufacturing's previous role as chief provider of exporter earnings. In contrast to the points made earlier, they would argue the following.

1   The argument that it is difficult, or at least a long-term process, to increase income from profits, income and dividends is no longer correct because much of the capital needed to provide the investment from which such income is derived can be raised abroad, in the country of investment.

2   Greater stress would be put on the fact, which is generally acknowledged, that the UK's competitiveness in private services is good and improving.

3   While it is true that services are less internationally traded than manufacturing, this is changing. Evidence can be found in both *Daniels* (1986) and *Thrift* (1986) for the rapidly increasing globalization of certain services.

4   Contrary to the arguments above, there need not necessarily be an overwhelming concentration on financial services. In recent years tourism, civil aviation and construction services have all demonstrated their potential as export-earners.

5   While there certainly are potentially problematic distributional implications in a concentration on services, concentration on manufacturing is not without its implications either. In particular, as we have seen from

Chapters 3 and 5, in employment terms manufacturing is more important for men and services for women. A focus on manufacturing, therefore, can be interpreted as a concern for 'jobs for the boys', while the part of the economy where most women work is seen as less 'real' and intrinsically dependent (Phillips, 1983).

6.3.3   The debate at regional and local levels

Export-base theory has been used to argue the importance of manufacturing to *regional and local* economies. Remember that the underlying argument is that an area (in this case a region or locality) needs to export to grow. It needs basic industries on which the growth of the rest of the regional/local economy ultimately depends. At sub-national level, however, different considerations come into play. Fothergill and Gudgin (1982) spell out very well the complexities of this at regional and local level within the UK:

> Basic industries, we recall, are those which sell their product outside the area, thus bringing in income from outside; dependent industries are those which sell their product to the local market – either to consumers, or to the basic industries themselves. Because the size of the local market depends on the income brought in by basic industries, the growth of the dependent sector will be determined by what happens to the basic sector.
>
> Of course, this is an oversimplification. In practice income is brought into an area by other routes, as well as by basic industries. For example, central government spending on pensions and social security benefits brings money into an area, which in turn supports jobs in dependent industries, such as retailing and public transport. In addition certain industries which serve the local population, such as health and education, are supported directly by public expenditure – mostly financed by central government – rather than by local consumer spending. And dependent industries themselves provide their employees with the income which will support still more dependent jobs.
>
> None of these points invalidates the basic-dependent split. What they do mean is that in the short and medium term, perhaps a decade or even more, the link between changes in the basic sector and changes in the dependent sector can be tenuous. If a steelworks closes, for example, this is likely to be followed fairly quickly by a second-round loss of jobs in those local firms which relied on the steelworks for business, such as haulage contractors. The reduction in earnings from employment will be partly offset by unemployment benefits and by redundancy payments, so local consumer spending and the jobs which depend on it, in shops and public houses for example, will not fall so dramatically.
>
> Even if some of the businesses dependent on the local market do feel the pinch, it may be some time before this begins to affect their employment, and the closure of the steelworks will of course make no immediate difference to local schools and hospitals. Children still have to go to school, whether or not their fathers are in work. The second-round loss of jobs may therefore not be very large at first. In the long run however, if the closure of the steelworks is not offset by the growth of a new basic industry, the size of the local dependent sector will begin to fall. Some people will move elsewhere in search of work. When they move, the demand for local consumer services will fall

again, as will the demand for school places and hospital beds. Employment in
the dependent sector will thus eventually be reduced to a level which can be
supported by the new lower level of basic employment in the area. (pp. 34–5)

The issue, then, is which are basic and which are dependent sectors. This
will clearly be a different mix from at national level. Certainly, as *Daniels*
(1986) argues, in principle basic sectors could very well include quite a
wide range of service industries. Moreover the impact of growth or decline
in the basic sector, however defined, will depend in part on the 'geography
of the multiplier effect', which was examined in section 2.

At *regional* level within the UK, in fact, most of the empirical evidence
so far points to manufacturing as being 'more basic' than services.
Fothergill and Gudgin (1982) come to this conclusion after their detailed
comparison of employment levels, while Harris (1987) demonstrates the
importance of manufacturing in interregional trade. If there is less interregional trade in services, the implication, he argues, is that individual
regions can depend less on services for exports.

However, there are nonetheless possible replies to these arguments.
First, the total level of interregional trade is not necessarily a foolproof indicator, for there are imports as well as exports and these may balance out.
What a region needs is *net* exports. One criticism of export-base theory has
been its ignoring of these complexities, and in particular its lack of recognition of the importance of activities which substitute for imports. Secondly,
and again a critique of the theory itself, flows of manufacturing goods say
nothing about the destination of profits. To analyse this the whole question
of branch plants and intra-company trading would have to be investigated.
Thirdly, there is clearly need for investigation of individual industries, since
there will be differences within the broad categories of manufacturing and
services. Producer services on the whole will have more potential than
consumer services at this level, but even within consumer services tourism
might be a major export-earner for a region. *Daniels* (1986) certainly provides evidence of trade in services between regions. Fourthly, however,
this raises the whole question of conceptualization. Where does the export
sector stop? How do you classify an activity which serves an exporting
activity? (And certainly many services would be vital here.) In the end, as
ever, the categorization depends on one's initial assumptions. From the
point of view of export-base theory it is possible to argue that, since the
business of a city is to export, all industries are ultimately basic in these
terms. Starting from the other end of the argument, it would be just as easy
to see all firms not as exporting, but basic in the sense that their ultimate
aim is the support of the local population. Fifthly, although over the UK as
a whole manufacturing sectors may at the moment seem more basic at regional level, this is not necessarily the case for each individual region: the
most obvious examples are the South East and the South West. Again,
there is need for more detailed investigation.

Finally, it should be noted that this theory says nothing about interregional relations other than trade. It does not consider other aspects of uneven

development, such as the geography of control, of quality of jobs or of wage-levels.

But if, on the whole, the evidence at regional level is that manufacturing looks likely to continue to be needed to perform a key role, the same is not necessarily true at *local* level. At this smaller spatial scale, services may very well perform an exporting role.

Activity 6.3

(a)   Why might local areas be more likely to survive by exporting services than are regions?

(b)   Give some examples of local areas within the UK which do have a service sector (or sectors) as the basis of their economy. (*Fothergill* et al. (1986) and *Wood* (1986) give examples of this.)

(c)   What kinds of implications might this have for the social structures of those places? (Think also of *Hall* (1985), *Thrift* (1986), *Lane* (1982) and *Massey* (1988).)

Examples abound of local areas with service industries as their basic, that is exporting, sectors. Some services may bring in income from quite a wide geographical area, sometimes including from outside the country. Towns with an important financial or professional services sector and resorts and historic towns which attract a lot of tourist trade are obvious examples. Retirement centres, too, may draw on wide areas. Each of these basic service sectors will have different implications for the local employment and social structure. Services which sell to a regional population may well cluster in the major town. Indeed *Fothergill* et al. (1986) suggest this may be the future economic base for many of Britain's cities:

> A linear extrapolation suggests that by the early decades of the next century few manufacturing jobs will be left in Britain's largest cities. Following the manufacturing-led model of urban decline . . . it would be tempting to suggest that cities might disappear entirely. A more likely outcome is that cities in future will be smaller and function primarily as service centres for their hinterlands rather than as centres of industrial production.

The social implications of such a future would vary greatly between cities. *Cooke* (1987), examining the internationalization of producer services, points to the emergence of a new world-scale urban hierarchy. And as *Thrift* (1986) points out, while a small number of elite world cities is emerging, of which London is one, 'other cities get only the leftovers, the manufacturing jobs and the lowlier service jobs. Thus the international services economy increasingly by-passes many cities and many workers.' For such cities, the future would be difficult. *Hall* (1985) asking 'whether . . . the inner cities in the older industrial regions have any economic future at all' talks of 'low-paid assembly industry', 'low-paid work in service industries associated with recreational or tourist developments' and 'some regional-scale office developments, mainly involved in routine data-processing'. In London, on the other hand, the development of a major international service sector is clearly under way. Financial services are now the second biggest sector in terms of employment (after education and health). The issue here is distributional (*Massey*, 1988). In London, as in some other world cities, the distribution of income within the workforce has become more polarized. This increasing inequality of incomes is true of the country as a whole, but earnings variations are sharpest of all in London: 'the divergence between manual and non-manual earnings, and between the highest and lowest paid in each group, is sharper in London than in the rest of the country' (Incomes Data Services, 1987).

At the level of the major city, however, export-base theory has come in for particularly severe questioning. As a very general rule, exports are likely to be proportionately less important the larger and more complex the economy being considered (Tiebout, 1956). And Blumenfeld (1955), putting this point together with the conceptual difficulties of categorization mentioned above, argues that the whole concept ought to be turned on its head for major urban regions. It is, he says, business and consumer services serving the urban area which 'enable it to substitute new "export" industries for any that decline as a result of the incessant vicissitudes of economic life. These services are the constant and permanent, hence the truly "basic" and "primary" elements of the metropolitan economy.'

6.4 What is an economy anyway?

6.4.1 Crowding out?

The discussions of deindustrialization by Singh and others, both concerning the definition of deindustrialization and concerning its causes, set the problems of the British economy, and of manufacturing, squarely in an international context. The decline of British manufacturing is seen to lie primarily in a loss of competitive power on the international stage.

There is, however, another view. This alternative approach, primarily though not exclusively elaborated in the work of Bacon and Eltis (1976), focuses much more on the problems of the *internal* structure of the UK economy. It is an explanation often referred to as 'the crowding-out thesis', and its argument is precisely that the explanation for the decline of UK manufacturing and the economy more generally lies in the restriction of opportunities for the profit-making sectors by the growth of other parts of the economy.

Instead of basic and dependent sectors, the distinction which is crucial to this view is that between marketed and non-marketed sectors. The marketed sector is that part of the economy where the output is sold on the open market; the product of the non-marketed sector is distributed through some other mechanism. The systems of publicly provided health and education fall within the non-marketed sector because their output is paid for out of taxes rather than through individual market purchases at the point of sale. The argument is that the non-marketed sector has expanded and that the marketed sector has been starved of resources and therefore of the potential for growth. The non-marketed sector has 'crowded out' the marketed one.

There are various mechanisms through which this crowding out is hypothesized to occur: through depriving the marketed sector of sufficient sources of labour; by depriving it of sources of investment; and through the impact of taxes levied to finance the non-marketed sector but reclaimed through higher wage demands. Each of these has been debated. On employment, the argument is that the increasing demand for labour by the expanding non-marketed sector has restricted the supply of workers to the marketed sector. In reply, opponents of the thesis point to evidence we have already examined in Chapter 3: that the expansion of the non-marketed sector has mainly been in public sector services and that the majority of workers taken on have been new recruits to the national workforce, rather than poached from elsewhere. Overwhelmingly it has been women who have been recruited to these expanding areas; the economic activity rate among married women has risen markedly (see Chapter 2). The declining marketed sector, on the other hand, employed mostly men.

The argument that the expansion of the non-marketed sector has deprived the marketed sector of funds for investment has also been disputed by pointing to evidence which indicates no shortage of money for investment and, anyway, an increase in manufacturing investment in the 1960s (Cairncross, 1979). Indeed, the counter-argument goes, it is not that the decline of private-sector manufacturing has been caused by lack of funds for investment but the opposite: that its decline and low levels of profit have been what has deterred investments. The City, with its worldwide arena of investment opportunities, could find more profitable outlets elsewhere for its funds.

On the basis of the crowding-out thesis, inflation, low investment (and therefore low productivity growth) and the poor balance-of-payments record of British manufacturing are all products of these shifts in the internal structure of the economy.

In terms of policy prescriptions, while Singh and Thirlwall argue for more investment in manufacturing to improve the quality of its output, Bacon and Eltis argue that the crucial factor is to cut back on the non-marketed sector. It is important to stress that this interpretation of the economy (though not the policy prescriptions) is not confined to those from a 'conservative' camp. Bacon and Eltis resemble the regulationists (see Chapter 1) in their focus on the national economy and its internal structure and dynamic as the essential unit of analysis. It was pointed out in Chapters 2 and 4 that Aglietta and the regulationist school also argue that the difficulty of increasing productivity in the consumption goods sectors, and particularly those which in the post-war years operated collectively through non-market mechanisms, was squeezing out from the economy the possibility of making sufficient profit. It was in this light that they interpreted cutbacks in public sector services and privatization of parts of the sector which was previously public. Cutbacks in public sector services reduce the crowding-out effect, while privatization involves a direct transfer from the non-marketed to the marketed sector, thus expanding the sphere in which it is possible to make private profits and also potentially reducing the labour-intensity of such services as the discipline of the profit motive makes itself felt in measures designed to cut costs. While for the 'crowding-out theorists' such policies are the key to reviving the economy, for the regulationists they are one among a whole gamut of changes necessary to overcome the problems posed by the increasing rigidities of Fordism and allow the continuation of capitalist accumulation.

The question which these theories are in the end all addressing is: what is the necessary cornerstone of the economy? The answer given is: private profit. That only what is profitable to the private sector is wealth-creating; that only on the basis of profits once made can other things, such as non-profit-making services, be afforded. Specifically, without profit made from marketed goods and services, no surplus can be generated and no non-marketed goods and services, therefore, can be provided. What has happened in recent decades is that an increasing percentage of the output/ profit of the marketed sector has gone into the non-marketed sector, thus squeezing off its growth through the mechanisms mentioned above.

At this point, there are a number of important issues to consider:

1   In itself, as with the basic:dependent distinction, the marketed:non-marketed distinction has nothing to do with the distinction between manufacturing and services.

2   Nor, indeed, is it related in a one-to-one fashion with the division of the economy into public and private sectors. While most of the non-marketed sector may be public, not all of public sector production is non-marketed, though in services it mainly is. Indeed it is frequently a matter of political contention the degree to which the public sector should behave like the private sector and make profitability its overriding goal. Moreover, the non-marketed sector is quite wide. It includes not only public sector services but also, for instance, the armed forces.

This issue is important. In much of the debate over Bacon and Eltis it has been assumed that marketed = private sector and non-marketed = public sector. (Indeed some of their argument presupposes a need to 'motivate' the private sector through high levels of profit in the marketed sector.) But there is no need at all for this to be the case. The public sector can include both marketed and non-marketed activities, and the degree to which it does so will vary with political circumstances.

3   As in the case of other theories, government policies based on this approach would have distinct geographical implications. Chapters 2 and 3, *Hall* (1985) and *Allen* (1988) indicate what these might be.

Activity 6.4

(a)   In comparison with other sectors of the economy, the geography of employment in certain public sector services is very even in relation to population. Which services? And why?

(b)   How might the geographies of publicly and privately provided consumer services differ? And why? What might be the geographical impact of privatization of such services?

6.4.2   What is wealth?

Underlying all these issues, however, are more fundamental ones, which bring us back to issues of definition and conceptualization. Issues such as: how does one define **profitability**? what is the wealth of a society?

The Bacon and Eltis thesis does not in itself make clear how to decide what is and what is not profitable. At first sight this may seem obvious, but consider the following issues:

●   Over what time-horizon is profitability to be measured? Are we talking of short-term or long-term viability? And what difference might it make? (*Cooke* (1987) points to contrasts here between Japanese companies on the one hand and UK and US ones on the other.)

●   Over how wide a segment of the economy is profitability to be calculated? For example: in a railway system should profitability be calculated for every individual line or for the system as a whole? Should every sector in the economy be individually run for profit or should some (transport and energy are obvious examples) be seen more as contributing to the profitability of the economy as a whole? At present in the UK the railway system is expected to make a profit, but roads are not.

●   What kinds of costs and benefits should be included in the calculations? For instance, should social costs and benefits be included as well as private ones?

What all these questions make clear is that the issue of whether or not a particular economic activity is profitable is not a simple, clear-cut one. The decision about how to calculate profitability is, either implicitly or explicitly, always the result of the application of social and/or political criteria and priorities. Like the definitions of 'full employment' and 'unemployment' (Chapter 2), the definition of profitability is socially constructed and can vary both over time and from one society to another.

Both issues are clear from a consideration of private and social costs and benefits. In the discussion of uneven development in Chapter 2 it was pointed out that one of the causes of the shifting patterns of development over time is that firms exhaust the advantages of already industrialized areas and move off to less developed ones. Those firms make their calculations of profitability on the basis of their own, private, costs and benefits. But there will also be **social costs and benefits**. Perhaps most obviously, physical infrastructure, from roads to sewerage to lighting, which has already been paid for in the older area will be abandoned or under-used while more public money will have to be spent on laying out new infrastructure in the areas to be developed. But the boundary between public and private is not fixed. At one extreme infrastructure may be publicly provided and subsidized; at the other it may be entirely up to the private sector, as with railways in nineteenth-century Britain, to build and run it. Nor does the boundary remain fixed for the calculations by individual firms. In different countries companies are required to contribute in varying ways to compensate for any 'social' costs of their decisions to invest or disinvest: that is, some of those costs are privatized. Moreover, the way in which profitability is calculated may well vary depending on whether an activity is in the public or private sector. Public bus companies, for example, traditionally cross-subsidized between profitable and non-profitable individual routes. That system came under threat with deregulation/privatization.

Finally, putting together the last two questions in the list above raises the issue of those parts of the economy which, although not in themselves profitable, are essential to the running of other, profitable, sectors. That is, even if they are not profitable directly in financial terms, they are in some sense '**productive**'. One obvious example would be major parts of the education and health services, or publicly subsidized transport infrastructure and services. Gough, for instance, writing in the 1970s of public expenditure as a whole, argued:

> The single most important conclusion that emerges is that an increasing proportion of the total are productive expenditures, producing inputs for the capitalist sector. The share of social services, infrastructure and accumulation expenditures is growing, while that of unproductive . . . expenditure is declining. It is wrong, therefore, to regard the growth of the state as an unproductive 'burden' upon the capitalist sector; more and more it is a necessary precondition for private capital accumulation. (1975, p. 80)

This notion of sectors being '**indirectly productive**' opens the door to much wider considerations. Since the economy is so interrelated, where can one then draw the line between what is productive and what is not? We cannot answer that question here. Suffice it to say that the issue has provoked long-running and still continuing debates within many of the major theoretical traditions. Moreover, some activities which are considered productive in one kind of economy, say a capitalist one, might not look so productive in another, and vice versa.

In the end, however, the question which the issue raises is: what is economic growth *for*? It is against that criterion that 'productiveness' must be judged, and the answer will consequently vary between societies. It might be argued that the purpose of an economy should be the enhanced reproduction of society. If that were the case the production of food, health and education, for instance, would be seen, at this stage of development, as more productive than for example the production of luxury consumer goods. What Bacon and Eltis and Aglietta, from their supportive and critical positions respectively, are arguing is that in a capitalist society profit is the motor and the measure of wealth. Moreover in western capitalist economies, such as the UK, that means profits made through the private sector and in private capitalist, not public, hands. Bacon and Eltis would argue that such profit is needed precisely in order to be able to do all the other things. But that in turn opens up all the questions with which this section began. Is that profit to be calculated in relation to the economy as a whole or in relation to each individual economic activity? Is it short-term profit which is to be maximized or long? And should the profit be under the control of private individuals and corporations, or be in public hands? The answers to the questions 'what is wealth?' and 'what is productive?' clearly also depend on what kind of economy and society one is talking about.

6.4.3   The economic and the social

So what *is* an economy? What is the difference between an economy and a society? In much discussion a distinction is made between 'the economic' and 'the social'; indeed all the theories discussed so far in one way or another work with such a distinction. It is important, therefore, to examine this great divide and to explore what are commonly seen to be the boundaries between the economic and the social. This can be done from a number of different directions.

Take the notion of work. In a society such as ours there are a number of different purposes to the activity of 'work'. From the point of view of the economy as a whole, the work put in must in some sense enable the society to continue and if possible improve or develop. It is what is necessary for the reproduction of society. From the point of view of an individual, work can be the means of providing daily needs, a basic source of income and/or a source of satisfaction and of communication with others.

Consider just two of these definitions: work as a means whereby society can continue and develop, and work as a source of income for individuals. These two definitions do not only characterize the purpose of 'work' differently; they also in fact refer to different things. The second definition only refers to paid employment, while the first refers to all the work which is necessary to keep society going.

The point, in relation to the discussion here, is that most definitions of 'the economic' include only that work which is paid. Yet much work goes unpaid;

work which is clearly necessary for the reproduction week after week, year after year, of society as a whole. The London Industrial Strategy (GLC, 1985), in its study of the economy of the capital city, estimated that out of 280 million hours work done keeping London going every week, only 100 million hours is paid for. 180 million hours – that is almost two-thirds of the work – is unpaid labour. Much of this unpaid labour is, of course, domestic labour in the home which, because it is not paid employment, is not usually treated as part of the economy. It usually goes uncounted. In fact in the Census of 1891 housewives were counted as employed in domestic service. This was a Census recently dubbed by a modern (male) commentator as 'perhaps the most eccentric of censuses'. But was it? It depends on how we want to conceptualize the economy and the relationship between the economic and the social.

What is clear is that the non-waged economy is intimately linked to the waged. It has already been seen that there are many who argue that an activity does not necessarily have to be individually profitable to contribute to the production of profit in the economy more widely. Such indirectly productive activity may not even enter into the paid economy. There has been a major theoretical debate in recent years analysing how in this sense domestic labour is productive in the context of the wider economy. It performs tasks which are necessary for the waged economy to function, from child-rearing (producing future workers) to housekeeping (maintaining current workers). Equally with many public services, for instance, domestic labour could be said to be indirectly productive. In the UK at the moment it seems to be acceptable that men in paid work should often rely on the labour of others (usually women) for a vast range of support services which are provided free of charge. And yet we can read: 'our modern economy cannot afford, nor can our democratic ideology tolerate, the existence of a large section of the population living by the efforts of others' (Myrdal and Klein, 1968, p. 26). Who in that quotation is living by the efforts of whom, do you think?

In fact, in that quotation, the parasitic section of society supposedly 'living by the efforts of others' is women doing domestic labour in their homes. The fact that they are not paid means that their work is not even noticed. Here, then, we have yet another major division of economy and society, equally significant and equally important to conceptualize correctly. Coote (1981), linking the conceptualization of full employment to the conceptualization of work, writes in complete contrast to the above quotation that it has been argued: 'that "women have not in our recent history ever had full employment". But of course that is true only in relation to paid employment. Most women are already *over-employed*' (p. 5).

Domestic labour is also, of course, productive of wealth in its broader conception, which goes beyond the production of financial profit, to include the fuller reproduction of society. Care for people who will never enter the paid labour force (people over retiring age are the most obvious example) when it is carried out in the home is productive only in this wider sense.

The operation of the domestic sector can affect the profit-oriented sector in other ways, too. More women earning a wage in the paid-labour sector can increase the demand for consumer durables, for instance. On the other hand the fact that many women have to fit paid labour around the demands of domestic work means that they are more likely to accept part-time jobs and that their choice within the job market is in many ways restricted. Thus, for instance, once committed to part-time working, people can afford, for reasons both of time and of money, to travel less far to work. This restricts their geographical range of choice and increases the monopoly power of local employers. Thus as Chapter 4 pointed out, the organization of domestic labour affects the way the waged labour-market functions, and women's jobs remain low-paid. This exclusion from full participation, in terms of either time or skill, of a section of the potential labour force represents a loss to the economy as a whole.

Further, the existence of an unpaid domestic labour sector means that it is hard to establish commercially viable, socialized provision. Laundries have difficulty being commercial because their 'competition' comes from unpaid labour. Unsubsidized child-minders and crèches are so expensive (because labour-intensive) that they often exclude most sections of society where (the women's) wages are too low to make paying for child-minding a possible option. In turn, the lack of provision of such facilities, combined with the apparent inability of most men to do their share of domestic labour, reinforces women's lower participation and weaker bargaining position within the waged labour markets – which makes it more difficult to pay for crèches and suchlike. The difference here between need (the social concept) and demand (the economic concept) is clear. To break the circle subsidized provision would be needed (there is another solution which we shall come to later) and this would require public expenditure in some form.

Here we again run into questions of what is productive and what is wealth-creating. If public expenditure on work such as this, because it is not immediately as an individual, economic activity financially profitable, is defined as unproductive and as a drain on the wealth-creating sector, then the constraints on it will be severe. The implication is the reinforcement of low pay and inequalities within the waged-labour sector, and the continuingly disadvantaged position of women in that sector. Contrarily, such moves can both give greater weight, ideologically, to women's work in the home and yet at the same time increase its invisibility. Married women not working for a wage are less likely to be considered 'really' unemployed:

> I say 'real' in quotes because the official unemployment rate has never accurately reflected the numbers of people seeking work. This is because in Britain (unlike other countries which include all those people who are actively seeking work in the figures, whether or not they are claimants), to be classified as unemployed you actually have to be claiming benefit. The use of registration as the criterion has always meant that women have been strongly underrepresented in the official count ... over the past few years the official definition of unemployment has been narrowed. (Beechey, 1987a, p. 31)

In spite of all these mutually reinforcing logics, however, the boundary between the paid and unpaid sectors, just as between the public and private sectors, is not immutable. Apart from the fact that it varies dramatically between different countries, it has also changed over time within the UK. Chapter 3 showed how Gershuny and Miles argue that particular *service functions* can be performed in a range of different ways, thereby reflecting, and affecting, the wider organization of the economy. The London Industrial Strategy, which has a whole section called 'Battles around the Boundaries', points out, for instance, that laundry was once a private service, that it then became commercialized (and occasionally municipalized), only later through the development of domestic technology to become a home-based service again:

> The determination of what are social and private responsibilities has always been a political issue. It has never been a static unchanging matter which can be taken for granted. Public health, education, libraries, parks, mother and baby clinics and the rest were all seen as a scandalous waste of money and fiercely resisted. (GLC, 1985, p. 201)

The clearest examples have perhaps been in wartime, when women were needed in industry: then all kinds of policies were devised for helping to cope with housework and child-care.

Over the present period, too, the boundary has been shifted. Parts of some previously public services – care of the young, the elderly and the convalescent, making dinners for schoolchildren – have been moved back into the unpaid sector in the home. The ideological shift was encapsulated by a 1983 Inland Revenue decision to tax employer subsidies to workplace nurseries. In other words, nurseries were to be seen as a taxable perk, like company cars, rather than an (indirectly productive?) sector allowing parents to join the paid labour force. Privatization of consumer services has involved renegotiation of the boundaries between all three sectors (private, public and domestic). Reduction in public care for the elderly is a case in point. Some of it will now be done by the private sector (and thus be productive in terms of profit). But the private sector cannot serve those who cannot pay; in those cases the work will be done in the domestic sector, where it will be counted as unproductive. Meanwhile within the remains of the public sector, discussion will continue over whether or not such activities should be expected to 'pay for themselves'.

All this raises again the issues of calculation mentioned in the last section in the discussion of profit. Discussing recent changes in health, education and transport, the London Industrial Strategy concluded:

> All these things have one thing in common. They appear to save money in the account books of the state, or the balance sheets of private firms, but they do so by taking no account of the unpaid time of ordinary people. If we calculated economy in terms of reducing all society's labour time, then cottage hospitals, local schools, better bus services, would still be with us today, and all queues would be shorter. Imagine the change in the organization of health care if all travelling time and queueing time had to be paid for at the going rate. (p. 201)

There is a now growing body of literature which argues that this household sector is in a crisis as serious as that of manufacturing – though of course it will show up in a different way (Coote, 1981; Phillips, 1983; Beechey, 1987a). In part this crisis results from the changes just mentioned, but there are also other, longer-term, factors in play. On the one hand the main workers in the domestic sector, women, are increasingly entering the paid labour force. While most married women thereby take on the 'double shift' of paid and unpaid work, the time for the latter must inevitably get squeezed. On the other hand, changes in demographic structure, especially the increasing proportion of elderly people, are adding to the potential workload.

A whole range of 'policies' have been proposed to deal with this crisis. Firstly, the boundary between paid and unpaid work could be re-thought yet again. On the one hand increased financial aid could be made available to those doing the work in the home – increased child benefits and support for those caring for elderly dependants come to mind. This could be conceptualized either as (partial) payment for necessary work or as aid to reduce the necessity of joining the formal, paid-labour market. The other way of shifting the boundary would, of course, be to provide more facilities through the public sector. Secondly, a range of policies for other sectors of the economy could help make domestic work easier. The food sector, retailing and transport are perhaps the most obvious examples. Crèches in shopping centres, pensioners' luncheon clubs, teleshopping and the expansion of door-to-door delivery services, better public transport, and the encouragement of local 'convenience' shopping outlets (perhaps organized into federations, perhaps linked into major central supermarkets, to help keep costs down through bulk-buying etc.) – all these would lighten the load of the unpaid domestic sector. Thirdly, a start could be made towards encouraging a more equal division of domestic labour. Stronger legislation to equalize pay between men and women would reduce the 'obviousness' of the fact that it should be the woman who stays at home. There is a whole range of other things which could be done: some shopping centres have introduced nappy-changing facilities in the 'Gents'.

Perhaps the most significant policy is a reduction in working hours, in particular the shorter working-day and the shorter working-week (this is the 'other solution' referred to above). Previous chapters have analysed the rise in unemployment, in casualization and in part-time work (see also *Hudson*, 1988). What these things indicate, it has been argued, is a need to reorganize paid work (Beechey, 1987a), and in particular to spread it out more equally between members of society. This would not only reduce the burden on those who do a double shift of paid work and domestic labour, but would also help towards combatting men's under-achievement in the home, give all workers more access to home-life and their children, and make more real that vision of a 'leisure society' which is occasionally held out.

Such ideas currently run up against a whole range of objections, but central among them is the notion of what is a 'real job' (see Chapter 2). It is not just that only paid work is seen as 'real work', but that a real job is seen as a full-time one. Part-time work is currently deprived of many of the statutory rights which pertain to full-time jobs, and we have seen a number of times how part-time work throws the data collectors into confusion. The same, it has been argued, can be said about the increasing 'flexibility' of work. *Hudson* (1988) documents some of the current rationale for this flexibility. But instead of being flexible to suit only the demands of the workplace, perhaps it could be flexible also in relation to the needs of the home. And instead of being reduced to the status of the 'periphery' of the labour force, flexibly organized work, like part-time work, could have the rights and status of full-time work, where hours could anyway be reduced and flexibility increased (Beechey, 1987a). Such changes might also mean re-thinking once again what is meant by 'full employment'.

These questions of how 'work' should be organized, how it should be divided between paid and unpaid, indeed how we define it, are maybe just as important questions for the future as what should be the balance between manufacturing and services. Of course, to make these issues the priorities would mean – again – reconceptualizing both the economy and the relation between 'the economic' and 'the social'.

Summary

- A number of major issues have been addressed:
  - which sectors can be the motor of the economy?
  - what are the characteristics of an export base?
  - what in the future might be the main sources of paid employment?
  - what options are there for the distribution of work, paid and unpaid?
  - and what are the social implications of different decisions on all these issues, including their geographical implications, for instance at regional and local levels?
- Consideration of these questions has raised the issue of what are the most relevant divisions of the economy. A number of different ones have been considered, each of them cross-cutting with the others, and each allowing a different perspective on 'the economy'. The following divisions have been mentioned:

marketed	–	non-marketed
manufacturing	–	services
basic	–	dependent
productive	–	non-productive
public	–	private
waged	–	unwaged

For some of these divisions the definition may vary between societies and between theoretical approaches; in many the boundary is debatable, for all of them which activities fall into which category changes over time within any one society. Economic categories are social constructions.

Activity 6.5

This Activity is designed to help you review the chapter; you may like to try part of it after first reading the chapter and use the rest to help structure your revision. Where possible, bring in arguments/evidence from other chapters.

Take each of the following divisions in turn:

manufacturing	–	services
productive	–	unproductive
public	–	private
paid	–	unpaid
marketed	–	non-marketed
basic	–	dependent

and recap:

- if and why they are important (for instance in theoretical and/or policy debates)
- the debate about how to conceptualize them
- how their boundaries may shift over time
- the social cleavages/distinctions which they mark
- their different geographies
- the implications of policies which prioritize different categories.

Further reading

The issues discussed in this chapter are, to one degree or another, matters of public debate, and one way to pursue them is to keep pace through the media with current events, and to place the issues of the day in a wider context (for example to place arguments over working hours, or the imposition of six-day working weeks, in the context of the discussions in section 6.4.3).

There are numerous books which consider the shape of the British economy and its future. Two examples are Andrew Gamble's *Britain in Decline: Economic Policy, Political Strategy and the British State* (London and Basingstoke, Macmillan; 1981) which points to the often deleterious impact on the economy of the international role of much of British finance and industry, and *Whatever Happened to Britain?* by John Eatwell (London, Duckworth and BBC Publications; 1982) which also places the UK economic changes in a longer historical context. Other books are listed in the bibliography.

There is also an increasingly important feminist literature on the economy. Anne Phillips' *Hidden Hands: Women and Economic Policies* (London, Pluto Press; 1983) is a good introduction. Veronica Beechey takes up the issues around part-time work in *Unequal Work* (London, Verso; 1987). These and other debates can be pursued by looking at journals such as *Feminist Review*.

References

AGLIETTA, M. (1979) *A Theory of Capitalist Regulation: The US Experience*, London, New Left Books.

AGLIETTA, M. (1982) 'World capitalism in the eighties', *New Left Review*, No. 136, pp. 25–36.

ALLEN, J. (1988) 'The geographies of service', in Massey, D. and Allen, J. (eds) (associated Reader).

AMIN, S. (1976) *Unequal Development*, Brighton, Harvester Press.

ANDERSON, J. and COCHRANE, A. (eds) (1989) *A State of Crisis* (Restructuring Britain Reader), London, Hodder and Stoughton/The Open University.

ATKINSON, J. (1984) *Flexibility, Uncertainty and Manpower Management*, Institute of Manpower Studies, Report 89, Falmer, University of Sussex.

ATKINSON, J. (1985) 'The changing corporation', in Clutterbuck, D. (ed.) *New Patterns of Work*, Aldershot, Gower.

ATKINSON, J. and GREGORY, D. (1986) 'A flexible future: Britain's dual labour force', *Marxism Today*, April, pp. 12–17.

ATKINSON, J. and MEAGER, N. (1986) *New Forms of Work Organization*, Institute of Manpower Studies, Report 121, Falmer, University of Sussex.

BACON, R. and ELTIS, W.A. (1976) *Britain's Economic Problem: Too Few Producers*, London and Basingstoke, Macmillan.

BARRAS, R. (1984) *Growth and Technical Change in the UK Service Sector*, London, The Technical Change Centre.

BEAUMONT, P. (1987) *The Decline of Trade Union Organisation*, Beckenham, Croom Helm.

BEECHEY, V. (1983) 'Woman and employment', Units 10 and 11 of *The Changing Experience of Women* (U221), Milton Keynes, The Open University Press.

BEECHEY, V. (1987a) 'It's off to work we go?', *Marxism Today*, May, pp. 28–32.

BEECHEY, V. (1987b) *Unequal Work*, London, Verso.

BELL, D. (1973) *The Coming of Post-industrial Society*, London, Heinemann.

BELL, D. (1980) 'The information society', in Forester, T. (ed.) *The Microelectronics Revolution*, Oxford, Basil Blackwell.

BLACKABY, F. (ed.) (1979) *De-industrialisation*, London/Heinemann/National Institute of Economic and Social Research, Economic Policy Papers 2.

BLUMENFELD, H. (1955) 'The economic base of the metropolis, critical remarks on the "basic:non-basic" concept', *Journal of the American Institute of Planners*, Vol. XXI, pp. 114–32.

BODDY, M., LOVERING, J. and BASSETT, K. (eds) (1986) *Sunbelt City? A Study of Economic Change in Britain's M4 Growth Corridor*, London, Oxford University Press.

BONEFIELD, W. (1987) 'Reformulation of state theory', *Capital and Class*, No. 33, pp. 96–127.

BOWLES, S. and EDWARDS, R. (1985) *Understanding Capitalism: Competition, Command and Change in the US Economy*, New York, Harper & Row.

BRANDT REPORT (1980) *North-South: A Programme for Survival*, The Report of the Independent Commission on International Development Issues under the Chairmanship of Willy Brandt, London, Pan Books.

BRAVERMAN, H. (1974) *Labour and Monopoly Capital: The Degradation of Work in the Twentieth Century*, New York, Monthly Review Press.

BUCK, N. (1985) 'Service industries and local labour markets: towards an anatomy of service employment', Regional Science Association Annual Conference, September.

BURAWOY, M. (1979) *Manufacturing Consent: Changes in the Labour Process Under Monopoly Capitalism*, Chicago, University of Chicago Press.

CAIRNCROSS, A. (1979) 'What is deindustrialisation?', in Blackaby, F. (ed.).

CASEY, B. (1987) 'The extent and nature of temporary employment in Great Britain', *Policy Studies*, Vol. 8, No. 1, pp. 64–75.

CENTRE FOR ALTERNATIVE INDUSTRIAL AND TECHNOLOGICAL SYSTEMS (CAITS) (1986) *Flexibility: who needs it?*, London, Polytechnic of North London.

CLARKE, J. and CRITCHER, C. (1985) *The Devil Makes Work: Leisure in Capitalist Britain*, London and Basingstoke, Macmillan.

COCHRANE, A. and ANDERSON, J. (eds) (1989) *Politics in Transition* (Restructuring Britain), London, Sage/The Open University.

COCKBURN, C. (1983) *Brothers: Male Dominance and Technological Change*, London, Pluto Press.

COCKBURN, C. (1987) *Women, Trade Unions and Political Parties*, London, Fabian Research Series 349.

CONFEDERATION OF BRITISH INDUSTRY (1985a) *Managing Change: The Organisation of Work*, London, Confederation of British Industry.

CONFEDERATION OF BRITISH INDUSTRY (1985b) *Change to Succeed: The Nationwide Findings*, London, Confederation of British Industry.

COOKE, P. (1985) 'Radical regions? Space, time and gender relations in Emilia, Provence and South Wales', in Rees, G., Bujra, J., Littlewood, P., Newby, H. and Rees, T.L. (eds) *Political Action and Social Identity: Class, Locality and Ideology*, London and Basingstoke, Macmillan.

COOKE, P. (1987) 'Spatial development processes: organized or disorganized?', in Thrift, N. and Williams, P. (eds) *Class and Space: The Making of Urban Society*, London, Routledge and Kegan Paul, pp. 306–29. Reprinted in Massey, D. and Allen, J. (eds) (1988) (associated Reader).

COOTE, A. (1981) 'The Alternative Economic Strategy: a new starting point', *New Socialist*, No. 2, Nov/Dec, pp. 4–7.

CREIGH, S., ROBERTS, C., GORMAN, A. and SAWYER, P. (1986) 'Self-employment in Britain: results from the Labour Force Surveys, 1981–1984', *Employment Gazette*, Vol. 94, No. 5, pp. 183–94.

DAMESICK, P.J. (1986) 'Service industries, employment and regional development in Britain', Institute of British Geographers, *Transactions*, New Series, Vol. 11, No. 2, pp. 212–26.

DANIELS, P.W. (1986) 'Producer services and the post-industrial space-economy', in Martin, R. and Rowthorn, B. (eds) pp. 291–321. Reprinted in Massey, D. and Allen, J. (eds) (1988) (associated Reader).

DANIELS, P.W., LEYSHON, O. and THRIFT, N. (1986) *UK Producer Services: The International Dimension*, Working Papers on Producer Services, No. 1, University of Liverpool.

DICKEN, P. (1976) 'The multi-plant enterprise and geographic space', *Regional Studies*, Vol. 10, No. 4, pp. 401–12.

DICKEN, P. (1982) 'The industrial structure and the geography of manufacturing', in Johnston, R.J. and Doornkamp, J.C. (eds) *The Changing Geography of the United Kingdom*, London, Methuen.

DOERINGER, P. and PIORE, M. (1971) *Internal Labour Markets and Manpower Analysis*, Lexington, VA, Lexington Books.

DUNFORD, M.F., GEDDES, M. and PERRONS, D. (1981) 'Regional policy and the crisis in the UK: a long-run perspective', *International Journal of Urban and Regional Research*, Vol. 5, No. 3, pp. 377–410.

FINE, B. and HARRIS, L. (1985) *The Peculiarities of the British Economy*, London, Lawrence and Wishart.

FOGARTY, M. (1986) *Trade Unions and British Industrial Development*, London, Policy Studies Institute.

FOTHERGILL, S. and GUDGIN, G. (1982) *Unequal Growth: Urban and Regional Employment Change in the UK*, London, Heinemann.

FOTHERGILL, S., GUDGIN, G., KITSON, M. and MONK, S. (1986) 'The deindustrialisation of the city', in Martin, R. and Rowthorn, B. (eds) pp. 214–37. Reprinted in Massey, D. and Allen, J. (eds) (1988) (associated Reader).

FRANK, A.G. (1967) *Capitalism and Underdevelopment in Latin America*, New York, Monthly Review Press.

FREEMAN, C. (1987) *Technology Policy and Economic Performance: Lessons from Japan*, London, Frances Pinter.

FREEMAN, C., CLARK, J. AND SOETE, L. (1982) *Unemployment and Technical Innovation*, London, Frances Pinter.

FRIEDMAN, A.L. (1977) *Industry and Labour: Class Struggle at Work and Monopoly Capitalism*, London and Basingstoke, Macmillan.

FROBEL, F., HEINRICHS, J. and DREYE, O. (1980) *The New International Division of Labour: Structural Unemployment in Industrialised Countries and Industrialisation in Developing Countries*, Cambridge, Cambridge University Press.

GARTMAN, D. (1979), 'Origins of the assembly line and capitalist control of work at Ford', in Zimbalist, A. (ed.) *Case Studies on the Labour Process*, New York, Monthly Review Press.

GERSHUNY, J.I. (1978) *After Industrial Society? Emerging Self-service Economy*, London and Basingstoke, Macmillan.

GERSHUNY, J.I. and MILES, I.D. (1983) *The New Service Economy: The Transformation of Employment in Industrial Societies*, London, Frances Pinter.

GILLESPIE, A. and GREEN, A. (1987) 'The changing geography of "producer services" employment in Britain', *Regional Studies*, Vol. 21, No. 5, pp. 397–411.

GODDARD, J. and COOMBES, R. (1987) *The North-South Divide: Local Perspectives*, Centre for Urban and Regional Studies, University of Newcastle upon Tyne.

GOUGH, I. (1975) 'State expenditure in advanced capitalism', *New Left Review*, Vol. 92, pp. 53–92.

GOULD, A. and KEEBLE, D. (1984) 'New firms and rural industrialization in East Anglia', *Regional Studies*, Vol. 18, No. 3, pp. 189–201.

GREATER LONDON COUNCIL (1985) *London Industrial Strategy*, London, GLC.

GREEN, F. and SUTCLIFFE, B. (1987) *The Profit System: The Economics of Capitalism*, Harmondsworth, Penguin Books.

GUILIANO, V.E. (1985) 'The mechanisation of office work', in Forester, T. (ed.) *The Information Technology Revolution*, Oxford, Basil Blackwell.

HAKIM, C. (1987) 'Trends in the flexible workforce', *Employment Gazette*, Vol. 95, No. 11, pp. 549–60.

HALL, P. (1981) 'The geography of the fifth Kondratieff cycle', *New Society*, Vol. 55, No. 958, pp. 535–7.

HALL, P. (1985) 'The geography of the fifth Kondratieff cycle', in Hall, P. and Markusen, A. (eds) *Silicon Landscapes*, London, Allen and Unwin, pp. 1–19. Reprinted in Massey, D. and Allen, J. (eds) (1988) (associated Reader).

HAMNETT, C., McDOWELL, L. and SARRE, P. (eds) (1989) *The Changing Social Structure* (Restructuring Britain), London, Sage/The Open University.

HARRIS, L. (1985) 'British capital: manufacturing, finance and multinational corporations', in Coates, D., Johnston, G. and Bush, R. (eds) *A Socialist Anatomy of Britain*, Cambridge, Polity Press.

HARRIS, R.I.D. (1987) 'The role of manufacturing in regional growth', *Regional Studies*, Vol. 21, No. 4, pp. 301–12.

HEPWORTH, M.E., GREEN, A. and GILLESPIE, A. (1987) 'The spatial division of information of labour in Great Britain', *Society and Space*, Vol. 19, pp. 793–806.

HILL, S. (1981) *Competition and Control at Work*, London, Heinemann.

HOBSBAWM, E.J. (1968) *Industry and Empire: Economic History of Britain since 1750*, London, Weidenfeld and Nicolson.

HOWELLS, J. (1984) 'The location of research and development: some observations and evidence from Britain', *Regional Studies*, Vol. 18, No. 1, pp. 13–29.

HUDSON, R. (1988) 'Labour market changes and new forms of work in "old" industrial regions', in Massey, D. and Allen, J. (eds) (associated Reader).

HUDSON, R. and WILLIAMS, A. (1986) *The United Kingdom*, Western Europe Economic and Social Studies, London, Harper and Row.

IETTO-GILLIES, G. (1987) *The Internationalization of the UK Economy: An Empirical and Comparative Analysis*, Occasional Paper in Economics, No. 9, London, South Bank Polytechnic.

INCOME DATA SERVICES (1986) *Flexibility at Work*, No. 360, London, IDS.

INCOME DATA SERVICES (1987) 'Earnings variations are sharpest in London', *Labour Market Supplement on London and the South East*, December, p. 11, London, IDS.

JACOBS, J. (1970) *The Economy of Cities*, London, Cape.

KALDOR, N. (1966) *Causes of the Slow Rate of Economic Growth of the United Kingdom*, Cambridge, Cambridge University Press.

KAPLINSKY, R. (1984) *Automation: The Technology and Society*, Longman, London.

KEEBLE, D. (1976) *Industrial Location and Planning in the United Kingdom*, London, Methuen.

KEEBLE, D. (1980) 'Industrial decline, regional policy and the urban-rural manufacturing shift in the United Kingdom', *Environment and Planning A*, Vol. 12, pp. 945–62.

KUMAR, K. (1978) *Prophecy and Progress: The Sociology of Industrial and Post-industrial Society*, Harmondsworth, Penguin Books.

LABOUR RESEARCH (1983) 'The manufacturers', New Technology Special, Vol. 72, No. 11, pp. 290–92.

LABOUR RESEARCH (1986) 'The growing army of self employed', Vol. 75, No. 2, pp. 13–15.

LABOUR RESEARCH (1987) 'Unions face fall-out from industrial decline', Vol. 76, No. 9, pp. 13–15.

LACEY, R. (1987) *Ford: The Men and the Machine*, London, Pan Books.

LANE, T. (1982) 'The unions: caught on the ebb tide', *Marxism Today*, September, pp. 6–13. Reprinted in Massey, D. and Allen, J. (eds) (1988) (associated Reader).

LASH, S. and URRY, J. (1987) *The End of Organized Capitalism*, Cambridge, Polity Press.

LEE, C.H. (1986) *The British Economy since 1700: A Macro-economic Perspective*, Cambridge, Cambridge University Press.

LIPIETZ, A. (1987) *Mirages and Miracles: The Crises of Global Fordism*, Verso, London.

LITTLER, C. (1982) *The Development of the Labour Process in Capitalist Societies*, Heinemann, London.

MACINNES, J. (1987) *The Question of Flexibility*, Research Paper No. 5, Department of Social and Economic Research, University of Glasgow.

MANDEL, E. (1975) *Late Capitalism*, London, New Left Books.

MARSH, P. (1982) *The Robot Age*, London, Abacus Books.

MARSHALL, J. (1985) 'Research policy and review 4: Services in a postindustrial economy', *Environment and Planning A*, Vol. 17, pp. 1155–67.

MARSHALL, J.N., DAMESICK, P. and WOOD, P. (1987) 'Understanding the location and role of producer services in the United Kingdom', *Environment and Planning A*, Vol. 19, pp. 575–95.

MARSHALL, M. (1987) *Long Waves of Regional Development* London and Basingstoke, Macmillan.

MARTIN, R. (1986) 'Thatcherism and Britain's industrial landscape', in Martin, R. and Rowthorn, B. (eds) pp. 238–90.

MARTIN, R. (1988) 'Industrial capitalism in transition: the contemporary reorganization of the British space economy', in Massey, D. and Allen, J. (eds) (associated Reader).

MARTIN, R. and ROWTHORN, B. (eds) (1986) *The Geography of De-Industrialisation*, London and Basingstoke, Macmillan.

MASSEY, D. (1979) 'In what sense a regional problem?', *Regional Studies*, Vol. 13, pp. 233–43.

MASSEY, D. (1984) *Spatial Divisions of Labour: Social Structures and the Geography of Production*, London and Basingstoke, Macmillan.

MASSEY, D. (1988) 'Uneven development: social change and spatial divisions of labour', in Massey, D. and Allen, J. (eds) (associated Reader).

MASSEY, D. and ALLEN, J. (eds) (1988) *Uneven Re-Development: Cities and Regions in Transition* (Restructuring Britain), London, Hodder and Stoughton/The Open University (associated Reader).

MASSEY, D. and MILES, N. (1984) 'Mapping out the unions', *Marxism Today*, May, pp. 19–22.

McDOWELL, L., SARRE, P. and HAMNETT, C. (eds) (1989) *Divided Nation: Social and Cultural Change in Britain* (Restructuring Britain Reader), London, Hodder and Stoughton/The Open University.

MEAGER, N. (1986) 'Temporary work in Britain', *Employment Gazette*, Vol. 94, No. 1, pp. 7–15.

MENSCH, G. (1980) *Stalemate in Technology*, New York, Ballinger.

MILES, I. (1985) 'The new post-industrial state', *Futures*, Vol. 17, No. 6, pp. 588–617.

MILLWARD, N. and STEVENS, M. (1986) *British Workplace Industrial Relations 1980–1984*, Aldershot, Gower.

MORGAN, K. and SAYER, A. (1985) 'A "modern" industry in a "mature" region: the remaking of management-labour relations', *International Journal of Urban and Regional Research*, Vol. 9, pp. 383–403. Reprinted in Massey, D. and Allen, J. (eds) (1988) (associated Reader).

MYRDAL, A. and KLEIN, V. (1968) *Women's Two Roles: Women and Work*, Second edition, London, Routledge and Kegan Paul.

NATIONAL ECONOMIC AND DEVELOPMENT COUNCIL (1985) *Changing Working Patterns and Practices*, London, NEDC.

OBERHAUSER, A. (1987) 'Labour, production and the state: decentralization of the French automobile industry', *Regional Studies*, Vol. 21, No. 5, pp. 445–58.

OFFE, C. (1985) *Disorganized Capitalism*, Cambridge, Polity Press.

PAGNAMENTA, P. and OVERY, R. (1984) *All Our Working Lives*, London, BBC Publications.

PECK, J. and HAUGHTON, G. (1987) *Training and the Contemporary Reconstruction of Skill*, North West Industry Research Unit Working Paper No. 19, School of Geography, University of Manchester.

PERRONS, D.C. (1981) 'The role of Ireland in the new international division of labour: a proposed framework for regional analysis', *Regional Studies*, Vol. 15, No. 2, pp. 81–100.

PERRONS, D. (1986) 'Unequal integration in global Fordism: the case of Ireland', in Scott, A.J. and Storper, M. (eds) *Production, Work, Territory: Geographical Anatomy of Industrial Capitalism*, London, Allen and Unwin, Ch. 12.

PHILLIPS, A. (1983) *Hidden Hands: Women and Economic Policies*, London, Pluto Press.

PIORE, M.J. and SABEL, C.F. (1984) *The Second Industrial Divide: Prospects for Prosperity*, Basic Books, New York.

POLLERT, A. (1987) *Flexible Patterns of Work and Ideology*, Women and Employment Conference, September.

PRAIS, S. (1976) *The Evolution of Giant Firms in Britain*, Cambridge, Cambridge University Press.

PRICE, R. and BAIN, G.S. (1983) 'Union growth in Britain: retrospect and prospect', *British Journal of Industrial Relations*, Vol. 21, No. 1, pp. 46–68.

PROWSE, M. (1987) 'Manufacturing: a decline which may have gone too far', in *The Thatcher Years: The Policies and the Prospects*, A Financial Times Publication.

RADA, J. (1981) *The Impact of Micro-Electronics: A Tentative Appraisal of Information Technology*, International Labour Office, Geneva.

RAINNIE, A. (1985) 'Small firms, big problems: the political economy of small businesses', *Capital and Class*, No. 25, pp. 140–68.

RAJAN, A. (1985) 'Service industry: consumer or creator of national wealth?', *Futures*, Vol. 17, No. 1, pp. 52–6.

RAJAN, A. (1987) *Services: The Second Industrial Revolution*, London, Butterworth.

RHODES, J. (1986) 'Regional dimensions of industrial decline', in Martin, R. and Rowthorn, B. (eds) pp. 138–68.

ROBERTSON, J., BRIGGS, J. and GOODCHILD, A. (1982) *Structure and Employment Prospects of the Service Industries*, Research Paper No. 30, London, Department of Employment.

ROBINSON, O. (1985) 'The changing labour market: the phenomenon of part-time employment in Britain', *National Westminster Bank Quarterly Review*, November, pp. 19–29.

ROBINSON, O. and WALLACE, J. (1984) 'Growth and utilization of part-time labour in Great Britain', *Employment Gazette*, Vol. 92, No. 9, pp. 391–7.

ROTHWELL, R. (1982) 'The role of technology in industrial change: implications for regional policy', *Regional Studies*, Vol. 16, No. 5, pp. 361–70.

ROWBOTHAM, S. (1973) *Hidden from History*, Pluto Press, London.

ROWTHORN, B. (1986) 'De-industrialisation in Britain', in Martin, R. and Rowthorn, B. (eds) pp. 1–30.

ROWTHORN, R.E. and WELLS, J.R. (1987) *De-industrialization and Foreign Trade*, Cambridge, Cambridge University Press.

SABEL, C.F. (1982) *Work and Politics: The Division of Labour in Industry*, Cambridge, Cambridge University Press.

SARGENT, J.R. (1979) 'UK performance in services', in Blackaby, F. (ed.).

SAYER, A. (1982) 'Explaining manufacturing shift: a reply to Keeble', *Environment and Planning A*, Vol. 14, pp. 119–25.

SAYER, A. (1985) 'Industry and space: a sympathetic critique of radical research', *Society and Space*, Vol. 3, No. 1, pp. 3–29.

SCHOENBERGER, E. (1987) 'Technological and organizational change in automobile production: spatial implications', *Regional Studies*, Vol. 21, No. 3, pp. 199–214.

SCHUMPETER, J. (1934) *The Theory of Economic Development*, Cambridge, Mass., Harvard University Press.

SCHUMPETER, J. (1939) *Business Cycles*, New York, McGraw-Hill.

SCOTT, A.J. and STORPER, M. (1987) 'High technology industry and regional development: a theoretical critique and reconstruction', *International Social Science Journal*, No. 112, pp. 215–32.

SCOTT, A.J. and STORPER, M. (1988) 'The geographical foundations and social regulation of flexible production systems', in Wolch, J. and Dear, M. (eds) *Territory and Social Reproduction*, London, Allen and Unwin.

SHUTT, J. and WHITTINGTON, R. (1987) 'Fragmentation strategies and the rise of small units: cases from the North West', *Regional Studies*, Vol. 21, No. 1, pp. 13–23.

SINGELMANN, J. (1978) *From Agriculture to Services*, London, Sage.

SINGH, A. (1977) 'UK industry and the world economy: a case of deindustrialisation?', *Cambridge Journal of Economics*, Vol. 1, pp. 113–36.

STONE, M. (1984) 'Competing with Japan – the rules of the game', *Long Range Planning*, Vol. 17, No. 2, pp. 33–47.

TARLING, R. (1981) 'The relationship between employment and output: where does segmentation theory lead us?', in Wilkinson, F. (ed.) *The Dynamics of Labour Market Segmentation*, London, Academic Press.

THIRLWALL, A.P. (1982) 'Deindustrialization in the United Kingdom', *Lloyds Bank Review*, Vol. 144, pp. 22–37.

THRIFT, N. (1986) 'The geography of international economic disorder', in Johnston, R.J. and Taylor, P.J. (eds) *A World in Crisis? Geographical Perspectives*, pp.

12–67, Oxford, Basil Blackwell. Reprinted in Massey, D. and Allen, J. (eds) (1988) (associated Reader).

THRIFT, N. (1987) 'Manufacturing rural geography?', *Journal of Rural Studies*, Vol. 3, No. 1, pp. 77–81.

TIEBOUT, C.M. (1956) 'The urban economic base reconsidered', *Land Economy*, Vol. XXXII, pp. 95–9.

TOWNSEND, A. (1986) 'Spatial aspects of the growth of part-time employment in Britain', *Regional Studies*, Vol. 20, No. 4, pp. 313–30.

TOWNSEND, A. (1987) 'Regional policy', in Lever, W.F. (ed.) *Industrial Change in the United Kingdom*, Harlow, Longman.

URRY, J. (1987) 'Some social and spatial aspects of services', *Society and Space*, Vol. 5, pp. 5–26.

VAN DUIJN, J. (1983) *The Long Wave in Economic Life*, London, Allen and Unwin.

WALKER, R. (1985) 'Is there a service economy? The changing capitalist division of labour?', *Science and Society*, Vol. 49, pp. 42–83.

WALLERSTEIN, I. (1974) *The Modern World System*, 2 vols, New York, Academic Press.

WILD, R. (1972) *Management and Production*, Harmondsworth, Penguin Books.

WILLIAMS, K., CUTLER, T., WILLIAMS, J. and HASLAM, C. (1987) 'The end of mass production?' Review of M.J. Piore and C.F. Sabel (1984) *The Second Industrial Divide: Prospects for Prosperity* (New York, Basic Books), *Economy and Society*, Vol. 16, No. 3.

WOOD, P. (1986) 'The anatomy of job loss and job creation: some speculations on the role of the "producer service" sector', *Regional Studies*, Vol. 20, No. 1, pp. 37–46. Reprinted as 'Employment change and the role of the producer service sector' in Massey, D. and Allen, J. (eds) (1988) (associated Reader).

WORLD BANK (1987) *World Development Report 1987*, London, Oxford University Press.

Acknowledgements

Grateful acknowledgement is made to the following sources for permission to use material in this text:

Text

Fothergill, S. and Gudgin, G., *Unequal Growth*, 1982, Gower Publishing Group; *Extract 1*: from Lacey, R., *Ford: the Men and the Machine*, copyright © Robert Lacey 1986. Reproduced by permission of Curtis Brown Ltd., London and William Heinemann Limited; *Extract 2*: from Marsh, P., *The Robot Age*, 1982, Sphere/Abacus; *Extract 3*: Gapper, J., 'New town looks to the young and skilled', *Financial Times*, 18 January 1988; *Extract 4*: Shutt, J. and Whittington, R., 'Fragmentation strategies and the rise of small units: cases from the North West', *Regional Studies*, Vol. 21, No. 1, 1987.

Figures

Figure 2.5: Keeble, D., *Industrial Location and Planning in the United Kingdom*, 1976, Methuen & Co. and Martin, R. 'Thatcherism and Britain's industrial landscape', in Martin, R. and Rowthorn, B., *The Geography of De-industrialisation*, 1986, Macmillan Education, Ltd.; *Figure 3.3*: Hudson, R. and Williams, A., *The United Kingdom*, 1986, Paul Chapman Publishing; *Figure 3.4*: Damesick, P.J., 'The service industries, employment and regional development in Britain: a review of recent trends and issues', *Transactions*, Vol. 11, No. 2, 1986, Institute of British Geographers; *Figure 4.1*: adapted from *World Development Report, 1987*, copyright © 1987, The International Bank for Reconstruction and Development/The World Bank, Reprinted by permission of Oxford University Press, Inc.; *Figure 4.2*: adapted from Falk, R., *The Business of Management*, 1961, Pelican by permission of the author and Wild, R. *Management and Production*, 1972, 1980, Penguin Books, copyright © Ray Wild, 1972, 1980; *Figure 4.5*: Marsh, P., *The Robot Age*, 1982, Sphere/Abacus; *Figure 5.2*: Atkinson, J., *Flexibility, Uncertainty and Manpower Management*, 1984, Institute of Manpower Studies/Manpower Ltd.; *Figures 5.6 and 5.7*: Massey, D. and Miles, N., 'Mapping out the unions', *Marxism Today*, May 1984.

Tables

Table 3.1: Buck, N.H., 'Service industries and local labour markets: towards an anatomy of service employment', Regional Science Association Annual Conference, September 1985; *Tables 4.1 and 4.3*: Lee, C.H., *The British Economy Since 1700: a Macroeconomic Perspective*, 1986, Cambridge University Press; *Table 5.1*: Lash, S. and Urry, J., *The End of*

Organized Capitalism, 1987, Basil Blackwell; *Tables 5.2 and 5.3*: Shutt, J. and Whittington, R., 'Fragmentation strategies and the rise of small units: cases from the North West', *Regional Studies*, Vol. 21, No. 1, 1987; *Tables 5.4 and 5.5*: 'Unions face fall-out from industrial decline', *Labour Research*, Vol. 76, No. 9, 1979; *Table 5.6*: Milward, N. and Stevens, M., *British Workplace Industrial Relations 1980–1984*, 1986, Gower Publishing

Photographs

pp. 142 and 143: From the collections of Henry Ford Museum and Greenfield Village.

Author index

Aglietta, M., 32–4, 82, 88, 138, 146, 164, 182, 236, 249, 252
Allen, J., 91–135, 184–228, 239, 250
Amin, S., 29, 30
Atkinson, J., 201–4, 207, 212, 225

Bacon, R., 247, 248, 250, 252
Bain, G.S., 215
Barras, R., 101, 135, 236, 238
Bassett, K., 132
Beaumont, P., 215, 227
Beechey, V., 148, 207, 212, 228, 256, 257, 259
Bell, D., 92, 104, 105–7, 108, 109, 114, 116
Blackaby, F., 15, 89
Blumenfeld, H., 247
Boddy, M., 132
Bonefield, W., 226
Bowles, S., 139
Boyer, R., 138
Braverman, H., 147, 150, 183
Breheny, M., 89
Briggs, J., 97, 105, 207
Buck, N., 99, 126
Burawoy, M., 148

Cairncross, A., 248
Casey, B., 204, 209, 210
Clark, J., 28, 112
Clarke, J., 119
Coakley, J., 44
Coates, K., 228
Cockburn, C., 149, 219, 282
Combes, R., 78
Cooke, P., 188, 189, 191, 192, 228, 246, 250
Coote, A., 253, 256
Creigh, S., 208
Critcher, C., 119
Croasdale, M., 44
Cutler, T., 150, 157, 171, 172, 173

Damesick, P.J., 115, 124, 126, 129, 132
Daniels, P.W., 126, 130, 234, 235, 239, 243, 245
Dicken, P., 61, 234
Doeringer, P., 211
Dreye, O., 30–1, 40
Dunford, M.F., 82, 85

Eatwell, J., 259
Edwards, R., 139

Eltis, W.A., 247, 248, 250, 252
Engel, E., 104
Evans, T., 44

Fine, B., 21, 33, 44
Fogarty, M., 192
Fothergill, S., 60–1, 69–70, 90, 188, 232, 244–5, 246
Frank, A.G., 29, 30
Frankel, B., 135
Freeman, C., 28, 85, 112
Friedman, A.L., 148
Frobel, F., 30–1, 40

Gaffikin, F., 90
Gamble, A., 259
Gapper, J., 181
Geddes, M., 82
Gershuny, J.I., 95–6, 101–2, 106, 108–13, 115, 235, 255
Gillespie, A., 125, 129, 130
Goddard, J., 78
Goodchild, A., 97, 105, 207
Gorman, A., 208
Gough, I., 251
Gould, A., 194
Green, A., 125, 129, 130
Green, F., 146
Gregory, D., 212, 225
Gudgin, G., 60–1, 69–70, 90, 188, 232, 244–5, 246
Guiliano, V.E., 152

Hakim, C., 206, 208, 228
Hall, P., 83, 83–5, 89, 246, 250
Harris, L., 7–44, 44, 134
Harris, R.I.D., 236, 245
Hart, D., 89
Haslam, C., 150, 157, 171, 172, 173
Haughton, G., 150
Heinrichs, J., 30–1, 40
Hepworth, M.E., 130
Hill, S., 140
Hobsbawm, E.J., 137, 144
Howells, J., 129
Hudson, R., 49, 127, 148, 168, 178, 207, 211, 212, 224, 226, 256, 257

Ietto-Gillies, G., 20

Kaldor, N., 237
Kalinsky, R., 157, 168, 177

Keeble, D., 55, 57, 58, 62–5, 66, 73, 130, 194
Kitson, M., 60–1, 69–70
Klein, V., 253
Kondratiev, 27, 29, 83–4, 108–9, 112
Kumar, K., 92, 123, 135

Lacey, R., 143
Lane, T., 222, 224, 239
Lash, S., 186, 188–92, 222, 224–5, 228
Leadbetter, C., 227
Lee, C.H., 144, 154, 159
Leyshon, O., 130
Lipletz, A., 44, 138, 174–5, 177, 182
Littler, C., 150, 183
Lloyd, J., 227
Lloyd, P., 90
Lovering, J., 132

MacInnes, J., 211
McQuaid, R., 89
Mandel, E., 85, 113–14, 114–16, 117–18, 119, 123
Marsh, P., 164–7, 168, 169, 170
Marshall, J., 130
Marshall, J.N., 124, 126
Marshall, M., 82, 86, 90, 187
Martin, R., 58–9, 60, 65, 80, 82, 89, 98, 128, 164, 170, 178, 183, 189, 239
Massey, D., 44, 45–90, 89, 90, 126, 189, 191, 192, 222, 223, 224, 229–59
Meager, N., 203, 209
Meegan, R., 89, 136–83
Mensch, G., 28–9
Miles, I.D., 95–6, 101–2, 108, 110–13, 235, 255
Miles, N., 222, 223, 224
Millward, N., 204, 218, 221
Monk, S., 60–1, 69–70
Morgan, K., 89, 179, 183, 239
Myrdal, A., 253

Nickson, A., 90

Oberhauser, A., 175–6
Overy, R., 144

Pagnamenta, P., 144
Pahl, R., 228
Palloix, C., 138
Peck, J., 150
Perrons, D., 82, 85, 153, 164, 170, 175
Petit, P., 135
Phillips, A., 244, 256, 259
Piore, M., 138, 145–6, 147, 150–1, 163–4, 168, 171, 176, 182, 199, 211
Pollert, A., 211, 212

Prais, S., 194
Price, R., 215
Prowse, M., 238

Rada, J., 177
Rainnie, A., 194, 195, 200
Rajan, A., 100, 101, 135, 234
Reeve, D., 90
Rhodes, J., 47, 48, 50
Roberts, C., 208
Robertson, J., 97, 105, 207
Robinson, O., 100, 207
Rothwell, R., 85
Rowbotham, S., 148
Rowthorn, R.E.(B.), 15–16, 18, 89, 97

Sabel, C., 138, 145–6, 147, 150–1, 163–4, 168, 171, 176, 182, 199
Sargent, J.R., 242
Sawyer, P., 208
Sayer, A., 65, 66, 89, 177, 179, 183, 197, 239
Schoenberger, E., 176
Schumpeter, J., 28, 112
Scott, A., 168–9, 176
Shutt, J., 193, 196–9
Singelmann, J., 105
Singh, A., 47, 50, 242, 243, 248
Soete, L., 28, 112
Stevens, M., 204, 218, 221
Stone, M., 172
Storper, M., 168–9, 176
Sutcliffe, B., 146

Tarling, R., 196
Thompson, K., 183
Thirlwall, A.P., 231–2, 243, 248
Thrift, N., 22, 43, 73, 130, 237, 243, 246
Tiebout, C.M., 247
Topham, T., 228
Townsend, A., 178, 208

Urry, J., 126, 186, 188–92, 222, 224–5, 228

van Duijn, J., 44
Veblen, T., 138

Walker, R., 116, 135
Wallace, J., 207
Wallerstein, I., 29–30
Wells, J.R., 15–16, 18
Whittington, R., 193, 196–9
Wild, R., 156
Williams, A., 49, 127
Williams, J., 150, 157, 171, 172, 173
Williams, K., 150, 157, 171, 172, 173
Wood, P., 124, 126, 183, 234, 236

Subject index

Key concepts are printed in bold and the page number in bold indicates where this
concept is defined.

accumulation of capital, *see* capital
accumulation; *see also* flexible
accumulation
agglomeration diseconomies, 63–5, 130
agglomeration economies, 75, 130, 237
assembly-line production, 11, 13, 33, 140–3,
155–7
assumptions, underlying, 2, 93
automation, 33–4, 39, 41, 67, 70, 76, 164–70,
170–1, 176–7

branch plants, 20, 30–1, 34, 40, 41, 58, 76,
78, 84, 118, 131, 178, 233–4, 245

capital accumulation, 23, 32–5, 84, 114, 139–
40, 147, 150
capital goods, 81, 158, 162–3
capitalism, 113–20, 139–40, 146–7, 164,
189–92; disorganized, 5, 186, 188–92, 195,
224, 225–6; late, 114–19; organized, 188–
92
central regions, 55, 58, 76–7, 79, 177
change: absolute, 50–2, 52–3, 55–7, 59–60,
77–9; relative, 50–1, 53, 60, 73–5, 101
cities: conurbations, 60–1, 70; free-standing,
61, 69, 128, 186; industrial, 5, 61, 186, 199;
inner, 60, 69, 84, 246; outer areas of, 60;
small, 60–1; world, 129, 246–7; *see also*
urban decline
City, the, 19, 21, 22, 23, 33, 38, 41, 76, 77,
134, 242, 243, 248
competition, international, 25–6, 42, 66, 72,
172, 247
concentration of ownership, 116, 132, 193–4,
199–200
concepts, 1, 46, 50, 87–8, 93, 120, 230
conceptualization, 4, 6, 35, 46, 55, 67, 76–7,
94, 95, 111, 138, 146, 174–5, 253, 256, 257
consumer goods, 74–5, 81, 104, 106, 109–10,
115, 151, 158, 162–3, 172, 175, 252, 254;
industries, 81, 118, 122, 171, 187
consumer services, 126, 130, 236, 240, 245,
255; intermediate, 110
costs and benefits, 250–1; private, 251;
social, 251
crisis, 38, 81, 110, 138, 150–1, 155, 163, 172,
174–6, 188–9, 256
crowding-out thesis, 247–50

cumulative causation, 74, 239
cycles, 27–8, 39, 48, 82–3, 88
cyclical change, 26, 27, 29, 213–14

data, *see* evidence
decentralization, *see* spatial decentralization
deindustrialization, 3, 4, 15, 18–19, 31, 46,
47–55, 57–9. 59–60, 61, 92, 222, 232; does
it matter?, 231–47
demand, 104, 106, 109–10, 111, 117, 126,
130, 151, 234–5, 254
de-skilling, 140, 141–3, 147–8, 150
determinism/historical inevitability, 85, 88,
104–5, 145–7, 150–1
direct foreign investment, 9, 16, 20–1, 23,
24–5, 26, 30, 178
diseconomies, *see* agglomeration
diseconomies
diversification, 116, 132
division of labour, 30–1, 40, 42, 48, 77, 86,
110, 116–17, 132, 191; domestic, 256;
gender, 148–9; hierarchical/unequal, 77;
inter- and intra-sectoral, 86, 187; sectoral,
78, 111–12; sectoral spatial, 78–9; **social,**
77, 93, **100**, 116, 118; **spatial, 77**–9, 86,
132, 175, 176, 189, 241; **technical,** 77, 81,
116, 138, **140**–3, 147, 149, 155; *see also*
international division of labour, new
dominance: numerical, 80, 213, 232;
structural, 114, 146, 213

economic activity rate, 49–50, 65
economic concentration, 116, 132, 199–200
economies: of scale, 167, 237; of scope, 167,
168–9; *see also* agglomeration economies
economy: definition, 252–7; national, 1, 3, 6,
12–13, 26, 32, 47–50, 153, 247–50; non-
waged, 253; real, 240; waged, 96, 98, 253–
7; *see also* information economy;
international economy; open economy;
post-industrial economy; self-service
economy
elasticity of demand: income, 235; price, 235
employment: full, 2, 33, 34, 41–2, **48**–50, 53,
60, 257; socially acceptable levels, 48–50;
total, 48 9, 51 2, 97
engine/motor of economic growth, 50, 92,
155, 231(**232**)–40, 243

en-skilling, 148, 168; *see also* de-skilling; re-skilling; skill
enterprise, *see* firms
entrepreneurs/entrepreneurship, 28–9, 84–5, 86
equilibrium, 32, 73–4
establishment, *see* plant
evidence, viii–ix, 2, 27–8, 32–3, 47–54, 55–7, 58–9, 60–1, 70, 84–5, 87, 93, 101, 103–4, 106, 109, 111, 155–63, 192–3, 204–11
explanation, 2, 28, 30–7, 62–8, 68–71, 71–2, 72–9, 84–6, 93, 109, 117, 119, 130–4, 153, 188–9, 201–4, 224–5
export-base theory, 241–7; debate at national level, 241–4; debate at regional and local levels, 244–7
exports, 17–20, 23–4, 50, 95, 137–8, 241–2, 244–7
externalization, of services, 100, 116, 131, 195

financial/portfolio investment, 16, 21–2, 23, 24–5, 40
financial institutions, 16, 19–20, 21–2, 24, 32, 33–4, 41, 98, 105, 123, 125, 126, 130, 134, 242, 243, 247
firms: flexible, 201–4, 204–13; large, 186, 192–200, 218; small, 32, 172, 177, 186, 192–5, 195–9
Fisher/Clark thesis, 104–5, 107, 118, 235
flexible accumulation, 82
flexible manufacturing systems, 164–73, 176, 177
flexible specialization, 33, 41, 82, 138, 163(164)–73, 178–9, 211, 212, 214; geography of, 174–81; neo-Fordism and, 163–4
flexibility: 5, 185, 200–13; functional, 170, 201–3; numerical, 170, 201–3; of work, 257
Fordism, 4–5, 33–4, 80–2, 85, 121, 138, 139–63, 167, 174–5, 177–8, 225, 232; geography of, 174–81; *see also* neo-Fordism
foreign trade, 16, 17–20; *see also* exports; imports
fragmentation: of labour market, 185; of large firms, 186–7, 192–200; of markets, 151, 171–2; of tasks, 82, 140, 147; strategies, 195–200
franchising, 194, 196–7
full employment, *see* employment, full
functions: control, 4, 75–6, 77, 132, 133, 194, 196, 199–200; managerial, 4, 77, 140; professional, 126; R&D, 84–5, 106, 116,

125, 126, 129, 234; scientific and technical, 77, 126

geographical, *see* spatial
globalization, 138, 239, 243
goods, *see* capital goods; consumer goods; intermediate goods
greenfield sites, 74, 239

headquarters, 58, 76, 130, 132
heartland technologies, 112, 122
hegemony, 33, 34, 146
high-tech industries, 58, 85, 129, 130, 165–70, 177, 194, 216, 233–4

imports, UK position in, 17–20, 245
income elasticity of demand, *see* elasticity of demand, income
indirectly productive sectors, *see* sectors/parts of the economy
inequality, regional, 55–60, 74–7, 94, 127
information economy, 106, 107, 112, 116
innovation, 27–9, 39, 84–5, 109, 112, 236–7; social, 39, 110, 122; technical, 42, 236–7, 238; waves of, 111–13
institutional tradition, 138, 140, 145–6, 150–1, 163, 164
intermediate goods, 81, 158–60, 162–3
intermediate services, 126
international division of labour, new, 30–2, 39–40, 174–5
international economy, 3, 9, 30–1, 32, 34, 36–8; comparisons, 5–6, 8–9, 15, 16, 241–2; impact on Britain, 1, 5, 9, 12–13, 16; UK in, 5, 8, 18, 22–6, 29–42
international reserves of labour, 31
internationalization, 3, 23–4
investment, 20–1, 115, 248; *see also* direct foreign investment; financial/portfolio investment

Japanization, 169–70, 172, 178, 179–81, 211, 225
jobless growth, 54, 59, 101, 236
jobs: managerial, 59, 77, 201; professional, 77, 92, 102, 107, 201; quality of, 59, 238; 'real', 50, 95, 240, 244, 256–7; scientific and technical, 59, 77, 102, 106; *see also* labour; occupations
just-in-time systems, 169–70, 176, 177, 234

Kanban systems, *see* just-in-time systems

labour: availability, 66; casual, vii, 5, 118, 178, 205, 212, 256; costs, 31, 32–3, 40, 65, 66–7, 71, 74, 82, 139–40, 174, 177, 207;

domestic, 253; green, 65, 74, 79, 174, 177, 224; homeworkers, 185, 205; organized, 67, 69, *see also* trade unions; **part-time**, vii, 2, 50, 100, 105, 118, 119, 132, 178, 200–1, 205, **206**–8, 219, 226, 254, 256, 257; reserves, 31, 63, 65; self-employed, 202–3, 208–9; **temporary**, 185, 200–1, **208**–11; unpaid, 252–7; *see also* division of labour

labour market, **201**, 211–12, 225, 238; dual, 211–12, 225; external, 203, 205, 210–11; flexible, 34, 82, 196–7, 211, 212–13; fragmented, 185; internal, 202, 210–11; restructuring, 200–11

labour movement, 212–13, 225–7, 239

labour process, 32, 41–2, 80, 85, 138, **139**, 148–50, 152–3; flexible production technologies and changing, 164–70; fragmentation in Fordism, 82

labour productivity, 13, 54, 140–3, 144

land, availability, 70

licensing, 194

linear model, 105, 112, 118, 119

location factors, 62–5, 68–9, 79, 132–3, 191–2, 204

locational change, 58, 131–2

London, 1, 29, 33, 55, 70, 125, 128; control functions, 75–9, 132; dominance of, 75–7, 133–4; greater, 81, 84; inner, 61; polarization of incomes in, 246–7; *see also* City

long-wave theories, 3, 26–7, 27–9, 35, 39, 42–3, 82–8, 108, 146, 151, 191; and regulationist theories, debate, 87–8

machinofacture, 147

management–worker relations, 179

manufacture, 119, **147**

manufacturing, 1, 2, 4, 5, 17–18, 31–2, 41, 56, 58, 65–7, 69–70, 109–10, 153, 155–8, 186, 192–200, 203, 216, 236–7; and service sector, 109–10, 238; as engine of growth, 232–5; decline of, vii, 3, 15, 31–2, 46, 47, 50–3, 56–7, 60–1, 70, 92, 97, 105, 118, 124, 177, 192, 214, 231–2, 238–9, 242, 247, *see also* deindustrialization; geographical changes, 55–62; what's happening to UK?, 45–90

market fragmentation, 151, 171–2

market saturation, 151, 171–2

mass consumption, 80, 144, 178

mass market, 171

mass production, 4, 33, 80, 82, 109, 138, 144, 145–6, 152, 155–8, 168; crisis of, 136–83

methodologies, 62–71, 71–2

multilateralism, 3, **24**–6, 37

multinational companies, 2, 20, 24–6, 30–2,

40, 41, 116, 117, 189

multiplier effects, 75, 232–3; technological, 75, 233, 240

national economy, *see* economy

neo-Fordism, 5, 33–4, 41, 80, 82, 85, 121, 138, 163–73, 170–3, 174, 225–6; geography of, 174–81; and unionism, 225–6

newly industrializing countries, 25, 123, 174–5

niche markets, 168, 172, 197

north–south divide, 3, 4, 57, 58–9, 60, 124, 127–9

occupational structure, vii, 102, 107

occupations: blue-collar, 101–2, 107, 121, 219; manual, 106, 216; non-manual, 107; white-collar, 102, 103, 106, 107, 114–15, 121, 132, 214, 219

open economy, 3, **9**, 22

output, 47, 53–4, 59–60, 94, 96, 101, 105–7, 151, 154, 157, 158–63, 237

ownership, *see* concentration of ownership

participation, labour-force, 148, 254

part-time employment, *see* labour, part-time

periodization, viii, ix–x, 2–3, 10–14, 26, 62–8, 71–2, 80, 88, 121, 170–1, 175–6, 188, 189–92

peripheral regions, 57, 58, 74, 76–7, 79, 82, 174–5, 191

plant: large, 185, 186, 196; relation between large and small, 196–9; small, 185, 196; *see also* branch plants

polarization, 132, 211; of incomes, 247

population, decentralization of, 69, 186

portfolio investment, *see* financial/portfolio investment

post-industrial economy, 4, **92**–3, 100, 103–8, 113–14, 122–3, 127–34, 235; towards a, 91–135

primary products, 15, 17, 19, 174, 242

private sector, 60, 115, 128, 130, 131–2, 207, 216, 220–1, 242, 249, 255

privatization, 82, 115, 208, 215, 227, 249, 251, 255

process production, 155–8

producer services, 126, 130–1, 234–5, 239, 245, 246

production, process, *see* mass production; process production; small-batch production

productive sectors, *see* sectors/parts of the economy

productivity, 104, 105, 109, 110–11, 140, 144, 235–6, 237

profitability/profit motive, 28–9, 69, 74, 79, 115, 118, 119, 126, 131, 139, 248, 249, **250–2**, 255
propulsive industry, 232–5, 239
public expenditure, 249
public sector, 60, 85, 98–9, 101, 124, 128, 132, 195, 209, 216–17, 219, 224, 249, 255

R&D, *see* functions
regional convergence, 177, 187–8
regional decentralization, 63–8, 74, 76, 131
regional divergence, 74–5, 186, 188
regional policy, 33, 63–4, 66, 67, 68, 71, 79, 231, 236
regional specialization, 78, 222
regions, *see* central regions; peripheral regions
regulationist theories, 3, 27, 32–5, 35–6, 37, 41–3, 87–8, 121, 139–41, 144, 146–7, 163–4; and long-wave theories, debate, 87–8; mode of regulation, 32, 80, 138, 144; regime of accumulation, 32–5, 80, 115, 179
re-skilling, 148, 168
reproduction of society, 115, 253
research and development, *see* functions
restructuring, vii, 16, 41, 65–7, 111–13, 116; of labour market, 200–11
rural areas, 4, 60–2, 82, 129, 199

scale: economies of, 167, 237; returns to, 237–8
scientific management, 140–4
sectoral specialization, 77–9, 81, 187; *see also* division of labour, sectoral
sectors/parts of the economy, 4, 51–3, 85, 86, 93, 97, 104–5, 110, 122–3, 154, 194–5, 203, 216, 236; **indirectly productive, 251,** 253, 255; **productive, 251;** unproductive, 251; *see also* private sector; public sector
self-service economy, 108–12, 115, 122
service economy, 4, 101, 108–13, 238–9
service functions, 96, 255
service industries, 4, 96, 97–101, 110, 114–15, 118, 123, 124–5, 133, 186, 207–8, 231, 233–4, 237, 238
service occupations, 96, 101–3, 205, 207
service products, 96
service sector, 15, 60, 94–105, 108, 119, 207; rise of, 91–135
services: definition of, **94**–6; rise of employment in, 2, 15, 60, 92; trade in, 19–20; *see also* consumer services; producer services
simple co-operation, 146
skill, 40, 147(**148**)–50, 168, 185; changes, 214; craft, 146, 147, 150, 157, 168;

designation of, 5, 41; multi-, 185; semi-skilled groups, 59, 149, 201; *see also* de-skilling; en-skilling; re-skilling
small-batch production, 155–63, 168
social costs and benefits, *see* costs and benefits, social
social division of labour, *see* division of labour, social
spatial division of labour, *see* division of labour, spatial
spatial fix, 189–91, 199–200
spatial: concentration, 57, 178; dispersion/dispersal, 57, 129, 187, 189–91, 199, 222–4; decentralization, 4, 34, 58, 63, 65, 66, 68–9, 81–2, 127, 131, 174–7, 186, 191; reconcentration, 199
specialization, 116, 118, 196; *see* regional specialization; sectoral specialization
standardization, 4, 115, 118, 167, 170, 171–2
structural change, 2, 3, 8, 10–14, 28, 33, 36, 37, 38–42, 93, 114, 119, 120–3, 126, 191, 222
supply, 126, 130
system, 27, 80, 87, 93, 107, 114, 119, 121–3, 155

Taylorism, 140–1, 146–7, 152–3, 174–5; *see also* Fordism
technical division of labour, *see* division of labour, technical
technological/technical change, 67, 70, 85, 108–9, 110, 112, 117, 164, 236–7
temporary labour, *see* labour, temporary
theories, evaluation of, 1, 29, 31–2, 34–5, 36–42, 133–4, 150–1, 191–2, 210–13, 245
theory/theorizing, viii–ix, 1–2, 28, 62–5, 66–7, 69–70, 71–2, 75, 79–89, 93, 104–7, 110–11, 138, 145–57, 188–92
Third World, 25, 30, 31, 40, 41, 82, 164, 174, 177
trade unions, 32, 34, 41, 52, 67, 71, 74, 82, 149, 178, 179–81, 185, 212, 213–27, 218–24, 239
turning-point, viii, 5, 46, 47, 79–88, 92, 121, 122–3

unemployment, 12, 13, 15, 28, 31, 48–50, 58, 63, 79, 212, 256
uneven development, 3, 46, 72(**73**)–9, 86–8, 94, 124–9, 133, 188, 189–91; form, 75–8, 81–2; pattern, 5, 36, 73–5, 81, 188
unproductive sectors, *see* sectors/parts of the economy
urban decline, 68–71, 246
urban–rural shift, 4, 60–2, 82

wages, 139–40; real, 144; social, 144, 153
welfare state, 13, 80, 81, 144
women, 65, 81, 100, 105, 148, 207, 219–20, 222, 226, 244, 253–4, 256
workforce: core, 5, 201–4, 205, 226; peripheral, 5, 201–4, 205, 210, 212, 214, 257
working class, vii, 239
world-system theories, 27, 29–32, 35, 36, 37–8, 39–40, 42–3, 121